CARGOES AND
HARVESTS

DONALD CULROSS PEATTIE LIBRARY
PUBLISHED BY TRINITY UNIVERSITY PRESS

An Almanac for Moderns

A Book of Hours

Cargoes and Harvests

Diversions of the Field

Flowering Earth

A Gathering of Birds:
An Anthology of the Best Ornithological Prose

Green Laurels:
The Lives and Achievements of the Great Naturalists

A Natural History of North American Trees

The Road of a Naturalist

CARGOES AND HARVESTS

BY

DONALD CULROSS PEATTIE

MAPS BY
BEATRICE SIEGEL

TRINITY UNIVERSITY PRESS
San Antonio, Texas

Published by Trinity University Press
San Antonio, Texas 78212

Copyright © 2013 by the Estate of Donald Culross Peattie

ISBN 978-1-59534-160-0 (paper)
ISBN 978-1-59534-161-7 (ebook)

Trinity University Press strives to produce its books using methods and materials in an environmentally sensitive manner. We favor working with manufacturers that practice sustainable management of all natural resources, produce paper using recycled stock, and manage forests with the best possible practices for people, biodiversity, and sustainability. The press is a member of the Green Press Initiative, a nonprofit program dedicated to supporting publishers in their efforts to reduce their impacts on endangered forests, climate change, and forest-dependent communities.

The paper used in this publication meets the minimum requirements of the American National Standard for Information Sciences—Permanence of Paper for Printed Library Materials, ANSI 39.48-1992.

Cover design by BookMatters, Berkeley
Cover illustration: Zocha_K/istockphoto.com

CIP data on file at the Library of Congress.

17   16   15   14   13 | 5   4   3   2   1

CONTENTS

ILLUSTRATIONS

CARGOES AND HARVESTS

CHAPTER I

PLANT POWER

PLANT power means to a nation what horse power means, or water power, fuel power, sea power, man power and brain power. It is the treasure that buys a nation's independence and supremacy. To obtain it men have gone forth with the sword and conquered neighbors more rich in fertile lands, great forests, precious dye plants, or healing herbs. Plant power has made and unmade the boundaries of kingdoms, sent men upon gigantic voyages of discovery, kindled great sciences. Plant power means world power.

In the mastery over Nature we men advance day after day and in the brilliance of our achievements we carelessly arrogate to mankind's muscle and mind authority for all the creative work of the earth. And yet our dependence is absolute upon a single substance—chlorophyll. This, the coloring matter pervading most plants, is the green blood of the world. It is the silent factory through which the lifeless elements of earth, air, and water pass and emerge as such life-sustaining products as sugar

1

and starch and such indispensables as wood, fiber, tannin, and rubber.

For the food we eat, the clothes we wear, the coal or fagots we throw on our fires owe their origin to plant growth. It is said that directly from plant products flows half the wealth and commerce of the world. Even our meat, furs, leather, wool, silk, feathers, bones, animal fats and fertilizers, are produced by creatures which live on plants or prey on others that are herbivorous. And the inorganic world of metals, gases, oils, minerals, and the energy sources like water power, indispensable as they are, are overwhelmed by the thousands of useful members of the vegetable kingdom.

Latent in fertile land lies a treasure which throughout history has furnished to those who could wrest away its possession, the basis for power, culture, and all the higher civilization. India, for example, has been from prehistoric dawn a prize for which men have worked and warred and greatly adventured. Her natives, it is true, have never held world leadership. But into the laps of India's conquerors have poured precious silks, wools, leathers, and ivories, whose source, fundamentally, lies in the country's varied and abundant vegetation, while directly from plant life flows the wealth of India's wheats and rice, her fruits, tannins, timbers, spices, dyes, hemps, cotton, flax, tea, coffee, sugar, oils, and drugs. The last of the conquerors of India is England. What took her to India? The spice trade. What keeps here there, despite the immense distance between the province and the homeland and the

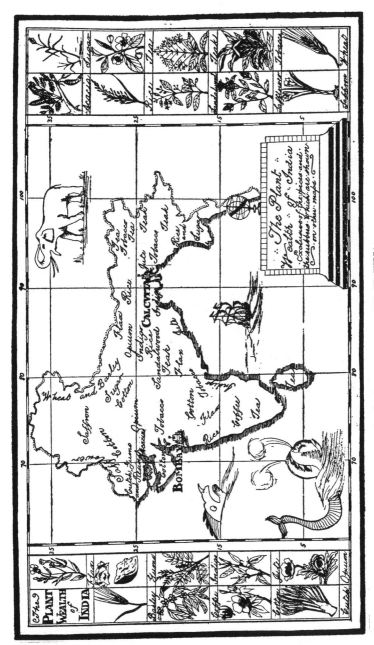

THE PLANT WEALTH OF INDIA

troublous jealousy of other nations, and the restless hostility of many Indians? Predominantly it is the wealth to be wrung from her forests and fields.

There are many Americans who regret our annexation of such a coveted and distant oriental possession as the Philippines. But having annexed it, we may as well study it and know its plant resources, as American scientists at Manila are doing. If it be true that the Japanese cast covetous eyes upon the Philippines it is probably not, as many people suppose, that they wish to expand their crowded population into them, for experts say that the Japanese dislike the climate of the Philippines and even of their own Formosa, which they have never colonized extensively. What the Japanese may well want is a grip upon the sugar fields, the rice paddies and the coconut groves of our island possessions, not to mention the precious tropical timbers, the gums and resins of Philippine woods.

The sources of plant power open to man's exploitation are several. In the first place there is the native vegetation of his country—that inherited boon which he has done so little to earn and spends so lavishly. A towering forest of useful trees is a potential mine of gold. But the man living beneath its shade must know how to turn it to his use and profit. The natives of many of the rich tropical rain forests have not exploited the wealth in their grasp, beyond the satisfaction of primitive needs, because they had not the imagination nor the science. With the coming of the white man a thousand new uses and needs have been discovered for plants of which he had previously never even heard the names. Books with titles like *The Useful Plants of Australia, The Useful Plants of Nigeria, The Useful Plants of Guam* tell the story of the service which economic botany renders mankind.

But beyond the random abundance provided by Nature, man may, by taking thought, add to his harvest through agriculture. A forest may be cut down and the gold mine thereby be worked out, but the wealth from agriculture is perennial; it is not a squandering of capital but an investment giving inexhaustible dividends. Cultivation, improvement by breeding, research, experiment and human perseverance play over the field, illuminating its problems. Above all, the introduction of species from other lands gives to an area, no matter how circumscribed by political boundaries, varied and ever-developing resources. Once only a few spots on the western coast of South America were blest with the trees that yield quinine. But did the other nations acquiesce in Nature's chance distribution of the genus Chinchona? On the contrary the Dutch and the British sought out the precious trees to transplant to their own colonies. To-day Peru's chinchona forests, almost exhausted by the shortsighted policy of destructive exploitation, are scarcely remembered as the source of the drug, while the Dutch have made their Javanese plantations the throne of the quinine trade.

And what unguessed rewards await our discovery? We are using but an insignificant fraction of the species of the world; at any moment we may find, among the hundreds of thousands of plants now considered useless, some which will solve a shortage, make a better substitute, or even create a new demand. As we pass a weed by the roadside to-day we may be ignoring that for which the world will clamor to-morrow. During the War there were to be seen receptacles bearing requests to deposit peach pits for use in making gas masks. Here was an unpredicted economic value placed upon a hitherto useless part of a plant. Or, to take an even more striking example, sugar in the classic diet was probably supplied only by honey and fruits. Then, in medieval days came the Arabs bringing sugar from the Orient. At once a new demand was created, one which is still increasing. All this time the Europeans were growing the humble beet. Only in the eighteenth century did a German chemist, Marggraf, discover sucrose in beets, and his pupil Achard showed how to extract it. And so, instead of a new demand, came a new plant to supply an old demand. Since then such countries as Germany, France, and northern United States, unable to raise one blade of sugar cane, have become prosperous sugar-producing regions, and have magnetized to their boundaries fresh sources of plant power.

Through the study of the indigenous flora harvests may be reaped from lands naturally poor in economic plants as we reckon them to-day. Even deserts, subarctic regions, swamps and salt marshes are capable of plant exploitation. Either through reclamation or the discovery of uses for their native flora these waste places will certainly be turned to use. A salt marsh grass of England is now utilized as a paper plant, lichens of arctic regions are suggested as dye plants and are indeed used to-day for litmus and the dye of Harris tweeds. Desert plants are gathered for tannins and rubber; swamps are dragged for Sphagnum moss; the sea beach is raked for kelp and wrack grass as fertilizers. As the world's population grows, as the obvious sources of food, clothing, timber, oil, and fertilizer become scarcer and the human race settles down to a program of economy instead of waste, lands now accounted of no use are bound to be exploited and to draw in their direction the centers of plant power and world influence.

No country is more instructive in this regard than Holland. It contains no natural drainage, practically no forests or important wild economic plants, and the climate is cool and cloudy. Yet the Dutch have utilized all of their land except bogs and acid heaths and have reclaimed thousands of acres from the sea. In the small grains, vegetables, hemp, hops, oilseeds and flax they have made themselves preëminent; they are, in fact, the gardeners of Europe. The Dutch cultivation of ornamental plants, too, particularly bulbs, is proverbial. But the genius of the Dutch for agriculture is not confined by the boundaries of their own land. In the East Indies they have taken a lead in the expert growing of tea, coffee, rice, sugar cane, spices, drugs and fibers, and to-day it is perhaps safe to say that in proportion to the population and area of Holland and its possessions this little country has as firm a grip upon plant

power as any nation in the world. Other countries
depend also on metals, animal products, water power,
coal or oil for their wealth; but Holland has had to
build up her power without much aid from these
sources; her commercial advantages rest upon the
crops she grows.

In contrast with the promise of latent possibilities
in our natural resources stands forth discouragingly
the reckless destruction of obvious treasures, and
agricultural stupidities such as the one-crop system,
and the inability to take up new crops or adapt to
new demands. The United States has stopped just
short of these pathways to poverty. Just in time
we have learned to save the remainder of our forests,
to rotate our crops, to introduce new plants and to
compete in fresh fields. Two more centuries of
thoughtless living would have ruined us. New countries like Australia and Brazil present fascinating
possibilities in plant exploitation and reveal also the
pitfalls of heedless destruction and unscientific cultivation. But they, too, will strive toward the upbuilding of their plant resources, natural and
introduced.

The part which the character of plant life has
played in the destiny of nations is closely linked with
plant power. Regions favored by abundant pas-
turage, fine wheat fields and the like, are apt to be
coveted by dwellers in regions with sparser or less
useful vegetation. Migrations, wars and conquests
naturally center about such regions. How many
hundreds of battles have been fought for the possession of fertile regions like the Po valley, or that

of the Ganges, the Nile delta, the wheat lands of North Africa! It will be remembered from the school-days' study of Cæsar how the Helvetians found their mountain valleys too crowded to grow the cereals necessary to support their population. When they poured out on the Rhône valley they upset the balance of power in Gaul, until Cæsar's legions drove them back.

In the classic world the grain supply, above all the wheat supply, was the key that unlocked the doors of wealth and power, for Italy and Greece were not self-supporting. When the Spartans destroyed the fleet which kept open the communication between Athens and the wheat lands of Thrace, they had won the war. When a Roman general with the imperial bee in his bonnet wished to concentrate his power, he took Egypt or "Africa" for his base of supplies. For he knew that if bread and circuses were what the mob wanted, he must get the bread first, in the wheat fields of North Africa. The circuses were easy to stage when a rich agricultural province was in the royal grasp. To-day North Africa is not the world's granary, but it is still the bread box of Mediterranean Europe. Even America owes this country an incalculable debt, for it was there that the great durum wheats were discovered.

To hold the power that lies in wheat a nation must have large areas and deep, rich soil. Russia, Argentina, Canada and the United States wield the influence in our time. But they did not always do so; perhaps they may not do so in the future. For if wheat is a profitable mistress for a nation to serve, it is also a fickle one. The fecundity of wheat lands is apparently exhaustible. When wheat is sown in virgin soil it usually makes a splendid growth for many years. Then gradually the yields become poorer until competition with vigorous new wheat lands deals the death blow to the old regions. It is said that this is what happened to Italy. The "sickening" of her wheat soils brought about continuous "hard times." Combined with the insidious competition of slavery, this drove the sturdy old Roman yeomanry to abandon Italy to slaves and landlords and to open up new farming districts in Africa, Spain and Gaul. Just what makes a "wheat-sick" soil is not certain. Some say it is exhaustion of the foods of the soil, for wheat takes but never gives of the precious nitrates and phosphates; others have thought that diseases—fungus and nematode parasites—settle in the region and drive out wheat culture; still others deny that "wheat-sick" soil exists. In any case it is undeniable that wheat power passes from one locality to another.

Foodstuffs like wheat, vital in the maintenance of life, have ever been and must always be dominant in the economics of human existence. But there are other plant industries which have had more checkered careers. In the sixteenth century the spice trade was probably the most lucrative ocean-borne commerce in the world. The price was high, partly because the cost of transportation was high, and partly because the wild sources were becoming scarce. But the craze for spices was of somewhat fictitious economic importance. The users of spice belonged to the uppermost stratum of society and as every one aspired to be reckoned in this class the demand was enormous. Under these conditions the price grew fabulously out of proportion to the intrinsic worth of the commodity. Consequently overproduction flooded the market and the prices fell to their present trifling rates. Can any one now conceive great nations going to war—as some three centuries ago they did—over the nutmeg question?

Nowadays tea, coffee and tobacco occupy a large proportion of the wealth invested in agriculture. It is imaginable that their story may repeat that of the spices. Some other beverage may be prepared for our tables or some other leaf fill our pipes. In Spain chocolate holds sway, in Paraguay *yerba maté* is drunk in place of tea, and in Arabia *khat*[1] is prized as highly as coffee. It was but three hundred years ago that the spice trader felt the star of his trade to be fixed—one may well wonder about the permanency of all but the absolutely essential crops of our times.

In connection with the waxing and waning of plant industries, there arises the powerful element of rivalry. Time after time nations have sought to keep for themselves the profits and benefits to be derived from the exploitation of plant products. In the history of the spice trade the Phœnicians, Arabs, Venetians, Portuguese and Dutch all sought successively to seize this important form of plant power and hold it by fair means or foul—chiefly the latter. Their attempts did not succeed, because a great

---

[1] *Catha edulis.*

trade cannot permanently be stifled by one corporation or nation, but an acute rivalry resulted.

So, too, the woad dye plant grown in Europe was undermined by better and cheaper indigo from India; the Ceylonese captured the coffee trade for a while until a disease drove it out; they then put in their claims for a share in the tea business, and with the Chinese and Javanese they dispute supremacy. Brazil has now made a successful attempt to supply the New World with coffee and the Old World coffees are no longer needed on our shores. On the other hand, England in British Malaya and the Dutch in Java are endeavoring, on the whole successfully, to render themselves independent of the former powerful supremacy of Brazil in the rubber trade. Egypt, India, China and Brazil, and, in fact, every warm portion of the globe, would like to break the grip of our southern states upon cotton.

The hold of the South upon tobacco is another well-established matter, but neither tobacco nor cotton constitute monopolies—at least there is no forcible exclusion of other nations. In modern times the old piratical commercial methods are seldom possible, and secrets of plant industry are difficult to keep. It is now truly the best man who wins. The finest and cheapest product will win out, and every faculty of agricultural science—soil and crop improvement, transportation facilities, marketing associations—are in full play, while the great growing centers of the world jostle to be first to bring their wares to your door. It is true that the Dutch hold a monopoly on quinine, to which they cling, and

that the Japanese have a sort of feudal exclusive
right in the camphor forests of Formosa. But
these are vestigial exceptions; the plants that feed,
clothe and house us are fast approaching a condition
of free-for-all competition, and well it is that they
are. The Dark Ages of wasteful and exclusionist
production seem to be over, and the era of intelligence and humanity dawns.

CHAPTER II

THE SPICES OF IND

THE spice trade—what magic its name conjures! It raises in the mind a picture of adventurers and pirates, of swart Arabs and haughty Portuguese *conquistadores*, of islands incredibly distant and beautiful, sleeping in the blue Pacific, of the marts of great Indian cities, of dark, cruel deeds done in the odorous groves of the jungles. And no tale of the spices so colorful or exciting but it has its voucher in fact and history.

It is impossible in our age to realize, when one looks into an old-fashioned spice box, each canister holding its own flavoring, how fabulously precious were once deemed the condiments which to-day every one can so easily procure. In the Middle Ages a single pound of ginger would buy a sheep, and a pound of cloves was seven times as valuable; two pounds of mace were worth a cow. And pepper— can any one to-day imagine it as worth its weight in silver? Yet, when Alaric the Goth captured Rome, he demanded as his tribute five thousand pounds of gold, two thousand pounds of silver and two thousand pounds of pepper. In medieval England rents were sometimes paid in pepper, and among traders it passed as a commodity of standard value, just as

14

tobacco ranked as legal tender in colonial Virginia. Kings presented pepper to each other—a doubtful compliment, one would think now—yet in those days it was gratefully received. It is told that when Henry II of the Holy Roman Empire came to Rome, the streets were "fumigated" with cloves; and in China cloves were held in the mouth to sweeten the breath of one speaking to the Son of Heaven.

The fabulous value of spices in former times contrasts so strangely with their cheapness at the present that it may well be wondered how this may be accounted for. Spices in olden days were rare, they came from parts unknown, places whose names were haunted with mythical wonders and terrors, and from these attributes they partook of such a fascination and value as we might feel to-day about a food brought from Mars. Their pungent taste and delicious odor made no less of an appeal to the ancient and medieval mind. The diet in those days was far simpler, and so it came about that persons with epicurean tastes, jaded by the familiar, found in spices an especial relish. Inasmuch as spices cost so much they were accessible only to the wealthy. To serve spices on one's table implied a certain rank and caste in worldly affairs, such as some feel to-day is bestowed by *pâté de foie gras* or hearts-of-palmetto salad. As every one aspired to be deemed of this class, poorer persons made a show of serving spices in order to display prosperity, and so it came about that the demand ever increased, and an essentially fictitious value was placed on pepper, nutmeg, clove and cinnamon. Nor must it be forgotten that spices were used as preservatives of meat. It was generally believed, and in some cases rightly so, that if spices were put into food, decay would not set in. As there was then no adequate system of refrigeration, the spices were credited with an extraordinary, even an indispensable worth.

Our conception of spices has changed from that which was held in ancient times. When the Lord spake unto Moses, commanding him what spices should be used in the sacrificial ceremonials, there was, in all that list, but one substance which we should call a spice. To those ancients anything aromatic was a spice, so that gum resins, oils, and even animal fats came under this category. But by spice we mean a seasoning plant. We use in our kitchens to-day many more such than even Lucullus could display at his most tempting banquets, for the ancients, beside caraway, mustard and bay, minor wild spices of the Mediterranean, knew only pepper, cardamoms, turmeric, cassia bark and ginger. These were spices which the Persians brought from India—India, that land which was the eastern border on the map of the ancient cartographers. Of cloves, nutmeg and mace, which grew only in the Spice Islands as distant from India as was that land from Greece, the classic peoples knew nothing, for no traders had ever ventured so far into the great stream of ocean. The spices which the Persians did know and trade in they sold to the Phœnicians of Sidon and Tyre who peddled them up and down the Mediterranean coasts from Alexandria to Rome, cities where all the luxuries were in demand.

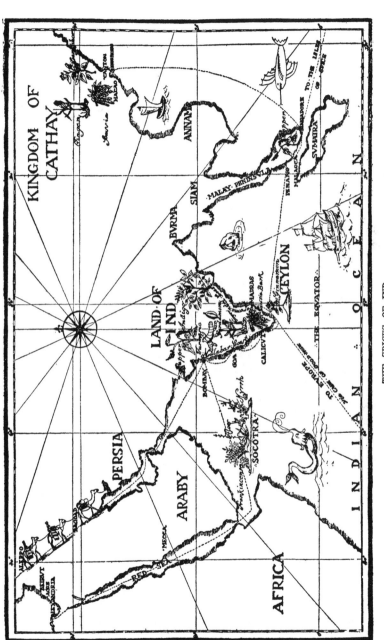

THE SPICES OF IND

Then came the Dark Ages, and when light broke again it was the Arabs who plied the Indian trade, and in Damascus, Aleppo, Acre, Beirut and Constantinople they sold the spices to the Venetians. Not Sidon and Tyre, but now Venice ruled the Mediterranean, and Venetian banqueters dined on spiced dishes under the shadow of San Marco's oriental dome. To the pepper, cardamoms, ginger and cassia bark of the classic age, were added cinnamon, cloves, nutmeg and mace, for the Arabs had ventured far to the East, to the Isles of Spice in the Pacific, and in the forests of Ceylon they had discovered the wild cinnamon, more esteemed than the related cassia bark.

Since all these precious commodities were brought by the Arabs, it became generally believed that Arabia was their native home, so little conception had the medievals of oriental geography. Spices of Araby are famous in story but they have no standing among historians. For it is doubtful if a single important spice is native in that arid country. It is the rich rain forests of the Far East which furnish the great seasonings. In later times travelers supposed that Malacca and Malabar were the home of cloves and nutmeg, while in reality these were but wholesale shipping points for these products brought from farther east. But to our distant ancestors there was no farther east. The Arabs saw to this; they were much too wily to let any one discover where the spices grew. They vouchsafed only vague generalities, and obscured even these in such tales of terrible sea monsters and beast-men that not the most venturous Venetian dreamed of daring the eastern seas.

One or two travelers, to be sure, had gone as far as India to see the pepper vine at home. But not until Marco Polo, a lad of fifteen years, left with his father and uncle for China did a truly daring or observant traveler see the Orient. When, years later, he returned, he brought with him tales of the ginger plantations of south China, and its camphor forests, of the cloves and nutmeg brought from distant isles to Malacca, and of the cinnamon groves of Ceylon and the pepper vines of Malabar.

His great book of travel, dictated while in prison, with its half-incredible stories of the spice treasures of the East, stimulated a host of merchants and explorers, and as every one knows it fired the mind of Columbus to seek a way around the world. A copy of Polo's book accompanied the great Admiral on his first voyage.

But it remained for the Portuguese, the sailors of the wild Atlantic, rather than the Venetians of the quiet little Mediterranean, to dare the terrors of the sea monsters. Inspired by Prince Henry the Navigator, the mariners of Portugal pushed each year farther down the coast of Africa. In 1497 Vasco da Gama rounded the Cape of Storms, astutely renamed the Cape of Good Hope by King Manuel, and reached Calicut on the west coast of the peninsula of India in a voyage of eleven months. Friendly relations were established with the rajah of Calicut, presents were exchanged with him in the name of King Manuel, and in the course of the voyages which followed, the Portuguese traders became known in every port on the Malabar coast. They came for the express purpose of capturing the spice trade, and it was pepper, ginger, cinnamon, and cardamoms which loaded the hulls of the returning vessels. The daring sailors and merchants did not content themselves with competing with Arab shipping. Whenever there was any doubt in their dealings with the Indians, or even with less cause, they turned their brass cannon upon the harbors and the palaces and brought the swarthy races to submission. It was with no disguise of their intentions that they seized that pearl of India's turban, the island of Ceylon. There grew the great cinnamon forests, and there the Portuguese meant to found their eastern empire—a brave little empire over half a year's journey from the homeland. By pitting the jealous princelings of Ceylon against each other the Portuguese, almost unnoticed, were soon in possession of the cinnamon monopoly. The potentates were glad enough to get off without being blown up, so when the Portuguese enslaved the natives of the jungle and forced them to gather the precious bark, the rulers did not demur. Under Portuguese law, no native was allowed to cut a single foot of bark or sell any except when ordered to do so by the conquerors. To disobey this rule was an offense punishable by death. The cinnamon collectors formed a special slave caste which it was impossible for a member of his descendants ever to quit. With the cinnamon monopoly assured, the traders of Lisbon could force upon Europe a price which is to-day almost unbelievable. In pepper too, they were supreme.

But the Portuguese were realizing that they had only begun to smell out the trails of the spice trade. They seized Goa, the last and greatest stronghold of the native spice export, and built a mighty warehouse and fortress. Under these walls lived three men of echoing fame. St. Francis Xavier came to bring the Gospel to the heathen, and here, too, dwelt Garcia da Orta author of the learned and charming *Drugs and Simples of India,* who was the first to treat, free of superstitions of Arab traders and European quacks, of the sources and values of the spices pouring from the new lands. It was of the wisdom of this scientist that Camoëns wrote an ode in celebration. The poet himself was the third of the great dwellers at Goa. Exiled from home, he wrote his epic of Portugal and the spice trade, and the wandering Ulysses of his song was Vasco da Gama, for *The Lusiad* was written to glorify the land which had wronged the poet. Portugal at that moment stood at the zenith of her glory. She was mistress of the seas, successor to Venice as maritime capital of Europe. Within the memory of Camoëns his fellow mariners had discovered Brazil, the Cape of Good Hope, the sea route to India and China. They held in their hands the pepper and cinnamon trades, at that time the most precious ocean-borne commerce in the world. To the inspiration which Camoëns drew from the exotic beauties of the spice lands, the Portuguese language owes much of its splendor of form and sound. When Robert Spruce was in the jungles of the Amazon three hundred years after Camoëns' death he heard *The Lusiad* recited by Portuguese soldiers.

Such are the glorious associations of the old gray fortress at Goa. Its conqueror, Alphonse d'Albuquerque took his fleet to the Malay straits and seized Malacca, key city of the Indian Seas. Lying as it does at the crossroads of all the great oriental sailing routes, Malacca was a priceless possession for the Portuguese. But these adventurers did not stop there. East they sailed until they found at last the islands which the Arabs had tried to hide from foreign knowledge for centuries. The Moluccas or Spice Islands are a group of mountains whose superbly wooded summits rise above the Pacific. On the little islands of Banda, Ternate and Amboyna grew cloves and nutmeg and mace, and thither at last came the Portuguese, their vessels scattered by typhoon, their approach contested by natives, Arabs and pirates. Undaunted, they mastered the islands, and the rajah of Molucca was forced to become the vassal of Manuel of Portugal. Factories were established in the Spice Islands and in Celebes and Gilolo. Java and Sumatra were Portuguese at least in name, and Borneo knew her galleys. Great was the wealth of the Portuguese East India Company and exorbitant the profits which it reaped. With slaves to gather the precious spices, without a rival in the India seas, the company poured into the lap of Lisbon such wealth as that old city had never dreamed on.

But it was written that Portugal should not rule

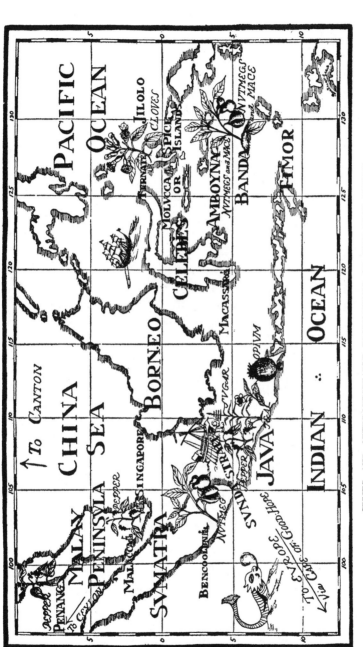

SPICES AND OTHER VEGETABLE PRODUCTIONS OF THE EAST INDIES

forever. The seeds of destruction were sprouting within. Her policy of excluding other nations from any share in the spice trade had raised against her a host of enemies any one of whom was more powerful than she. The hauteur of Portuguese officials, their grafting administration, and the cruelty with which they oppressed the natives led to their downfall. The religious fanaticism of the missionaries and the terrors of the Inquisition at Goa made few converts and many foes, so that without a well-wisher in the world the overseas empire was doomed to death.

Portugal's brief flame of genius had burned out. In 1581 her crown was united with that of Spain, and this, more than the attacks of the Dutch and English upon her spice fleets, eclipsed her greatness. For the larger of the united kingdoms had shown no interest in the East beyond an abortive attempt of Magellan to claim the Spice Islands. The Spanish preferred the trade winds and the Atlantic. What their galleons brought back was not spice, not even the capers, green peppers and vanilla of New Spain, but the ingots and the rubies plundered from the Aztecs and the Incas. To the Castilians it appeared easier and more profitable to rob the red men of their gold, and they had no stomach for the commercial turn which the Portuguese eastern spice trade had taken. In the year that Portugal became the ally of Spain her East India Company closed its doors for the last time, just as the Dutch company was rising to power.

Indeed, freed from Spanish oppression, the Dutch

genius was seeking room for expansion. Like ants following a trail of sugar to the bin, the Dutch merchants and privateers trailed the Portuguese around the Cape of Good Hope to India, nosed their way to Malacca, and stole on to the Spice Islands. One by one the Portuguese strongholds fell. Of their greatness there are left no visible evidences except the ruined cathedrals on the Malabar coast and the alien-sounding title of "Don" by which the Ceylonese princes address each other. These potentates watched with interest the contest between the Dutch and Portuguese for the isle of cinnamon. The chivalry, the pride and aristocratic bearing of the defenders appealed to their own natures, but it was without regret that they saw the Dutch triumph.

To-day the eastern possessions of Portugal consist only in a few obsolete ports in India, part of the sandalwood island of Timor, and the port of Macao. This city was founded in 1557, hard by Canton, and now represents the oldest European settlement in China. Its purpose was to provide a factory for the Canton spice trade in ginger and cassia bark. Here in a grotto dwelt Camoëns while he wrote half of his epic, and to his memory there is erected there the one monument in the East to a western literary figure. The Dutch tried once to capture Macao, but the gallant old city beat them off. To-day nothing remains of her glory, and her maintenance is drawn from gambling tables.

The era of Dutch greatness had now begun. At first Holland found an ally in England, but Queen Elizabeth soon realized that her real rival was not waning Portugal but waxing Holland. She changed sides in the alliance, and the Dutch went on alone in the eastern seas, fighting the Portuguese and the English shipping as they proceeded. In 1623 they surprised in time of peace the English spice factory at Macassar and slaughtered it to a man. For this Cromwell later forced the Dutch to pay three hundred thousand pounds. But it was cheap at that for it left Holland master in the East.

The Dutch East India Company, which had begun its career in armed attacks on Portuguese ships, now emerged as the foremost business corporation of its times. The profits which it reaped from spice enabled it to pay enormous dividends, and its credit was the best in Europe. But the gold mantle which this company wore had its seamy side. In cruelty the Dutch outdid the Portuguese. As traders, they were more obsequious to the native princes, they were more energetic in drumming up trade, and they showed no misplaced religious zeal. But their greed for monopoly was even worse, and their oppressive measures were inhuman.

The Dutch immediately grasped the effectiveness of slavery in the cinnamon forests of Ceylon. Woe to the village which did not furnish its quota of the bark. The men were tortured to death, or if they fled, the Dutch whipped the women. In the Isles of Spice they tried still another method. Fearing that the English would somewhere slip in and get cloves and nutmegs, the Hollanders, who could not possibly keep watch over the whole of the immense archipelago, decided to confine the spices to certain islands where they could be easily controlled. They went from one island to the next chopping down and burning all the spice trees until cloves were left only on Ternate and nutmegs on Banda and Amboyna. Java fell under their sway and they proceeded to lay a monopoly upon pepper, cochineal, cinnamon, indigo, sugar, tea and opium. Having robbed the Javanese of their most precious exports, they forced the natives to work these crops as slaves. The story of their cruelties, even to women, has few parallels in history.

This was the dark side of Dutch imperialism. Far away in the Netherlands themselves a strange new flower had come into bloom. Wealth and the Orient had breathed upon the land, and there sprang up in Holland a galaxy of painters, musicians, scientists, and poets. Looking back over the story of the spice trade it is evident that each nation which has held it—Persia, Phœnicia, Arabia in the golden age of Damascus, Venice and Portugal—has blossomed under its Midas touch. Suddenly beautiful buildings were erected, exquisite garments were seen in the streets, men lived in ease and that idleness which gives peace for great minds to dream and philosophize. Then when the precious trade passed away the great buildings crumbled, the poets were dumb, men once more had to scurry for their living. May we not ascribe to the spice trade and the new glories which it opened some of the greatness of Holland in the seventeenth century?

In that era Dutch shipping constituted four-fifths of the world's total. A fleet of six vessels from the

Isles of Spice brought home a cargo worth two million gulden or about as many dollars. It is no wonder that in days of such affluence the Dutch did not hesitate to burn thousands of pounds of spice on the docks of Amsterdam, when the market was overstocked and the price was in danger of falling.

But like Portugal, Holland's genius burned brightly only for a century. The Dutch East India Company found that it could not keep up its monopoly because the Chinese and Malay junks hung around its trade routes as numerous as bees, and the other European nations stole the spice trees. In 1770 Poivre, governor of Mauritius, a French island off the coast of Africa, succeeded in smuggling cloves and nutmeg out of the Moluccas to his own province. From thence the culture spread to Zanzibar and the West Indies. The Spanish took ginger from India for their West Indian possessions, and the English stole the secrets of the Spice Islands for India.

The tremendous forces of oriental commerce could not be controlled or monopolized by the petty exclusiveness of Dutch administration, and breaking these galling confines, the competing nations at the same time broke the bubble of Dutch profiteering. The East India Company which had in the seventeenth century been able to pay 40 per cent dividends, failed in the eighteenth for fifty million dollars. For half a century, in fact, it had been the mere ghost of a business corporation. Its moneys were derived only by forced contributions from the natives and by immense loans from banks.

Slower than Spain, Portugal and Holland, but wiser and more persistent, the expansive genius of England was finding itself at last in naval exploits. As early as 1601 the English had rounded the Cape of Good Hope, and in 1604 Sir Thomas Middleton's great trading fleet arrived in the spice countries. In 1600 Queen Elizabeth chartered the British East India Company, and at first spices were the great items on its invoices, though later tea, silk, and such precious commodities overshadowed those articles for which originally the British ships sought out India. The English were quick to see the strategic importance of the Malay Straits. In 1786 Captain Light founded Penang in order to get a grip on the pepper trade, and Sir Stamford Raffles revived Singapore which for several centuries has fallen into decay. To-day, it is said, in no port may be seen the flags of so many nations as fly in the harbor of Singapore. With its rise the Dutch pepper trade at Malacca declined, until at last Holland abandoned that city to its English neighbors. Hongkong the British built close to Canton to share the Portuguese trade, and from that day Macao set foot on a downward course.

Clashes between England and Holland were sure to come, and when they did England this time was the stronger. For a brief time all the Dutch possessions fell into English hands, and at Bencoolen in captured Sumatra, Sir Stamford Raffles planted ten thousand nutmeg trees. But the English returned to Holland by the Treaty of Vienna in 1815 practically all the islands, and kept for themselves

India, Ceylon and the Malay Peninsula. The nutmeg cultivation was then transferred to Penang, and the ancient Dutch monopoly of Ceylon cinnamon was honorably terminated. Slavery was abolished and in place of the reckless destruction of cinnamon trees there grew up, under the English, the splendid cinnamon plantations that one sees to-day. On that island nothing remains to remind us of the Dutch except the curious use of Dutch Roman law in the native courts, and an elaborate system of canals along which cluster Dutch cottages and quaint windmills. These only remain, and the hatred of Dutch cruelty.

The portions of the Orient under English rule have lost sight of the spice trade. For spices are no longer either necessary as preservatives, nor are they luxuries and badges of caste. Many parts of the world now grow spices, the competition is keen, the market is always full, and the price is correspondingly low. The spice trade has become a matter of small change, and to-day the English spice plantations, though owned and exploited by British capital, are manned by Chinese labor.

Not so the Dutch. In their island possessions they have remained preëminent in spices and through all the vicissitudes of competition and falling prices have clung to the once glorious trade. Holland has reformed her ways; the monopolies are over, honest officials are in power, and the artificial props of false prosperity are knocked down. In 1860, just after the appearance of *Uncle Tom's Cabin,* a novel,

Max Havelaar, by E. Douwes Dekkar was published, in which were exposed the evils of slavery in the Dutch colonies. The effect of the book was tremendous and it may be said to have virtually ended the shameful chapter.

Though our own country has never held any possessions among the Spice Islands, it has shared in the great trade. In the halcyon days of American shipping, between 1800 and 1860, our schooners by the score sailed the vast distance around the Horn, across the Pacific to the Moluccas, Canton and India. The pirates of "Sundy Strait" are still famous in the stories of New England sea captains who yearly brought home the cargoes of pepper and ginger that made vast fortunes for the great shipowners. Lucky are those that have tasted the preserve called "East Injy," in which ginger is the chief ingredient, made by the Salem housewife. And as one passes down a quiet street in old Gloucester, Marblehead, Portsmouth or Boston, and gazes at the stately houses with the tranquil fanlights one may imagine, with a fair chance of being right, that the wealth which built up the beauty and dignity of the house and its occupants was wrested in the sea of pirates and typhoons, from the half-forgotten, dark, romantic spice trade.

SUGGESTED READING

FIELDING, ROBERT O., *Spices, Their Histories,* 1910. Entertaining and vivid.

FERGUSON, A., *All About Spices,* 1889. Discursive work, relating both to the history and culture of spices,

32   CARGOES AND HARVESTS

ORTA, GARCIA DA, *Colloquies on the Simples and Drugs of India,*. Eng. tr. by Sir Clements Markham, 1913; from Lisbon ed., 1895, ed. Condé de Ficalho. Quaint and delightful.

THOMPSON, J. S., *The Chinese,* 1909. Chap. II, "The Portuguese and Camoëns in China." A charming glimpse of old Macao and the poet of the spice trade.

RIDLEY, HENRY N., *Spices,* 1912. Complete on culture and market of spices to-day.

JANK, JOSEPH K., *Spices: their Botanical Origin, their Chemical Composition, their Commercial Use,* 1915. A handy and informative book.

WILCOX, EARLEY V., *Tropical Agriculture,* 1916. Chap. XVI, "Spices and Flavoring." A convenient and scientific account of the production, market and nature of the important spices.

Encyclopædia Britannica. See articles on Cinnamon, Clove, Nutmeg, Pepper, India, Malay Archipelago.

CHAPTER III

QUININE—THE COMING OF A SAVIOR

IN the palace of the Viceroy of Peru, at Lima, the Lady Ana de Osorio, Countess of Chinchón, lay burning with a three-day malarial fever. The news that the wife of the viceroy was sick and like to die had spread over the countryside, in that year 1638, and it was heard by Don Francisco Lopez, the Corregidor of the town of Loxa. To Don Juan de Vega, her physician, the Corregidor sent a parcel of a curious reddish bark, directing him to administer it in powdered form to the countess. The physician tried it, and behold, the disease was arrested! Never before had it been known that there was a cure for malaria, in those days the most widespread of the dreaded parasites of humanity.

After the recovery of the good countess, she and her husband returned to Spain. With them they carried a quantity of the marvelous bark, and their physician, who accompanied them, also carried a store of the *quina* which he sold in Seville for a hundred *reals* a pound. In a short time the fame of the Countess' Bark, as it was called, had spread all over Spain. It attracted the attention of the Jesuits who eventually carried the precious substance to the ends of the earth, whence it came to be known as Jesuit's Bark. With it they even cured the Emperor of

China of malaria, and as a reward they were granted the site for a cathedral in Peking, which they hold to this day. Louis XIV bought the secret of the remedy from Sir Robert Tabor, an English physician, for two thousand louis, a handsome pension and a title. Tabor was reckoned a fraud by physicians, but quinine was at least one honest medicine in his cabinet.

It is difficult for us to imagine to-day what general rejoicing the cure for malaria awoke throughout the world. In those days no one knew the cause of the disease; it was thought to be night air or noxious vapors arising from freshly opened earth. By closing the windows at night people believed that these poisonous vapors could be excluded, and certain it was that they were less liable to malarial fevers when they did so. Even in the hottest countries people stifled in sealed rooms at night rather than risk the dread disease. They little suspected that by closing the windows they were keeping out the mosquitoes which spread the infection.

The genus Anopheles comprises numerous species of mosquito which are of world-wide distribution in equatorial regions, and in very warm, wet summers may be seen as far north as New York State, southern England and northern China. They may be recognized by their habit of "standing on their heads" when they bite, instead of humping themselves as the common Culex mosquitoes do. The bite of the Anopheles, deadly as it may be, is not nearly so irritating as that of the Culex, nor does the malarial mosquito sing so loud a war cry as the noisier common pest. But it is Anopheles that carries in its salivary glands the real evil doer, a microscopic animal living in the mosquito's body. When the mosquito sucks blood, she (for only the female bites) injects with the ordinary poison of an insect sting some of the malarial parasites. Entering the blood stream these terrible animalculæ live upon the life fluid, constantly incubating and hatching new generations of their kind, which increase in incredible numbers, until, unless checked, the sufferer generally dies. The sickness is recurrent, and brings chills, fever, depression and prostration.

What misery it meant to the human race to have an absolutely unchecked disease of this sort ravaging by far the greater part of the habitable world! It has been said that empires that had yielded to no human enemy have gone down before its assaults. The fall of the Roman rule had many causes, but malaria alone might well have been enough to effect it. In early classic times malaria was an unheard-of disease on the northern shores of the Mediterranean. Then the legions returned from the conquest of the hot and plague-ridden Nile valley. Soldiers with malarial fever lay on their cots in Italy and were bitten by mosquitoes from the Pontine marshes; the Italian mosquitoes became infected and bit healthy people who in turn became malarial. So, at least, it is conjectured. Presumably the New World, too, was free from malaria in pre-Columbian days. But with the coming of the white man countries which had previously been healthy were pestilence stricken. The disease, at one time local, was spreading rapidly over the world. And then came the marvelous discovery of the cure of the Countess of Chinchón, and suddenly men perceived a savior coming to the plague-stricken world.

Our knowledge of how first the use of the bark was discovered is but legend. Spruce, Markham, and other scientists who knew the Indians of the chinchona forests say that these never had any understanding of the properties of the bark and indeed would refuse to touch it; physicians prescribing it for Indian patients had to write it out for the apothecary as "vegetable alkaloid." On the other hand, there is a story that an Indian, ill of the fever, slaked his burning thirst in a mountain pool. Finding himself much restored, he drank again from the pool and by repeated draughts he at length completely recovered his health. Investigating the pool, he found it to contain fallen logs of the chinchona trees. He then taught his fellows to use the bark. The story is entertaining but unlikely. It is probably to some nameless Spanish chemist, experimenting with the alkaloids and essences of Peruvian plants, that we owe the happy accident of the discovery of the use of quinine in malaria.

But it must not be supposed that in the general rejoicing which accompanied the finding of the new cure there was no opposition to Peruvian bark. The Protestants would not use it because it was "Jesuit's Bark," and all sorts of diseases and mysterious deaths were laid at its door. "It was condemned because 'it did not evacuate the morbific matter,' because 'it bred obstructions in the viscera,' because 'it only bound up the spirits and stopped the paroxysms for a time and favored the translation of the peccant matter into the more noble parts.' " [1]

In the end, however, Peruvian bark won for itself the place which the metaphysical and pedantic doctors would not grant it, and to-day it stands as one of the few absolutely specific medicines.

As the demand for quinine increased, the Count of Chinchón himself made a collecting trip in the Andes during which an immense amount of bark was taken. In his wake came a host of imitators to exploit and pillage the chinchona forests. In a short time there grew up a special low caste of natives in Peru, Ecuador and Bolivia known as *cascarilleros* or cascarilla gatherers. These people, rough nomads comparable to lumber-jacks but considerably inferior, wielded the axes which rang upon the trunks of the great chinchona groves and with large knives slit the precious bark from the logs and sold it as raw product.

To thinking people it was apparent by the opening of the last century that the supposedly inexhaustible chinchona forests were giving out. The increased demand clamored for the felling of trees more rapidly than nature could possibly replace them. And the methods of collection added terrific wastage. The lazy Indian rarely troubled to roll over a heavy log but merely stripped the easily available bark and left the rest to rot. In vast areas the chinchona forests were nothing but a memory where once they

---

[1] *Paris Pharmacologia*, quoted by Maddox, John Lee, *The Medicine Man*, 1923.

had been abundant. The last stands of the great trees were falling. In his shortsightedness the cascarillero preferred to hold a monopoly while the price soared, even though the end of the great resource was in sight. He guarded this monopoly with ferocity; the rumors about the fate of those who tried to invade the cascarilla collecting grounds are hard to believe, but they are told upon good authority.

It was while on his collecting trips in South America that the distinguished botanist Humboldt visited the chinchona forests and reported that twenty-five thousand trees were felled annually in one district alone. Scientists and doctors in Europe repeatedly petitioned their governments to take action to avert the extinction of the most precious single vegetable cure in the world. But the doctor and the botanist do not often receive such courtesy or attention at court as the general or the politician. So year by year the boon which meant a saving as vast as the waste caused by war was slipping through the hands of heedless humanity.

From time to time chinchona plants were brought to European cities, but only as curiosities. The first of them was seen in 1846 when the botanist Weddell raised one from seed in Paris. It was the French who made the first attempt to grow chinchona for medical purposes. A small plantation was started in Algeria, but probably from lack of water the trees all died. Not until the Dutch, those masters of intensive horticulture, bethought themselves of Java, was the right climate selected. The high, rainy mountain

QUININE FORESTS OF THE WORLD

slopes of the island, warm but not hot, were similar in physical respects to the Andean highlands where chinchona was native. As early as 1829 Blume, the great Dutch naturalist, had perceived the possibility of quinine production in Java and had tried to secure seeds from Bolivia, but they had died on the way.

It was only after incessant petitioning that the Dutch colonial authorities were induced by doctors and botanists to send an expert to South America to procure the precious seedlings. In 1849 this task fell on the rather unwilling shoulders of the elderly naturalist, Dr. J. K. Hasskarl, colonial botanist. The mission which this scientist undertook was a perilous one. Should it become known that he was seeking to subvert the channels of the chief source of livelihood among the dwellers of the chinchona districts, his life would hang upon a hair. It was understood, moreover, that the Dutch were openly laying plans for chinchona cultivation in Java, and the presence of a Dutch botanist in the Andes would certainly be looked upon with suspicion.

Hasskarl therefore assumed the incognito of a German naturalist, Herr Müller of Cassel, and sailed from Amsterdam in 1852. He crossed Panama during a terrible epidemic of yellow fever and arrived at Callao in Peru on a boat carrying a yellow-fever patient. A drunken port quarantine officer passed the case, and another and even more terrible mosquito-carried disease broke out in the country as an ironic heralding of the approach of Dr. Hasskarl on his vital mission. This scientist, with Dutch astuteness, enlisted the aid of the Peruvian Government itself, for at that time Peru desired exploration of its easterly region which it wished to colonize. He volunteered to return a report upon the natural resources of the country, and by this means he was able at the same time quietly to undertake the collecting of living chinchona trees. Arrived in the forests, after a perilous Andean journey, Hasskarl was faced with the task of collecting his material without arousing suspicion. That he did so is a credit to his tact, while his unerring accuracy in detecting the impostures thrust at him shows his keen scientific ability. He succeeded at last in possessing himself of seeds, which he sent by a trusted envoy to Holland; his seedlings he dispatched in two lots to Panama. It is well that he did not put all his eggs in one basket, for the first consignment died of neglect upon the wharves, but the second was put on board a Dutch merchantman and then in mid-Pacific was transferred to a warship which rushed the precious cargo to Java. As quickly as possible the plants were set out at Tjibodas in the warm, rainy highlands of that island.

It may have been thought the venerable naturalist's labors were over; but practically under compulsion from the Dutch Government he had now to undertake the direction of chinchona culture in Java. The hardships of his journey, the close application to his task of guarding the new plantation, the failure of many of the seedlings, were burdens too heavy for the old man. He returned in broken health to Europe and did not live to realize his dream of writing a botany of the Dutch East Indies. But if Hasskarl gave his life, he at least got blood-money for it. How much more fortunate he was in this regard than his English associates shall appear.

As time went on, the Dutch experiment proved enormously successful. At the present time the Dutch may be said to be practically the only exporters of chinchona in the world. They have about twenty-five thousand acres under plantation, and the quality of the bark they produce is the best.

Unhappy was the fate that followed the collectors of chinchona. Shortly after the return of Dr. Hasskarl, the Dutch thought it prudent to increase their supply and bought from Ledger, an Englishman who had obtained chinchona seeds from Bolivia with infinite difficulty, enough seeds to raise twenty thousand plants for the first year. For this they paid him only $185, with a promise that more would be forthcoming if the seeds grew. They grew as no one had ever dreamed they would. But not a penny more did Ledger ever get. In 1892 he was found living in poverty in New South Wales. After two years of constant petitioning by Sir Clements Markham, director of Kew Gardens, the Dutch, who were reaping millions yearly from chinchona, were persuaded to give Ledger an annual pension of $500. Ledger had given seeds to the Indian Government for nothing. And nothing was his reward, though Sir Clements Markham moved heaven and earth to appeal to the merest instincts of gratitude in the governing classes of India. Markham knocked on the door of an empty house.

But there had been persons in India to whom the quinine question was vital. Lady Canning, wife of the Viceroy of India, had long cherished the dream of establishing the chinchona tree in British India. Nowhere was it more needed than in that malaria-ridden land. When the Sepoy rebellion broke out, the malarial plague, like all others, trailed the camps of the armies and ravaged the land. It was then that Lady Canning was able to interest her government in the introduction of chinchona. Sir Clements Markham was intrusted with the supervision of the task. In April, 1860, taking with him Weir, an English gardener, a native boy and two mules, he started out from Crucero, Peru. At Acco-kunka he met ''a red-faced man about fifty years of age who gave his name as Don Manuel Martel.'' This man said he remembered Hasskarl in 1854 and he ''vowed that if he or any one else ever again attempted to take cascarilla plants out of the country he would stir up the people to seize them and cut their feet off.''

Martel's warning was evidently intended for Markham, whose careful efforts to conceal his mission appear to have been unsuccessful. Then on May 11 the arrest of Markham was commanded by the Alcalde of Quiaca instigated by Martel, whose son brought the order. The arrest exceeded the powers of the Alcalde, and Markham indited a note to this effect and dispatched it to the dignitary. He did not, however, tarry to discuss the Constitution of Peru, but quietly hastened forward with his plants. On the road to Sandia he was met by young Martel and his party. Markham, carrying his revolver in his hand, received civil treatment. He might have met with less respect had they known his weapon was empty.

At Sandia he found the whole neighborhood against him. He was prevented from hiring mules to go anywhere except to Crucero, where Martel was waiting for him. At last, however, he struck a bargain by exchanging his gun for mules. In order to escape Martel at Crucero, Markham then took a short cut. Through the wild, roadless country he went direct to the coast, sending Weir and the Indian boy to Crucero to throw Martel off the scent. The plants nearly froze crossing the Andes. Arrived at the coast of Islay, they were almost lost through an attempt to bribe their night watchman to bore holes in the cases and pour in boiling water.

Having safely transported the plants to India, Markham hopefully set them out. Mistakes were made and failures followed and it was determined to send for more plants. Casting about for aid, Sir Clements Markham recalled that there was at that time approaching the chinchona districts an expert botanist and tropical explorer named Richard Spruce whose botanical specimens were flowing into Kew from untrodden places. Markham sent a commission to Spruce to collect a fresh consignment of seeds and plants from the chinchona forest, and this errand Spruce took up. That he did it only half willingly may be inferred from a statement contained in his journal where he says that "when a plant has been ground to powder in the chemist's mortar, it has lost most of its interest, for *me* at any rate." The description fits chinchona bark very well. Spruce was no economic botanist; in fact, his chief interest was in tropical mosses. But, as it chanced, the moment was one when he was glad of the commission and the money.

While Markham was struggling with the chinchona plantations in India, Spruce was ascending the Amazon from its mouth to its source in a small canoe. Once, while seeking the headquarters of the Orinoco, he fell victim to malaria. In order to obtain a nurse he exchanged his Indian guide for the services of a native woman. She could see at a glance that the Englishman was going to die, so she went into the next room to wait for the end, and there she waited for many days. To her great disappointment, for he had money, the Englishman at last crawled out of his bed and continued his journey. After three thousand miles of travel in the Amazon, he arrived upon a memorable day within sight of the snowy peaks of the Andes. From those long-desired summits there blew at last a cool wind of healing, laden with the perfume of febrifugal forests. In the jungle he left his specimens and much of his kit, for the canoe could ascend no further, and trusting his possessions to his lazy Indian followers he pressed on across the divide. When he arrived in the capital of Ecuador he received Markham's commission to collect chinchona, and without resting from his tremendous journey he set about a fresh expedition to the source of the Jesuit's Bark.

It was no easy task to find a place where the trees

were still abundant. The cascarilleros were careful to conceal these localities, and when they vouchsafed any information it was invariably false. But Spruce was not outwitted, and he selected as the happiest hunting ground no other place than the slopes of Chimborazo, noblest of South American mountains. Having secured the competent aid of two fellow countrymen, Spruce was about to set out on his mission, when he was suddenly stricken deaf —precursor of the more terrible disaster which four days later overtook him. Almost a total paralysis fell upon him, and he had to be carried to the baths of Loja, there to seek recovery. Very slowly his health in part returned, and at the earliest possible moment, though bent practically double, Spruce dragged himself across the Chimborazo range. Through all this painful journey he was keenly alert to every plant, bird and insect, every beautiful view, and to the life of the Indians whom he encountered. He even found the time and strength to discover where lay the lost trail to the mountain lake wherein, as ancient records tell, the Incas sank their treasures to keep them from the Spaniards.

Arrived at last in a splendid forest of chinchona, Spruce found that the fruits were still young, and it was necessary, in spite of his ill health, to await their maturity. He describes the chinchona tree as one of striking nobility. Its glittering foliage and lofty stature made it visible amidst the densest forests. The country in which he found himself was invigorating, and Spruce's task at this point offered many delights.

But soon his errand in that neighborhood became known to the natives and their hostility took the form of mutilating the inflorescences of the trees just as their fruits were maturing. Every inducement, also, to lead him away, was held out. There were promises of larger fields elsewhere, but Spruce was not to be tricked like that unfortunate young man of whom he tells, the ambitious Portuguese youth who was deceived into buying a large quantity of bark. With the prospect of immediate riches he was allowed to marry his employer's daughter, and having borrowed heavily he took the bark to Liverpool. Only there did he learn that his ware was the bark of a tree related to chinchona and resembling it, but worthless as a febrifuge.

Spruce, forewarned by such examples, would not even allow his Indian guides to collect except in his sight. By a timely bit of bribery he got the local authorities to protect the precious inflorescences, and when at last the seeds were set he collected several thousand, and many living seedlings. Then he built a raft and on this he floated his cargo toward the coast. Once in the night the raft ran into snags, and for a few desperate moments it seemed that the fruits of all his labors would be washed away. But Guayaquil was reached at last in safety, and within a short time Spruce was able to vent a sigh of relief as he watched the home-bound ship bearing his prize toward the horizon of the Pacific.

Hardly had his mission been accomplished when fresh disaster overtook the unfortunate man. A reputable banking house in Guayaquil failed when the English cashier embezzled the funds. Spruce lost all his savings. He was left penniless, in broken health, thousands of miles from home. But the intervention of friends enabled him to return to England. He passed the remainder of his life in poverty, able to sit up at his microscope only a few minutes at a time, but devoting all his failing energies to disinterested scientific research. With difficulty Sir Clements Markham persuaded the British East India Company to recognize Spruce's services by a small annuity. The last years of the explorer's life were at least attended with honors. The greatest men of his time journeyed to his bedside for the privilege of a few moments' chat with the wonderful old man.

The chinchona plants were set out upon the Nilgheri hills in India. Their culture, however, was never wholly prosperous, and it became apparent that the wrong station had been selected for them. The undaunted Lady Canning called into conference the leading economic botanists of India and it was decided to send to Java for a fresh consignment of plants. While Lady Canning's emissary, Anderson, was engaged on this mission, she herself was stricken with malaria and died. The Javan enterprise was successful, and the plants were set out in Ceylon, where they have done moderately well.

At the present time India grows the largest part of its consumed product, and quinine can be had at any post office in India at prices possible to the poorest native. The Dutch, however, retain their monopoly and the great wholesale market for chinchona bark is still at Amsterdam. The United States has four important quinine factories and is a heavy consumer of the medicine. But though the Philippines might possibly be a favorable spot for growing the trees, no American has been so farsighted or so bold as to try to divert to his own pocket some of the millions which the Dutch now reap from the forest monarch with healing in its bark.

SUGGESTED READING

MARKHAM, SIR CLEMENTS R., *Peruvian Bark*, 1880. A long book but easy reading; gives information on almost all matters relating to quinine and a host of other subjects pertaining to Peru.

WATT, SIR GEORGE, *The Commercial Products of India*, 1908. See "Chinchona." A pithy account, with much botanical information; includes the story of Lady Canning.

SPRUCE, RICHARD, *Notes of a Botanist on the Amazon and Andes*, ed. Alfred Wallace, 1908. Two volumes, by the great explorer himself, of vivid adventures, containing a splendid and pathetic account of gathering quinine seeds at the foot of Chimborazo.

GORKOM, KARL W. VAN, *A Handbook of Chinchona Culture*, tr. by Benjamin D. Jackson, 1883. Popular account of Dr. Hasskarl and the Dutch expedition to Peru, with much cultural information.

LE WALL, CHARLES H., "The Romance of Drugs," *Am. Journ. Pharm.*, Vol. 96, pp. 266-268, 1924. Brief but entertaining.

WILCOX, EARLEY V., *Tropical Agriculture*, 1916. Chap. XVI, "Drugs." A concise and interesting report on the cultivation of the chinchona tree.

CHAPTER IV

THE AGE OF RUBBER

WHEN Columbus on his first voyage came to Haiti, he beheld there a group of Indians playing with balls that were elastic and bounced wonderfully. The great admiral marveled. Nothing like that had ever been seen in Europe; the Scotchman with his golf ball was not; the lithe English lad at the net did not exist. Now for the first time a white man, Columbus himself, beheld rubber.

To-day the importance of rubber and the variety of its uses are exceeded by nothing, unless it be steel. But steel has given wages to thousands of white men, while rubber has caused the enslavement of millions of red men and black. Listen to the roar of motor traffic in the street—at every moment, at every turn of an automobile wheel, rubber is being worn out. Just so were human lives ground down and worn out to procure it.

Despite the preëminent place in commerce of rubber to-day, a century ago men held it in slight regard. Slowly they learned to put it to its manifold uses. The Spanish conquerors of Mexico acquired from the Indians knowledge of waterproofing their clothes with it. Scientists in their laboratories made bottles and tubing of it. Priestly, the discoverer of oxygen, found that it would erase pencil marks, from which property is derived the word "rubber." But for a long time the exotic substance could find in daily affairs no place of real moment because rubber as it was then known was too sensitive to temperature; at freezing point it became brittle and broke up into granules and at only moderate heat it became sticky and then melted. Under use it wore out rapidly. Then in 1823 Mackintosh began to manufacture waterproof garments from rubber, and the monuments to his name seen on a rainy day have glorified it beyond the power of statues or obelisks. Sixteen years later Goodyear invented vulcanization. He discovered that by combining rubber with sulphur its freezing point was lowered and its melting point heightened so that at all ordinary temperatures it retained its essential properties; in addition to this its durability under wear was vastly strengthened and its elasticity increased.

From the moment that vulcanization became public knowledge the value of rubber leaped forward with a bound. The corners of the earth were ransacked for rubber-yielding plants. Indians and negroes who had never seen a white man now for the first time beheld the palefaces, the rubber prospectors who ventured into every jungle, no matter how miasmic or hostile.

Among the first trees to be tapped was the familiar rubber plant of Main Street bay windows. This darling of the parlor gardener is but a puny thing as grown in northern houses. But in the tropics it is a mighty tree, almost a forest in itself. Seen from a distance it appears to be a lofty grove under whose shadows the houses of men dwindle into insignificance. For, like its relative the banyan tree, it drops from its branches "props" which take root and sprout again, so that an ancient *Ficus elastica* looks like a tree with a hundred stems, or like a grove of trees all grown together. Immense height and immense spread characterize this superb, glittering giant of the vegetable world. In our own country, near Miami, Florida, are specimens twenty-five years old. But these are as nothing compared with the century-old rubbers of India, where the tree is revered and preserved by the generations passing like puffs of smoke beneath its shade. In Bengal and Upper Burma it chiefly flourishes, and there for a long time rubber was collected in quantity. But to-day so many other plants are known to give better and more rubber that *Ficus elastica* is no longer tapped.

Over two hundred species are now being exploited for their rubber. Nearly all plants with milky juice contain more or less rubber, though some contain very little and a great deal of detrimental resin or other adulterants difficult to eliminate. Time has been required to show what plants are most profitable, and in the process of learning by trial and error there have been failures and tragedies and vast national crimes.

Asia, Africa, and the Amazon—these are the world's three sources of rubber, and of these the

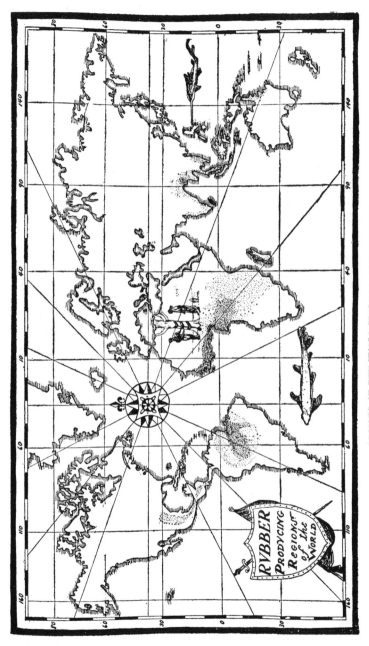

REGIONS OF THE WORLD WHICH PRODUCE RUBBER

blackest past and most unpromising future belongs to equatorial Africa. Only in the last decade of the nineteenth century, while the Great Powers were still scrambling for territory on the dark continent, did men begin to turn their attention to the wild rubbers. A large number of African trees, and more particularly vines, contain the desired latex, so that the whole continent, except the deserts and dry regions offered a field for the new exploitation. At first only small parties of white men with hired native laborers worked the great tropical rain forests. Soon, however, the secrets which the first rubber prospectors had tried to guard leaked out, and the business men of London, Paris, Berlin and Brussels grew alert to the possibilities of a new wealth to be wrung from the hot, forbidding jungles. In the course of the first six months in 1895 the production of Funtumia rubber from the British colony of Lagos increased twenty-five fold. Thousands of negroes, chiefly Fantis, were imported from the Gold Coast to work the trees. But at the end of two years the rubber export of Lagos had declined by a third. The natives, spurred on by greed and without any supervision or restriction, had slaughtered the very flower of the forest. They tapped the trees both at top and bottom in order to get more latex at once, with the result that the trees shortly died. They even cut down the vines and chopped them into bits to get the maximum amount of rubber. By 1897 there remained not a district in the great rubber forests of Ibadan and Jehu but had been completely ruined by the collectors. The colony of

Lagos, which during the rubber boom had undertaken vast public works intended to accommodate an increasing and wealthy population, was so heavily mortgaged that when the slump came it faced ruin. In order to save what remained of the squandered treasure it passed an act forbidding any rubber to be tapped for two years. This mild restriction resulted in benefits no less mild. The curtain had fallen over the glimpse of a glowing future.

Such is the story of West Africa, the underside, as it were, of Africa's great shoulder. Far worse were the events which next transpired, in Central Africa, in the valley of the continent's greatest river. The basin of the Congo had, so far, had a more fortunate history than West Africa which had suffered for three hundred years from slave raiding by Europeans and Arabs. But the English, at first the culprits, had finally put a stop to all that. The Congo basin, more distant, less accessible from the sea, difficult to penetrate, remained still free from the slaver's raids.

And now came the darkest days that cruelty and selfishness had ever blackened for Africa. The Congo Free State was set up as a sort of greater Liberia, a vast sanctuary for the downtrodden African races. This pious act was the idea of Leopold II, King of the Belgians. In appearance the Free State was merely guided and protected by this noble Christian monarch. In reality Leopold ruled the Congo by an unseen authority. White men and native mercenaries did his bidding in the Free State like the slaves they were. His empire, more actually a dictatorship than any other rule in the world, was utterly invisible. It was not recognized openly anywhere in Europe; the masses of the thinking world did not suspect its existence. It was not to be found on paper except in the secret orders issued to the holders of "concessions" in the Congo. It was, in short, nothing but a gigantic money-making conspiracy, intended to squeeze out of the lives of men and trees the millions which Leopold wished to add to his private fortunes and to those of the financiers who could win his favor.

It is now thirty years since that chapter of horror opened, and the echoes of it have almost died away. But it should not be forgotten. Many of the chief actors in the shameful proceedings are still living, and most of the splendid men who, by nothing in the world but moral courage, brought the crimes to an end are yet alive and deserve to be honored. The statements which men like E. D. Morel and Sir Harry Johnston gave to the world concerning the wickedness of Belgian machinations were at first considered incredible, and now that the storm has all but subsided people sometimes regard them as wild exaggerations. But they are probably only too true. It was true that any native village not furnishing, under the name of taxes, a certain quota of rubber and ivory was liable to the flogging or shooting of all its members. It is true that while the men of the village were away on rubber and ivory hunts the "authorities" took all the wives and children as hostages and held them, often in a condition of starvation, until the men could buy them back with the black milk which is rubber and the white bone which is elephants' tusks. It is true that hundreds of thousands of men, women and children had their hands cut off, that women, perpetually chained in files, were used as porters to carry loads of as much as sixty pounds apiece. It is true that the black mercenaries employed to "keep order" were chiefly recruited from the ranks of cannibals, and that when the men of a punished village had all been shot the soldiery were given the women and the children, and it is true that the indecencies, brutalities and mutilations were so unspeakable that they have only two or three times been trusted to print.

Rubber was the cause of the "hand-maimed host." Rubber was the cause of flogging old women to death. Rubber was the cause of the surrendering of children to cannibals. Rubber was the cause of the wealth and splendor of Leopold's palace in Brussels and of his pious gifts to churches. Rubber was the cause of the hushing of every scandal. If there is a hell and any plants grow there, rubber will be the king of them, and Leopold II with the infamous Governor Wahis will be found sitting under its shade.

The Congo reform movement, with its reports, was at first not credited. Then it was blackmailed, threatened and bribed. Then the rubber financiers contended that all these abuses had happened long ago and that the offenders had been punished and their places taken by good men. They said this in 1900. But in 1903 Morel's report, with the most scathing indictments yet issued, appeared and scandalized the world anew. The Belgians continued to declare that it had all happened long ago; "*nous avons changé tout cela.*" But the world would be fooled no longer. In 1909 the Belgian parliament itself denounced the king's influence in the Congo. England and America brought pressure to bear, and at last the infamous structure of Leopold's power crashed about his ears. He did not long survive his defeat. The Congo Free State, too, was declared at an end, and Belgium formally took it over to administer it by upright men of the public service, for whose conduct the government itself stood responsible.

But the great days of the African rubber trade seem drawing to eclipse. Not only are the trees and vines much depleted, but it is becoming apparent, now that time has elapsed sufficient to prove what are the best rubbers, that the Africas, as they are called, are intrinsically inferior to Pará. In addition to this is the drawback that the African native has proved a poor collector. He is incurable in his habit of adulterating the rubber to increase its weight; he cannot learn to keep dirt and bits of wood out of the latex; he cannot be trusted not to cut down trees, not to tap them too often, or tap them from the top. The galling confinement which a rubber collector's life imposes is not so well supported by the negro as by the more industrial half-breed of Brazil.

Considering the unsatisfactory condition of labor and the inferiority of the native rubber, it is difficult to see how Africa can keep step with Brazil

and southeastern Asia. Africa, of course, might try
to plant her own Pará. But in view of the keenness
of competition on the one hand and on the other of
the value of the richer African soils for growing
cotton, cacao and other crops, it is doubtful if this
plan will appeal to the practical investor. Only un-
foreseen turns in the path of Fate can open any
bright prospects for African rubber.

In a rain forest vaster than that of equatorial
Africa, on a river many times larger than the Congo,
the greatest rubber exploitation of the world has,
in the course of only a handful of years, sprung into
being. Brazil, before the rubber boom, had known
the hum of industry only on her Atlantic seaboard
where coffee had formed the backbone of her wealth.
The vast territory of Amazonas had yielded little of
importance save Brazil nuts and precious tropical
timber trees. With the expansion of rubber industrialism in Europe and America and with the discovery that *Hevea braziliensis* of the Amazon yields
the finest of the world's rubbers came the trans-
formation of the great valley. At first the necessary
labor was supplied by enslaving the Putamayo Indians, and slavery, like a black tide, rose up throughout the length and breadth of the Amazon until it
reached Peru, Bolivia, and Ecuador. Under the
poisonous fumes of the rubber-curing camps the red
men wilted and died, or fled to the innermost jungle
and fought desperately for their existence. In order
to obtain labor the rubber exploiters had to send to
the coffee districts of Brazil. At the time there was
a surplus of hands in the neighborhood of Bahia, and

thousands, with promise of better pay, were lured to the Amazon. These men were of a decidedly more intelligent and industrious class than the Indians and were of that hardy if not very refined triple hybrid, the Portugese-Indian-negro. They, it is true, were not exactly enslaved; they came of their own free will and theoretically they are equally free to go, though in reality they often find this impossible. The homesickness of those chained to the land has been the most pitiful, if not the worst feature of the lot of the *seringuero*.

"Seringuero" is the name of a worker of a rubber tract or seringæ. The seringæs of the Amazon all lie along the great river or its tributaries; they are of indefinite depth extending inward parallel to each other, but are narrow, since water frontage is in great demand. The owner of a concession, usually a Portuguese of half- or full-blood, employs a band of laborers to work the seringæ. To each workman he assigns a tract which is marked by means of a rude trail called an *estrada*. The seringuero is responsible for keeping his estradas clear of the swift growing tropical weeds, and on this trail he goes out each day on his round. One hundred and fifty to two hundred and fifty of the larger trees are usually to be found scattered along each estrada. The seringuero goes to each tree making an incision at the base and placing a cup to catch the latex. When he has tapped all the trees he works another estrada and then returns to the first one which by this time is ready to be worked again.

The blow which the seringuero deals the tree is

given with a short heavy ax called a *machadinho,*
which is made of not very sharp iron, steel never
being used because it is regarded as unlucky or poisonous to the tree. If this superstition has any foundation, it is probably the fact that the ignorant
seringuero has not the manual dexterity to use a
sharp steel instrument, which he would drive home
so deeply as to hurt the tree. The splendid tapping
knife used by the British in the eastern rubber plantations was tried out in Brazil and gave, in the hands
of the seringuero, only disastrous results.

The machadinho's blow upon the tree is a broad,
shallow one, upwardly oblique. It is not a clean
cut, as it tends to smash the surrounding tissues so
that the wound has difficulty in healing. As a result,
entrance is given to any of the horde of fungus parasites with which the damp, hot jungle abounds. The
list of diseases to which Hevea is heir is growing
steadily, and attempts to check them are, in the
nature of things, difficult.

When the rubber has been collected, the seringuero
proceeds to coagulate it over a fire. This fire is
generally made from the nuts of the *uracuri* palm,
which as they burn give off an especially creosoty
smoke that enters the rubber and lends to it some
of those properties for which Pará hand-cured
rubber is famous. The seringuero, squatting on his
haunches over the fire, dips a paddle into the cup
of latex, holds the paddle over the fire and slowly
turns it round and round until the rubber is cured.
He then dips again, and with the cured rubber as a
matrix he repeats his actions hour after hour until

he has coagulated a rubber ball of standard size. This process, slow and painful though it is, is largely responsible for the superiority of Amazonian rubber over all others. It is not a method which appeals to those who like to see work performed mechanically, quickly and in a wholesale way. Nor is it a method compatible with health or comfort. The constant squatting, with sunken chest, over the unhealthy fumes of the fire has led to the spread of occupational diseases in an acute form. All sorts of respiratory troubles are prevalent among the seringueros. In addition to the dangers of the curing process must be counted the unhealthy conditions of the forest, hot, wet, fungoid and malarial. The seringuero's house is ill protected from the torrential rains, is set close to the wet earth and during the winter is miserably cold. His food, consisting largely of starch and of canned goods purchased from his employer, is quite insufficient to keep any man strong in such a climate.

Such is the unenviable lot of the seringuero. In his relations to his employer he is hardly more fortunate. From him the seringuero has to buy all his supplies, including food, and on this not only has an exceedingly heavy freightage been charged, but the employer himself often reaps a profit of as much as two hundred per cent. Even at these high rates the seringuero generally manages to buy all necessary supplies. Indeed, during the great rubber boom of 1910 the laborers got so much for their rubber that they bought gramaphones and similar luxuries. But often in a lean year the seringuero cannot afford the food he needs for himself and family—usually a large one. That is quite all right, the employer assures him, his credit is always good. In this way the seringuero is betrayed into debt to his employer, and he is compelled by law to stay and work out the debt. The employer sees to it that he never succeeds. And under this cloak slavery walks abroad in the Amazon.

But the employer, the middle man who sells the rubber to the great exporting firms at Manaos and Pará, is not necessarily fortunate in his dealings. He himself is often mortgaged, body and soul, to the merchants on the coast from whom he procures his supplies. On the other hand, he frequently loses money to the seringueros, for it is a condition of the contract of employment that if the seringuero is sick, food must be provided for him until he gets well. A large number of workers are quite naturally on the sick list all the time. Furthermore, the seringuero frequently steals the rubber and sells it for a good price to the smugglers who ply up and down the backwaters of the rivers picking up this kind of trade. It is difficult to stop this form of stealing, and as yet little has been done to combat it.

In Pará, the one important city at the mouth of the great valley, there prevails a curious mushroom growth. The extremely poor and the extremely rich jostle together. Fortunes are easily made and as readily lost. Speculation, adventure, and competition are in the very atmosphere. By the great steamers it is less than a week to New York and Lisbon and scarcely more to London. Persons from all over the world walk the docks and promenade in the squares, buying, selling, consulting maps, taking passage up the river, or speeding home across the Atlantic. Pará is a frontier city comparable to Kimberley when the diamonds were discovered, or the Klondike when gold was found. In our country at the present time only oil causes the rushes, the booms and slumps, the stealing of claims, the feverish prospecting which accompany the rubber trade of Pará.

If it is true that the Amazon valley is the greatest wild reserve of the world's rubber, it is equally obvious that Brazil is faced with problems which cloud the skies of her future. There are the labor problem, the food problem, the transportation problem, the fungus disease problem, the revenue problem, the problem of competition with the British plantations in the East. As a solution for the labor problem it has been suggested that Hindus, Chinese and Japanese be imported to work the trees, as they have been in British Guiana. Intellectually superior, they ought to be better workers, and if interbred with the indigenous labor, they might harmonize the discordant elements. The trouble with this solution is that human beings cannot be deliberately mated like animals, and that Hindus and Chinese are clannish peoples who regard their blood as superior. And the natives are for a Brazilian Brazil. They no more wish the competition of oriental labor than California wishes it. They will not, in fact, tolerate it.

The food problem, it might seem, could be solved by having the native laborers grow their own vegetables. But in their slaving toil they have no time to do this. It is, moreover, exceedingly difficult to maintain a vegetable garden in a rain forest on account of the incursions of insects that emerge from the surrounding jungle, of nematodes that riddle the soil, and of fierce tropical weeds that spring up over night. A man who maintained a garden there could do little else. Also if the boats did not do a business in carrying food upstream they would lose so much money going up, and would have to charge so much higher rates for the rubber they took down, that the arrangement would work to the detriment of all. As to the transportation question, it might be thought that railroads were the answer. But railroads in the jungles cannot compete with the river which carries boats down by its current.

The Brazilians have often been advised to lift the heavy duty on rubber. But without the duty they cannot afford to pay for the administration and public works of the province, since rubber is the only really rich crop in the Amazonas. That Brazil will at last emerge victor from her difficulties is more than likely. But it does not take an expert to see that her future is full of those cómplex economic and social questions which make the warp and woof of history.

Utterly different in every regard is the picture of rubber culture in southern Asia. After the failure of *Ficus elastica,* it was decided to introduce the best rubber trees of other countries. This was an absolutely novel departure in the history of the trade. It seemed to many English capitalists incredible that rubber could ever be profitably grown. There were to be considered the cost of suitable agricultural land, the cost of planting, the years of waiting for return on the investment and the eternal cost of labor. Could British planters compete on such a basis with Brazil, where the trees grew wild on land needed for nothing else, where there was no need to wait for trees to come into bearing, and where labor cost a song; or could Africa with its slave labor be rivaled? A century earlier no one would have believed it possible; but the Dutch had pointed the way by showing that they could successfully compete with wild resources by plantations of chinchona, spices, oil palm and other vegetable treasures which formerly no one had dreamed of cultivating.

About 1875 the Indian Government sent Wickham to the Amazon to investigate Pará, Caucho, and Ceara rubber, and to bring back seeds and plants. The greater part of the material was sent to Ceylon and the rest to Singapore. The first to get a start was Ceara rubber. The coffee industry in Ceylon had just gone bankrupt, owing to the ravages of a fungus disease. Planters were pulling out their coffee and looking for something to put in its place. Ceara rubber was tried. But its yield was disappointingly poor and the price of rubber just then was low. Then in the Nineties Pará rubber, which had given poor results at first, was found to yield beyond expectation, and the few seeds available in the botanic gardens of Ceylon were knocked off for high prices at auction. More seeds were sent for, vast acreage was planted, and just as the trees came to bearing age (which happened sooner than had been forecast), the price of rubber commenced to soar. From that day to this Pará rubber has enjoyed favor in Ceylon, Bengal, the Malay Peninsula, French Indo-China, Java and Sumatra.

There has developed now a special class of East Indian rubber tappers, well paid, intelligent, and organized. They live in decent sanitary houses, cultivate their own gardens, buy food and clothing from private firms and tradesmen like the free men they are. The system of collection which they are taught to practice is in complete contrast with that used by the Brazilian seringuero; the incisions are not made by the heavy, bruising blow of an ax, but with a small hand knife of very sharp steel which makes, by an easy slice, a clean, precise cut which is as different from the opening in a Brazilian tree as a surgeon's cut from a shell wound. Trees are tapped regularly and left to grow untouched two years out of every three. Under plantation conditions the trees have no other growth to contend with for light and room, are freer of wound diseases, and may be tapped when two years old.

In short, the plantation condition of rubber in the East is what is generally called "model." Even the occupational diseases incident to the curing of rubber in Brazil are eliminated here by the use of acetic acid for coagulating the latex in tanks, instead of by the slow, painful, smoky handwork of the South American laborer.

With all these advantages, it might be supposed that plantation rubber would drive from the market the Brazilian trade, with all its evils and the rot at its core. But actual experience has shown that Brazilian Pará is essentially better than plantation Pará. For this a variety of causes has been assigned, such as the climate and soil conditions of the countries which plant their rubber, the early age at which the plantation trees must be tapped in order to meet expenses, and the poor coagulation properties of the acetic acid method as compared with the slow, careful system of smoking used in Brazil. This last point probably best tells the story. Slow, difficult and unhealthy the Brazilian method may be, but it is, so to speak, handwork; it gives an artisan product. The rapid, cheaper, healthier mechanical method employed in the East does not cure so well. Among other faults it produces an absolutely dry rubber, which is to say a poorer rubber, while the Brazilian cured rubber contains precisely the right amount of natural moisture. For all the finer uses of rubber, such as surgical supplies or inner tubes, in which great strength must be combined with extreme thinness and elasticity, only Brazilian Pará will do. This problem the plantations face. But ingenuity, sanitation and system are certain in the end to hold their own against the slipshod methods of wild rubber exploitation.

Such was the state of rubber production in the first decade of our century. And then came the terrible years of 1914 to 1918. In the course of a few months the curve of rubber consumption leapt skyward like a rocket. Automobiles, trucks, airplanes, submarines and all the trappings of war demanded rubber. The Allied nations easily kept in touch with the great tropical lands which furnished the indispensable commodity. Not so Germany and her allies. Shorn of the tropical colonies producing rubber, and supplied with domestic reserves sufficient to last but a year under peace-time conditions, they faced a crisis. The high councils at Wilhelmstrasse knew that they could no more carry on without rubber than without steel or coal. To seize it from the enemy or to buy it from Brazil was impossible—their hands were held. They were ringed with the iron wall of France and England.

Yet it was apparent to the Allies that throughout the four years of war Germany was managing to produce rubber. Some believed that the Germans were getting it from plants indigenous to the Kaiser's domains. The spindle-tree, Sicilian artichoke, sowthistle and a few others, had been suggested by the Germans before the War as possible sources in time of need. These species do indeed yield varying amounts of the precious latex, and the sow-thistle and artichoke can be cultivated intensively and harvested easily. But the amount of detrimental resin which accompanies the rubber of sow-thistle is so large that it is doubtful if the extraction of its rubber could ever be profitable. When the botanists of Berlin and Munich had marshaled every plant in the Emperor's realm which could be made to yield a drop of rubber, they had nothing to show but an assemblage of unprofitable weeds—a ragged company when compared to the great trees of the tropics flowing with the precious milk.

And yet, to the puzzlement of the Allies, the Germans were producing rubber. Since their defeat they have come forward with the explanation. They have told how they synthesized rubber in the laboratory—told all but one detail of the story. This last link is a guarded secret.

The great German chemists—and at the opening of the War Germany enjoyed a Golden Age of chemistry—set themselves to conquer the most difficult problem in applied science that had ever confronted them. How easy it appears from the empyrical formula to synthesize rubber! All you have to do is to combine ten atoms of carbon with sixteen of hydrogen, and there you have rubber! But to get them to combine, and in those proportions—there was the difficulty. The attempt had been made repeatedly, but the substance evolved always lacked either the elasticity, the waterproof property, or the vulcanizing power of real rubber. The only success achieved had been due to the admixture of more or less natural rubber. And of this the German supply was exhausted.

The first composite which the chemists of Germany turned out they called methyl rubber, but by the common soldier it was known as "war rubber." It could be cheaply manufactured, but it deteriorated so rapidly under use that it was soon discarded as hopeless. At his great factory at Leverküsen, Hoffmann made a new product, a piperidine rubber, as it was called. This time the artifact proved durable enough, but it was neither soft nor elastic. Still, so hard pressed was von Tirpitz for rubber, which was especially in demand for the great submarine fleets, that he accepted the makeshift. Hoffmann later evolved an improved form of this product, and claimed that it was as soft and elastic as Pará rubber and 20 per cent more efficient as an insulator of electrical currents. The results of testing this underseas were so satisfactory that the Imperial Government ordered the manufacture of it on a large scale.

It was all very well to talk about a large scale, but where were the materials to come from? Two things were indispensable, acetone and aluminum. Acetone, before the War, had previously been procured almost wholly from America, where it was manufactured from acetate of calcium. In looking about for a substitute source, the Germans decided upon the acetate of gray lime which it derived from the distillation of beech wood. The beeches of Germany and Hungary are famous for their beauty. The most mechanistic of the Germans must have regretted this shearing of Freya's hair, the crowning golden glory of northern forests. But the stern necessity of war drove home the ax, and the ancient beeches fell.. The only trouble with this source of supply was that the beeches of the Central Powers were scarcely sufficient, even if every tree were sacrificed, to meet the War's demands. For the big guns called for acetone, too, for their ammunition, and consequently the rubber makers had to look elsewhere for larger sources of supply.

Now the chemist went to the other extreme of the vegetable kingdom and called upon a microscopic organism. *Bacillus macerans,* which is found in rotten potatoes and can be grown in such a culture, possesses the power of converting alcohol into the acetone which was so much needed. This novel ally was summoned to the German's aid. But the difficulty here was that the bacterial action fluctuated violently and could not be controlled, and that potatoes were getting steadily scarcer.

Previous to the War Dubosc, a Frenchman, had shown how to produce acetic acid from acetylene. To get acetone it was only necessary to add calcium carbide, which could be manufactured in quantity. When the Germans tried this their problem was solved—as it happened by the researches of their foes. By the close of the War six hundred tons of acetone a month were turned out of the great laboratories.

But throughout the War the question of obtaining aluminum in quantity remained difficult. The airplanes laid special claim to it and consumed it rapidly. As a substitute for copper it was called for on every hand. Great ingenuity was displayed in obtaining it from the earth but the supply never met the demand.

But despite these endeavors, there remained to the synthesis of rubber the obstacle of slowness. How the Germans overcame this difficulty they refuse to disclose, but we have their word for it that it is a highly ingenious method. They have also repeatedly told us that the final product was in every way excellent. But whenever a captured airplane or submarine with German synthetic rubber upon it fell into Allied hands, the rubber did not fulfill the

German's claim for it. Quite evidently its vulcanizing powers were poor and it had not good properties of endurance.

It is generally admitted that the theoretical problems of synthesizing rubber were solved by the Germans during the War. But it was strictly a war-
time process and it has no practical value in peace.
The best proof of this is that the Germans have not
been able to continue the business. German synthetic camphor and German synthetic dyes are back
in the market after their eclipse of four years. But
German synthetic rubber is dead. It is too expensive.
Only the acute demand which war entailed enabled
the Germans to afford such a costly process.

On the Allied side of the trenches very little attempt was made to find rubber substitutes and none
at all to synthesize it. Natural rubber rose in price,
but it was still plentiful. To be sure, an interest in
the native rubbers of the United States developed.
It was plain that we would do as well to render our-
selves self-sufficient in this regard as in others. Our
government and various research institutions became
interested in wild rubber-yielding plants. As a
whole, we are more amply provided with them than
Europe, due chiefly to the presence in our flora of a
large number of that miscellany of plants called
"milkweed." It has been rumored that Edison has
gone to work on the problem of producing rubber
from milkweeds. The prestige of his name leads
many to believe that whatever he tries to do he will
accomplish; others doubt that even an Edison could
get enough rubber from milkweeds to compete with

the product of the forest kings of the Amazon. Whether or not this be so, is hard at this early date to say. But surely it is worth while to make the effort.

There is this to be said for milkweeds; they are herbaceous. In this country where hand labor is so expensive, we could not afford to collect and cure rubber by the difficult process by which the seringuero works, even if we grew tropical rubber trees, which quite surely we cannot do. We must have a rubber crop that will be a field crop, to be sown and harvested by machinery, if it is to be a money-making proposition. Moreover, no crop will succeed on any land which will support a better-paying crop equally well. If a rubber crop in this country is to be commercially exploited, it will have to be one which grows on poor soil where more profitable crops will not grow; and it will have to be one which grows fast and can be planted and harvested wholesale. Under present conditions other schemes are merely visionary.

There is one exception, and that is the case of the plant which yields guayule rubber. This composite, *Parthenium argentatum,* is a shrub of the desert areas of Mexico, and of Texas, New Mexico and Arizona. Guayule has had a peculiar history. It, too, was used for rubber balls by the Indians; their method of extracting it was to chew the plant. By thus breaking open the latex-bearing ducts, and by the admixture of saliva and the churning motion of mastication, they coagulated the latex into rubber. Samples of this prehistoric masticated rubber are frequently found in Mexico and our own south-western states, and are preserved in museums.

The plant from which guayule came was not, how-ever, even collected by a botanist until J. M. Bigelow discovered it in the famous Mexican Boundary Sur-vey of 1852. Not until 1904 did a clever American, William A. Lawrence, undertake the extraction of rubber from this shrub. His process was mastica-tion on a huge scale—not, to be sure, by employing thousands to chew it, but by macerating and coagu-lating it in huge mixing machines. The difficulties which have stood in the way of perfecting this ma-chinery have been discouraging, but after repeated trials success now seems assured.

Guayule is being exploited on an increasing scale. The difficulty has been that it must be hand gathered; for this purpose peon labor is generally employed. The crude methods by which the unintelligent gather-ers proceed have led to a dangerous waste. Instead of merely cutting the plant back and taking the stems and leaves, which allows the plant to spring up again the following season and permits a perpetual harvest, the peons pull it up by the roots because this requires no skill, although it is probably as much or more work. As a result, guayule is being extermi-nated in many places where formerly it was abun-dant. A more hopeful aspect of the case is the start which Americans have given to guayule by its culti-vation. As it takes readily to desert soils of little value for growing other things, it meets a prime re-quirement of an American rubber crop. There have been difficulties in the way of plantation guayule, but one by one we are overcoming them. Taken all in all, guayule is, at the present moment, America's "best bet" for a rubber crop.

Dr. Hall of California has made an interesting step in trying to bring some of the desert milkweeds into cultivation. As field crops they may prove even more successful than guayule. They yield also a fiber, both in the bast cells of their stems and from the silky down of their seeds, which may well prove a strong argument for their culture. *Asclepias subulata,* the plant which Hall recommends as furnishing the best all around prospects of American success, after three years growth can be harvested annually and perhaps even twice a year. Three hundred to five hundred pounds of rubber could be produced per acre. No attempt has yet been made to improve the rubber-bearing properties by selection, as has been done with Pará rubber, for instance. Such an improvement would be the first step in the profitable cultivation of desert milkweed, if its rubber content is to be raised above the present average of 3.1 per cent.

These experiments, sketchy as they have been, are the first signs of an intelligent attitude toward the upbuilding of a home-grown rubber industry. Many persons are utterly skeptical, but after all the experiment is barely begun. Not one plant in one hundred of the American species with milky juice has been tested.

The most recent aspect of the American rubber industry is the realization that American interests in the great tropical fields have been quite neglected.

The feeling is becoming prevalent that English capital has the rubber of the world largely in its hands. Our own country has no large tropical possessions which can produce rubber except the Philippine Islands. In the light of this state of affairs, Congress recently appropriated a large sum for the purpose of furthering American rubber interests, first by the study of the present market situation, secondly by a survey of rubber plants and production.

Such is the momentary status of rubber. It is in the position of most other crops ten thousand years ago—still gathered from the wild, since the planted crop has not yet driven the wild rubber from the market, still fluctuating violently in price, subject to booms and panics, barely emerging from a stage in which its exploitation has meant slavery, waste, and occupational ills.

When the wild sources of rubber become exhausted, a new order will prevail. And they will certainly be exhausted. When one and two hundred years ago Americans attacked the priceless treasure of the world's greatest temperate forest with ax and fire, they justified themselves by saying that our forests were inexhaustible. Now, in a mere tick of time, we are left with nothing but a pitiful remnant of what we once possessed. With the demand for rubber doubling and tripling, is it not foolhardy to think of the wild resources as inexhaustible?

When wild rubber is gone the plantation system will reign supreme. Then rubber will evolve out of the barbarous stage in which it finds itself to-day and, like timber production in Europe, will become the subject of forestry, or it may, as has been suggested in the case of milkweed, take a place in temperate agriculture. With these changes, it will relinquish its shameful rule in the realms of destructive exploitation, of slavery, and of profiteering and establish itself in the heart of civilized life. If mechanical invention and industrial expansion progress as they promise to do, rubber consumption will increase in a ratio that staggers imagination. Steadily and inevitably rubber is mounting the steps to a throne among the mighty powers of industry and history.

SUGGESTED READING

WILLIS, J. C., *Exploitation of Plants,* ed. by F. W. Oliver, 1917, Chap. IV, "Tropical Exploitation with Special Reference to Rubber." The most concise, lucid and suggestive of all the references. Deals with historical, cultural and industrial phases.

MOREL, E. D., *Affairs of West Africa,* 1902, and *Red Rubber,* 1906, introd. by Sir Harry Johnston. These books exposing the crimes of rubber production in Africa did much to bring on the Congo reform movements.

SPENCE, D., *The Rubber Industry,* ed. by Joseph Torrey and A. Staines Maunders, 1914. Introduction "Historical and Descriptive." Concise and packed with information on the conditions of Amazon life contrasted with the East Indian plantations.

LLOYD, F. E., "The Guayule—A Desert Rubber Plant," *Pop. Sci. Month.,* Vol. 81, pp. 313–330, 1912. *Guayule, a Rubber Plant of the Chihuahuan Desert,* Carneg. Inst., Wash., 139, Vol. 8, p. 213. The first

THE AGE OF RUBBER 79

reference is a popular, the second a more technical account of the American rubber shrub.

Dubosc, A., "Le Synthèse du caoutchouc en Allemagne," *Caoutchouc et gutta-percha*, Vol. 16, pp. 1055-1056, 1919. One of the few accounts of the secret German war rubber. The publication may be difficult to procure in this country except in college chemical libraries and the Library of Congress.

Hall, Harvey M., and Frances Long, *Rubber Content of North American Plants*, Carnegie Inst., Wash., 1921; *A Rubber Plant Survey of Western North America*, 1919. Technical studies in wild rubber crops of America; the summaries are simple in diction and important as generalities.

Wilcox, Earley V., *Tropical Culture*, 1916, Chap. XIII. "Rubbers and Gums." Authoritative and most readable accounts of history, varieties, and processes.

CHAPTER V

THE FIVE O'CLOCK CUP

"WHICH will you have," asks your afternoon hostess, bending over the three shining urns, "tea, coffee, or chocolate?"
Which shall it be, chocolate, divine drink of the Aztecs, the *chocolatl* of which Montezuma quaffed fifty cups a day? Or tea, that fragrant essence of the East, recalling with its faint bouquet, as only odors can, the thoughts of sages and the talk of almond-eyed maidens of far away and very long ago. Or shall it be coffee, black as the dark continent from whence it first came, coffee that should, as Talleyrand said, be

> *Noir comme le diable,*
> *Chaud comme l'enfer,*
> *Pur comme un ange,*
> *Doux comme l'amour.*

To-day all three drinks enjoy a universal popularity in America, though as a general thing men take coffee, women tea, and the children chocolate. In England and Russia tea is the drink; in Arabia and Turkey coffee reigns supreme; while in Spain and many a Spanish country chocolate holds sway.

It is not precisely by accident that European races

have chosen their beverages as they have. The dominance of England in the tea trade with China and India is quite reason enough why tea is the national drink. The Arab contact with Abyssinia, where coffee grows wild, has, as the Arabs would say, Arabified the darker drink. Stout Cortez it was who gave to Spain "the drink of the gods," the sacred *chocolatl*.

Prescott has painted for us the picture of the Emperor of the Aztec Court, tossing off his half-a-hundred daily cups of chocolate. He drank from a golden cup and stirred his drink with a tortoise-shell spoon. A corps of servants was at hand to prepare the mixture, dropping the pellets of chocolate into the cup, pouring on the water, macerating the chocolate with a sort of swizzel stick, and beating it to a froth before it was passed to the royal lips.

Attractive as the picture sounds, it must be said, with respect for historical truth, that Montezuma drank down this mixture stone cold, generally without sweetening but with the addition of vanilla, green peppers, or some other hot spice. And so we see that Aztec chocolate was as different from our chocolate as is their art from ours. To us their drink seems barbarous; to them ours would probably have appeared as a positive perversion of their national beverage.

We are asked by a Spanish chronicler to believe that the royal household consumed about 2,744,000 *fanegas* of cacao pods a year, half again as many bushels. This would be almost as much as the entire world consumption at the present time. We are not obliged to credit this statement, but it leaves us with a lively impression of the importance of chocolate in Montezuma's life.

Towns paying tribute to Montezuma gave chocolate as well as precious skins and feathers, shells, balsams, resins, perfumes, corn, pepper and quills of gold. From Soconusco in Guatemala two hundred bales were set down in *The Book of Tributes* as the required tax, together with four hundred cups for drinking chocolate. It is remarkable that to-day the chocolate of Soconusco is considered the finest in the world—so fine indeed, and so rare, that only a few great experts and connoisseurs know it.

It is difficult to account for the various grades of chocolate, the inner circles of excellence, except by a study of the botany of the genus Theobroma, which Linnæus, father of botany, so named because it means "Drink of the Gods." There are several wholly distinct species involved, but most of the commercial chocolate of to-day comes from *Theobroma cacao.* Cacao, too, is a Mexican word, and our word cocoa is merely a corruption of it, but it is properly interpreted to mean a special kind of chocolate—the pulverized seeds from which the nutritious but heavy fats have been extracted. Cacao should not be confused with *coca,* sacred plant of the Incas (*Erythroxylon coca*) from which we derive cocaine, nor with coconut, the palm of a thousand uses which Dr. Johnson insisted on spelling "cocoanut," to subsequent confusion.

But by whatever name it is called, the chocolate

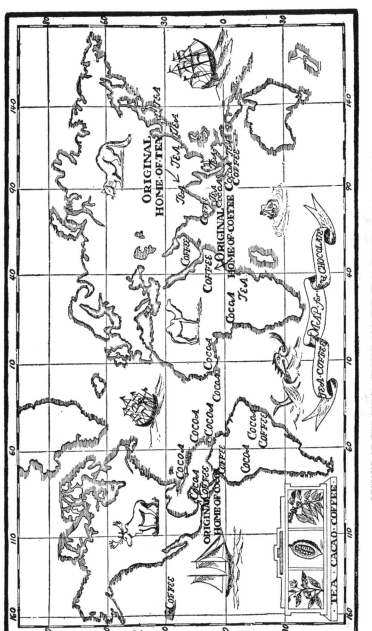

REGIONS OF THE WORLD WHICH PRODUCE TEA, COFFEE AND CHOCOLATE

tree is strangely fascinating, for its flowers burst forth from the trunks of the trees and later the long rugged pods, looking almost like squashes, hang from the boles as fantastically as though they had been nailed there.

It is not the privilege of most of us to gaze upon the chocolate tree, although the visitor to the famous old experimental gardens of the Department of Agriculture, on Brickell Avenue, Miami, Florida, may see a few. But what are these to the wondrous groves of chocolate in the true tropics, where for a thousand years the Indian has toiled and gathered the strange pods, and beat them upon the *metate,* the flat stone table. "She who sells prepared cacao," says Ximenes, Franciscan chronicler of things Mexican, "grinds it first in this way, breaks or pounds the kernels; the second time grinds it more, and the third time grinds it finer still, mixing it with grains of corn, cooked and washed, and this being done adds a little water in a jar. If a small quantity is added it makes a rich cacao, if too much no foam results, and in order to produce the very best it is made and preserved as follows:

"Namely, it is strained and after straining it is lifted in order to drain; foam is formed, and is set aside and the remainder sometimes becomes very thick, and water is added after grinding.

"The one who knows how to make it well, sells it good and fine, that only the Señores drink it; it is soft, foamy, brown-red and pure, without much paste. Sometimes they add aromatic spices and even honey from bees, and some rose water, but the cacao that is not good has much sediment and water and does not make any foam but only froth."

In ancient Mexico chocolate beans passed as currency; twenty beans were the smallest unit of purchasing power; four hundred made a *tzontle,* or eight of the smallest units; twenty *tzontles* made one *xiquipilli,* and so on through a long and unpronounceable system. It is said that on the Mosquito Coast of Panama chocolate beans are still passed as money. There is no real reason why they should not be, since if not too old they could perfectly well be sold for use. Beans of an inferior kind have been used in Mexico as alms for the poor.

Astute and economical were those good monks who gave chocolate beans instead of Spanish gold. Yet the Church at one time took a stand against chocolate. It is said that the Spaniards became so enamored of chocolate drinking, and in particular the Señoras of Chiapas that they would have it brought to them in the middle of the church service by their maid servants. The Bishop of Chiapas was shocked by this irreverence, since chocolate was not a drink mentioned in the Bible, and he exhorted his sisters to better piety. This proving vain, he forbade the custom. But a higher official of the Church, being himself perhaps a chocolate drinker, is said very subtly to have defended the drinking of chocolate during worship—how it is not now quite clear. At any rate the custom went on and it is said the Bishop of Chiapas was poisoned for his pains.

And there were others who sought to check the

rising favor toward chocolate. José de Acosta in 1614 wrote of it for European readers in this wise: "The chief use of cocoa is a drincke which they call Chocolate, whereof they make great account, foolishly and without reason, for it is loathsome to such as are not acquainted with it, having a skumme or frothe that is very unpleasant to taste, if they be not conceited thereof. . . ."

When Drake and Frobisher and their fellow pirates the Dutch fell upon the Spanish ships returning home with the ingots of the Aztecs, they were disgusted to find a large part of the cargo made up of bales of chocolate beans, and threw them into the ocean with epithets such as only sailors know.

The Infanta Maria Theresa, when she came as a Spanish princess in 1660 to wed the King of France, brought chocolate with her, carried by her Spanish confessors on whom the French looked with much suspicion, but in spite of prejudice she popularized the drink of the gods.

In England the first chocolate house was opened at Queen's Head, Bishopgate Street, London, in 1657, the same year that the first tea house appeared, and by seven years later the drink was thoroughly popularized. In that year, November 24, Pepys records: "To a coffee house to drink jocolatte, very good." By 1673 chocolate was the rage of the moment. "A lover of his country," one of the sort that delights to write ponderous sentiments to the papers, contributed to a periodical an article full of cant patriotism, demanding the prohibition of chocolate, as well as tea, brandy and rum, because the English spent good British gold on these foreign products instead of patronizing the home industries. Frederick the Great prohibited its use or importation in Prussia—why is not clear except that he opposed most innovations except the potato.

Despite every opposition chocolate has won its way over the earth on sheer merit. It contains the same stimulating alkaloids that tea and coffee have, but it is nourishing beside, which tea and coffee are not. In fact of the three great drinks chocolate is the only one that can lay claim to being a real food.

The greatest consumers of chocolate in the world are the Americans. Crude cocoa came to America at first, and was exchanged for fish by Gloucester fishermen trading with the West Indies. The following advertisement in the *Boston Gazette and Country Journal* for March 12, 1770, was the first indication of the future greatness of the chocolate trade in this country:

> To be sold by John Baker
> At his store in Back Street,
> a few bags of the best Cocoa,
> also choice Chocolate by the
> Hundred or smaller Quantity.

Such was the origin of the well-known firm that displays as its stamp the quaint painting, *La Belle Chocolatière.*

To-day chocolate is grown all around the Gulf of Mexico except in the United States, on the West Coast of Africa (a most inferior grade), in Ceylon, the Dutch East Indies, and in Polynesia, as one may note from the letters of Robert Louis Stevenson, who grew chocolate trees himself.

One island off Africa, the Portuguese possession of Sao Tome, is famous for its chocolate, where the story of the tree mingles with a dark tale of slavery. Labor conditions in the chocolate and palm oil groves of the island have been the subject of a special investigation on behalf of the negroes. Chocolate is one of those products which serve to remind us that slavery is common to-day in the dark corners of the earth.

The last great epoch in the story of chocolate is the invention of modern refined cocoa, which came in 1828 and is primarily an American drink. When made with water it forms a dilute beverage almost as thin as coffee or tea, as part at least of the substance actually goes into solution, instead of being merely solid particles in suspension as chocolate is. Undiluted cocoa is probably about as stimulating as chocolate, and certainly far less fattening, but cocoa in a diluted form is often given preference in the diet of children, because of the ease with which it may be digested. Certainly one cannot imagine giving to babes a cup of chocolate as the Spanish take it —as thick as molasses and more indigestible than a box of candy. Yet to the gourmet and the real connoisseur of chocolate, good chocolate means Spanish chocolate. And truth to tell you have not tasted chocolate till you know it as the Spanish serve it— even though you do not care to repeat the performance. You are drinking chocolate then, although not until the coming of the Spanish was the hot drink invented, in a form approaching the original draught which Montezuma quaffed from a golden goblet.

It produces a whimsical contrast to turn from chocolate, the almost sacred plant of the Aztecs, to coffee, which found its first use among Caucasians as a method of staying awake during religious ceremonials. Yet the fifteenth century Arabs who so employed it confess to this themselves. Legend will have it that the nature of coffee was first discovered when Abyssinian sheep browsed on the leaf and became so excited that they could not sleep that night. However that may be, *Coffea arabica* is a misnomer and might more precisely have been *Coffea abyssinica,* for coffee is native to that mysterious land whence come so many other fragrant shrubs, myrrh and frankincense above all.

It is strange that the Egyptians, who had considerable knowledge of Abyssinia, Ethiopia and Somaliland, where coffee grew wild, knew nothing of it. They traded in the incense plants of the lands, but either the natives of those lands and times knew nothing of the properties of the coffee shrubs or the Egyptians were not interested. It is most likely that the negroes never drank coffee; some tribes there are that merely chew the seeds.

It is most likely to some Arab trader, traversing the highlands of Abyssinia, that we owe the most sustaining of all nonalcoholic beverages. Chance or whimsical experiment taught him to brew an extract of the curious "bean." Good fellowship induced him to pass the secret to other men. And so it was that coffee made the pilgrimage to Mecca, to the delight of all the Faithful that were a little inclined to drowse during too long excerpts from *Al Koran*.

It is easy to believe that the orthodox were horrified, not so much that their brethren required a stimulant to keep them awake as that a barbaric drink should even touch the outer garments of sacred ritual. The Arabs, having no word for coffee, called it by a word that meant wine, and Mohammed had expressly forbidden wine to all the sons of Allah. It took some elaborate exegesis on the part of Mussulman theologians to get around this point, and Ahmed III tried to exterminate the mushroom crop of coffeehouses.

But in the end coffee triumphed through the dominions of the Crescent and to-day Mocha coffee, genuine Arabian Mocha, is the finest in the world, though it is claimed that not one American in many thousand has ever tasted one drop of the precious article. The production of this brand is extremely limited, and the demand for it in Turkey and Egypt is probably sufficient to consume every grain of genuine Mocha that grows. We drink what we are pleased to call Mocha, however, and as by that we mean a very fine grade of coffee we have assuredly small reason to grumble.

Perhaps were we offered a cup of Mocha as the Arab makes it we would even turn up our noses. For the coffees of the Near East require a strong stomach. They have spread into Greece quite naturally, and one may sometimes taste them in Greek restaurants in this country—served very hot and blacker than night, in tiny cups of which fully one half is solid coffee grounds, the upper part being half liquid and half grounds. Your Greek waiter, if he should see you surreptitiously trying to pour a little sugar into this dense brew, will snatch away the bowl with a shocked expression. It is worse, to him, than mixing water with fine old champagne. Under the name of drip coffee this general style of coffee is known in the old French quarter in New Orleans. And though one may not be used to such a drink, may even in fact find it repulsive at first, there is no denying that drip coffee wins the hearts of all who try it more than a few times. Just as Spanish chocolate and jasmine tea are the pick of the connoisseur, so the Turkish style of serving coffee does really give one a bouquet, a delicate, delightful, aromatic flavor which no other coffee can. This lies not so much in the superiority of the grade of coffee itself as in the mode of preparation. One feels inclined to sip at a little demi-tasse of Turkish coffee, to reflect on life, to talk lazily with one's host or guest—one feels that the tongue may be loosened and epigrams, witticisms and sage thoughts flow from the lips. One despises the ordinary watery cup that appears at breakfast, hastily made, hastily gulped before the commuter's train is caught, adulterated as it is with cream and sugar.

All these things one thinks—and then when bedtime comes one thinks of them again, and thinks and thinks. When dawn breaks after a sleepless night one is resolved never to touch the terrible brew again unless preparing to sit through a continuous performance of "Parsifal."

In this particular form it is probable that coffee first reached Europe, when coffeehouses opened in Constantinople, then Venice, then Marseilles—following the great trade routes by which so many strange products of the gorgeous East have entered Europe.

In 1672 an Armenian named Pascal opened the first Parisian coffeehouse, the haunt of the chess players. We may well believe *they* needed something to keep them awake. For fame no coffeehouse, perhaps, has ever surpassed Procope's establishment in the Rue des Fosses at Saint Germain, where gathered the ponderous Boileau, witty La Fontaine of the "Fables," Molière the uproarious, and Voltaire of the kind, cynical eyes who swept in his train the whole chattering flock of the Encyclopædists.

If Procope's house ever had a rival it could only have been that one where there foregathered Addison and Steele, those princely journalists, and Pope and Dryden, big men in a little age. The first London coffeehouse, however, was not this one, but another that opened in 1652 in St. Michael's Alley, when coffee sold for seven shillings a pound.

Coffee, like every innovation, has had its opponents, and Charles II looked on the coffeehouses as "hotbeds of seditious talk and slanderous attacks upon persons in high stations," meaning presumably himself. Persons who frequented the coffeehouses he anathematized, declaring that they "devised and spread abroad divers false, malicious and scandalous reports to the defamation of His Majesty's government and to the disturbance of the peace and quiet of the nation.'' Somehow the coffee shop survived, however, outliving even the displeasure of Louis XIV, though Louis XV defended coffee for love of Du Barry, whose delight it was. ''Racine and coffee will pass,'' wrote Madame de Sévigné of the rage for the young dramatist who had ousted the old Corneille from the seat of the mighty, and of the drink that was becoming almost more popular than French wine. As well might it have been said, ''Shakespeare and tobacco will pass,'' and no doubt in Elizabethan times in England there were many who thought just that.

Presumably coffee was one of the items in the universe of proscriptions in Puritan America, and certainly it cut no such figure even by Revolutionary times as did tea. It was not till 1833 that the first coffee mill was erected in this country, on what is now Washington Square, New York City. With time, however, coffee has become our drink. To-day the United States is the great coffee-consuming country in the world. We use one half the coffee in the world, and in the consumption per person we are exceeded only by Norway, Sweden and Holland, where the coffeepot brews daylong upon the back of the stove. Our supply comes chiefly from Brazil and Hawaii.

In sharp contrast stand out our neighbors to the north, the Canadians, who use less than a pound of coffee a year per person. The same is approximately true of all the white population in the British Empire, except South Africa, where the Dutch element throws the balance from tea to coffee once more.

When once coffee had firmly taken root in the popular taste, men began to wonder why Arabia should be allowed to produce all the crop, and in the centuries when the European nations were building their great empires the coffee plant was carried all over the tropical world. The Portuguese gave coffee to Ceylon, the Dutch brought it to the East Indies, the French to the West Indies. It is said that only two plants of the French shipment survived, and that from those two have been bred and inbred all the coffee trees of the Caribbean and Brazil. If this tale is true there have seldom been so many culti- vated descendants from a pair of parent plants, for to-day Brazil produces more coffee than all the other countries in the world put together.

Coffee is to Brazil what cotton is to our South, or corn to the Middle West. Coffee and business de- pression or inflation go together. Coffee keeps alive the banks, it runs the "great steamers white and gold that go rolling down to Rio"; it makes of Brazil a mighty empire. As nothing are her gold, her diamonds, her rubber forests and her precious stands of rosewood compared with the little red berries nodding among the shiny green leaves—the great coffee plantations of mountain slope and plain.

But the Brazilian grasp on coffee is of recent origin. Time was when Java led in the world's coffee production, and for a brief period it seemed as if Ceylon was to be the chief home of the potent berry.

A tragic story that, of a climate perfectly suited
to coffee, plenty of working capital, intelligent supervision, industrious native labor at cheap rates, a
clamoring market. And then came a microscopic foe.
Man is generally supposed to rule the world. But
he has many betters. The coffee leaf disease, related to wheat rust, proved one of them. It broke
out, no one knows how, in 1880, a tiny, rusty, leprous
spot upon the leaves, that sapped the life of the
foliage and brought it withered to the ground.
To-day the value of the coffee crop in Ceylon is
but one three-hundredth of what it had been on
the eve of the great disaster. Ruined and discour-
aged, Ceylonese planters turned to quinine, rubber,
chocolate, and at last to tea. In the end the great
coffee disaster worked good for the island. Ceylonese teas are to-day among the highest grades in
the world.

And tea is the world's choice among the beverages.
It cheers and comforts more millions of humanity
than any other one stimulant on the earth. We are
apt to forget this in America where on the whole
coffee predominates. But when we think of the
peoples who chiefly drink tea—Japanese, Chinese,
Russians and the white population of the British
Empire, we realize that the majority of humanity
is included in the census of tea drinkers.

The origin of the use of tea lies in the mist of
mythology, and probably no amount of speculation
will bring out the story of how first tea came to be
made. That "Old Man" that figures so frequently
in Chinese fairy tales, is said to have appeared to

peasants with a tea branch in his hand and commanded them to brew its leaves and drink of the brew. Another legend has it that Bodhidharuna, a Buddhist ascetic, introduced tea from India into China. A commoner story is that the mythical Emperor, Chinnung, gave tea to his people in 2237 B.C. We are approaching closer to history when we hear from the Japanese that a Buddhist abbot, Dengyo Daishi of the Hiei-Zan temple near Kyoto, brought with him on his return from China in 805 A.D. the cup that is now practically synonymous with things Japanese.

"Insensibly," says Sir Edwin Arnold in one of the longest sentences from his tireless pen, "the little porcelain cup becomes pleasantly linked in the mind with the snow-pure mats, the pretty, prostrate *musumes* (serving girls), the spotless joinery of the walls, the exquisite proprieties of the latticed *shojis,* adding to all these a charm, a refinement and distinguished simplicity found alike amid high and low, emanating, as it were, from the inner spirit of the glossy green leaf and silvery blossom of the tea plant—in one word belonging essentially to and half constituting beautiful, wonderful, quiet and sweet Japan."

The tea house, with us often more like a branch of the local ladies' club than anything else, is in Japan more than a restaurant or a social gathering place. It is a sort of secular temple, without a god, where tranquillity, good breeding and delight are enthroned.

The word *cha* (for tea, both in Japanese and

Chinese) may be heard on the lips of every one in Japan many times a day. The tea house is the *cha-ya; cha-dai* is tea money or *pourboire*. Girls are trained in the tea ceremonies from childhood; there are special teachers of the ceremonies, even professional tea hostesses who will take charge at large receptions or do the honors of a high-class inn.

There is a long list of properties necessary to a decently conducted tea ceremony, and among them are a special tea room which should be small enough to be covered by four and a half mats. The mats must be a spotless white. In the room there should be nothing else except one picture and one vase with a few flowers. The cups must be elegant and preferably antique with historical associations. The guests must wash their hands in water from a wooden tub, dipped with a wooden ladle before they drink, and they are to be assembled by the sound of wooden clappers.

The tea itself is to be the finest green powder, from a jar of good design. A few leaves are placed in the bottom of a cup and the "honorable hot water" is poured on them. Even the method of making hot water is important, and honorable *old* hot water is considered best—though by that the Japanese merely mean that the lid has begun to rattle on the kettle.

Picture the English governess of a noble family in Japan confronted thus with her national and necessary beverage—tea green instead of black, served boiling hot, without milk and sugar, in tiny cups. To sip at the demi-tasse, instead of gulping down the draught at once, would be a shocking breach of courtesy, meaning that she disliked her host's tea.

Only think of that to which the good lady was used —the casual ceremony of an English tea table, the big cups of heavy black tea, flooded with a small lake of cold milk, and sweetened, the leisurely sipping, the munching on marmalade sandwiches.

To the Japanese, to whom tea drinking is an almost reverent act, what a sacrilege is the English service! And indeed to the connoisseur of tea the oriental tea is the perfection of the leaf, a pure, pale infusion, aromatic as a flower, delicate and evanescent in taste.

It has been said of the drinking of tea that it has passed through three stages in the Orient, and if this be true it roughly parallels the use of tobacco among the Indians and early Europeans. At first its use was wholly religious. Later it took on a supposed medical aspect, then it passed into the realm of a luxury and finally became general as a sort of æsthetic pastime. By 1587, when Hideyoshi, the medieval hero of Japan, gave his great tea party, it became evident that tea drinking was universal even among the poorest classes.

Never was such a tea party. It lasted ten days and was attended by thousands of persons, for every one in the realm was invited and requested to bring any historic or curious or beautiful drinking or teamaking instrument he possessed. For a few days a vast museum of such instruments was assembled, and all men marveled.

So devoted to tea was Hideyoshi that he had a sort of tea censor and cupbearer, Senno Rikyu, who not only ministered at the tea ceremonials of the royal household but set the fashion and arbitrated disputes of tea etiquette for the rest of the empire. Of this man, who was also a famous artist, the Emperor asked his beautiful daughter in marriage. Senno Rikyu respectfully replied that his daughter was already betrothed. At this the Emperor gave a gesture of displeasure, and Senno Rikyu left his presence. It is related that he went to his apartments, gave to his friends the most perfect tea banquet that had ever been served in Japan, and then committed *hari-kari*.

In China, too, the imperial tea ceremony had its immutable observances. In the Bohea hills, even by 800 A.D., there grew special bushes reserved for the Emperor's use, on account of their wondrous essence, and so it came about that in the days of early tea importations to England, Bohea stood for an especially fine grade of tea. The name was bandied about among successively inferior grades which sought to cover defects by a name, until at last Bohea came to mean the poorest quality. It is good that those ancient emperors are asleep beneath the eternally murmuring pines of the cemetery at Jehol, and cannot know the degradation of the name Bohea.

There is little that the Chinese and Japanese did not know about the elaborate and finicky process of cultivating, picking, curing and packing teas, and for this reason it is hard to understand how it happened that Marco Polo made no mention of tea when traveling in a land where the tea industry must have represented a tremendous labor and investment of wealth. Yet tea was quite unknown to Europe until the Dutch brought it back from Java, although the Portuguese had come in contact with it in their commercial explorations earlier, and had ignored it. The English inherited the tea trade when the Dutch supremacy passed temporarily away, and for a time the British East India Company sought to make tea a monopoly.

In 1658 appeared the first notice of the public sale of tea on English soil, when the *Mercurius Politicus* of London ran this advertisement:

> That excellent and by all Physitians approved China Drink called by the Chineans *Tcha*, by other nations *Tay, alias Tee*, is sold at the Sultanese Head, a cophee-house in Sweetings Rents, by the Royal Exchange,
> London.

Thomas Garaway, the first English tea dealer, who founded Garaway's famous coffeehouse, offered tea for sale at as much as fifty shillings a pound, and it was this high cost that brought into existence the famous tea chests of Georgian times, among the daintiest and most nicely artificed objects of English craft.

Then in 1660, when Pepys recorded in his diary: "I did send for a cup of tee, a China drink, of which I had never drunk before," Parliament put its first tax on tea, eight pence a gallon on tea and chocolate alike—that tax which was to culminate in the immortal tea party in Boston Harbor.

As tea drinking slowly but steadily got under way in England and the demand grew for the best grades in fresh condition, there arose that famous class of merchant ships known as the tea clippers, built for speed, as graceful as racing yachts, which set some of the world's records for commercial sailing. In 1866 nine ships, all built by the same Scotch firm at Greenock, simultaneously cleared the harbor of Foochow, China, with a cargo of tea. They raced around the Cape of Good Hope, almost immediately losing sight of each other and only met again off the Lizard, the first landfall of England. The two leading ships, in a great westerly wind, then raced neck and neck, with every rag of canvas set, the whole distance to London. All nine ships docked on the same day, within two hours of each other, having completed the stupendous journey in ninety days. It had taken Vasco da Gama eleven months to beat around the Cape in search of the spices of Ind.

With the coming of steam and the opening of the Suez Canal the need for speed and the skill of the builder were just as much in demand as in the more romantic sailing days. The *Stirling Castle* made the trip from Woosung to London in twenty-eight days.

Nor is England the only nation whose tea trade is a chapter of romance. Russia, where tea is even more nearly the national drink, long got her supplies by a toilsome caravan journey with camels from

Manchuria through Mongolia and the desert of Gobi. One of the most daring exploits in commercial history was that of Captain Wiggins, who took tea from China around Siberia, through the Arctic Ocean, and landed it on the tundras of the north coast of Russia. When successful this course required four months instead of eighteen as did the caravan journey, but it was very costly, and the cost of tea in Russia was already so high that the lower classes could seldom enjoy the cheering cup. The trans-Siberian railroad went far toward making it available for all the Russias. To-day the only tea caravan routes are in Persia and Morocco.

Not all tea, however, comes to us from China. It was in 1820 that the discovery was made that tea grew wild in the hills of Assam, India, which were perhaps its original home. This very region had been marked out by Sir Joseph Banks (who sent the *Bounty* on its breadfruit expedition) as the region where tea might be grown, and though confusion for a time resulted because a botanist placed the wild Assam specimens in the genus Camelia (to which tea is related) it was still tea, in whatever genus it was placed. To-day India is one of the greatest tea-producing regions of the world, growing, for the most part, black teas rather than greens, as the English prefer them. Java, of course, is an old hand at tea growing, but Formosa is new at the game. Here the Japanese have fostered a tremendous industry. Practically all Oolong teas are grown in Formosa, and they are nearly all consumed in America.

The attempts of our own country to grow tea have had a peculiar fascination. Tea plants were first introduced by André Michaux, friend of George Washington, in Revolutionary times. This great French botanist, the greatest perhaps who ever set foot on American soil, gave us also the mimosa of southern gardens, and many other Old World ornamentals. At Charleston, South Carolina, he had a sort of plant introduction garden where he grew Old World plants, some that, planted by his hand, may still be seen to-day. Here also he kept the beautiful trees and shrubs brought from the high mountains of North Carolina, awaiting shipment to the Old World. Thirty-five years ago, in the ruin of his garden, there were several tea bushes still alive.

Michaux realized that the climate of South Carolina, warm and wet, was well suited to tea growing, and did his best to get the industry started, but the times were not ripe. South Carolina was still a crude, hard-fighting, struggling colony from which the Indians had not wholly vanished. The necessities were barely to be had. And tea is a luxury.

In 1848 tea was tried again in South Carolina by Dr. Jennins Smith, of Greenville. The plantation was within sight of the Saluda mountains, and stood at about one thousand feet altitude. Several heavy snows fell on the plantation, and yet it survived. It did not, though, find tea enthusiasts among the good cotton and rice farmers of the Palmetto State.

It was in 1858 that the Department of Agriculture,

or rather the Patent Office of which Agriculture was then an inconspicuous branch, took up the project of tea for the United States. Almost the first work of the Department was in connection with the problem of the introduction of tea, so that the present Office of Foreign Seed and Plant Introduction may perhaps lay claim to being the original nucleus of the Department of Agriculture. And Robert Fortune was its first agricultural explorer.

Sent to China in search of tea plants, Fortune collected these and a wealth of ornamental plant material beside. His adventures read like a novel, and culminated in a wild escape in a Chinese sailing junk pursued by pirates armed to the proverbial teeth. Fortune's crew fled into the hold, except one or two, who, cowering behind the rail, steered and tacked whilst Fortune himself among his tea plants beat off the enemy with his long American rifle.

His plants, safely returned to America, were widely distributed through the South and on the horticultural side were a marked success. That there is not yet a tea industry in the South has been due more to business reasons than lack of skill in tea growing.

As we are spending annually sixteen million dollars for tea, the Department of Agriculture has again interested itself in the great project of American tea planting. The Bureau of Chemistry has established near Pinehurst, North Carolina, a tea garden where experiments in cultivation, fertilizing, picking and preparation have been made that have for their science and skill and their triumph over difficulties attracted attention even in the tea-growing districts of the Orient.

The experiment remains, though, somewhat theoretical in its value. As yet the industry is too young to attract capital among Southern planters, who know a safe market for their staple crops. Even with abundant negro labor, the problem of labor cost is still an aggravated one for the American tea grower when he comes to compete with the Eastern teas. As yet we cannot do more than salute our native tea industry heartily and wish it success.

Among the hopeful signs of the future of American tea is the development of machine methods— the picking machines, the air fans to dry the tea, the rollers and sifters, cutters and packers, the driers and desiccators. In these last rests much of the finesse of tea manufacture. For green teas and black teas are not, as is generally thought, derived from different varieties of tea, but are merely differently cured. All teas are at first green. The black teas are merely more thoroughly oxidized. So, too, the black teas vary among themselves not so much from differences in the kinds of leaf as differences in picking. Orange Pekoe is the fine tea that it is because it represents only the buds of leaves. In this state the chemistry of the leaf is different enough to make a complete change in flavor. What we taste when we drink tea is the essential oil. It is the caffein that puts the stimulation into tea. Tannin, the other of the three great constituents of the leaf, is what determines the strength or weakness of tea.

But while the development of modern science is showing us the way to the selection of fine teas, and machinery is cutting the cost of preparation and incidentally improving the sanitation, the greatest of all tea countries goes on along very much the same lines of cultivation, harvesting and preparation which Confucius must have known.

Statistics on the production of tea in China will never be known, for the small farmer grows a little patch of tea for home use that rarely gets into a market. Still, there are districts, especially around Canton, where tea for the market is the dominant industry, where it makes up, indeed, the fabric of the lives of no one knows how many hundreds of thousands of humans.

The hand labor of old-fashioned Chinese tea production is enormous, requiring both skill and patience under unpleasant conditions. For tea must be grown where it is eternally hot and damp, where showers soak the pickers to the skin and a few hours later a tropic sun parches their lips. There is kneeling and back-bending; there is straining up on tiptoe.

The very spirit of the tea gardens of southern China has been conveyed to us in a poem, painted on silk by one Li Yihitsing, who tells the story of a girl who slaves amid the odorous leaves. The poem has been literally translated by some unknown Sinologue. It so completely breathes the spirit of the tea industry in its antique charm that it is given here in part, paraphrased from a rather too literal version.

Amid the ten thousand hills lies the roof of our house.
And to north and to south of the village, everywhere
   grows the tea.

From early to late, and ever in haste, I toil,
Each morning at dawn arising, to work in the fields of
   tea.

With the first dawn light I dress, only half fixing my
   hair,
And hastily seize my basket and go out while the mist is
   still thick on the hills.

The little girls and the old women, walking two by two,
Cry: "Which steep of Singlo will you climb to-day?"

And still the sky is dark, and the hilltops hid in mist,
Not yet, not yet shall I pick the buds and the leaves
   while wet with dew.

Ah me, I wonder for whom, for whom, we are forced to
   toil,
To pick the leaves that quench the thirst of some-one far
   away.

The girl thinks of some almond-eyed lady in a
far-away city, pouring the tea with slender fingers,
and is envious. Caught in the rain, and dried by
the sun, her dress is made to smell sweet with tea
flowers and she puts one in her hair.

We've picked enough, and the leaves are gone from the
   topmost bough.
Our baskets brim and each one talks of home.
Laughing we pass along where just against the pool
A pair of frightened mallards rise and fly away.

The pool has limpid water and there the deep-stemmed
    lotus grows;
Its little leaves are round as coins and only half ex-
    panded;
Going to the overhanging bank where the water is clear
    as a mirror,
I look down at my face and see the change in it.

My locks are all tangled; my face is covered with dirt.
In what house lives a girl so ugly as your slave?
I was not so ugly before I grew weary in the tea gardens;
I was not so ugly before the wind and the rain aged me.

The poem trails away at last, as inconsequent as
a tropic rain shower, as dainty as an ancient painting on silk, as aromatic as a cup of oriental tea with
the jasmine flowers slowly opening upon it and
shedding again for us the fragrance dried and long
forgotten.

SUGGESTED READING

KNAPP, ARTHUR W., *Cocoa and Chocolate, Their History
    from Plantation to Consumer,* 1920. Both for his-
    torical information and an exposition of the cocoa
    and chocolate industry this book is nearly complete.
BAKER, WALTER, & CO., LTD., *Cocoa and Chocolate,* 1907.
    A short and popular account, centering around the
    history of a famous company, but containing much of
    general information, especially on the chocolate cus-
    toms of the Aztecs.
DAHLGREN, B. E., "Cacao," *Field Museum Botanical Leaf-
    let,* No. 4, 1923. A brief, popular and authentic ac-
    count, touching on nearly all subjects pertaining to
    chocolate and cocoa.
MODI, J. JIVANI, "A Few Notes on a Flying Visit to Japan,"
    Pt. 3; "The Tea-cult of the Japanese," *Journ. Anthrop.*

Soc. Bombay, Vol. 12, pp. 671-686, 1922. A full account of the tea ceremonies, with many historical notes; at once learned and popular.

MITCHELL, GEORGE F., "The Cultivation and Manufacture of Tea in the United States," *U. S. Dept. Agr., Bureau Plant Indust.,* Bull. 234, 1912. For notes on the early history of tea in America and the recent government venture in tea this is the authority.

ANONYMOUS, "Description of the Tea Plant," *Chinese Repository,* Vol. 8, pp. 132-164, 1840. Not a common periodical but if it can be obtained it should be read for the sake of its notes on tea in China.

ANONYMOUS, "A Ballad on Picking Tea in the Gardens in Spring-time; in Thirty Stanzas," *Chinese Repository,* Vol. 8, pp. 195-204. The poem quoted in this chapter is here given in full in a literal if not very poetic form.

Encyclopædia Britannica, "Tea," 1910. The account of the tea clippers is portrayed here, very romantically for a reference book.

WILCOX, EARLEY V., *Tropical Agriculture,* 1916. Chap. VIII, "Beverages." A pithy discussion of the difficult processes of tea raising and marketing.

CHAPTER VI

THE VANISHING VEGETABLE DYES

WHEN Cæsar came to Britain he found the natives painted blue. This naïve form of adornment, accomplished with the aid of a plant called woad, is one of the indications that the dyeing process goes so far down the channels of human development that we cannot trace its origin. In all likelihood the art is older than the textile industry, for it is not hard to believe that imaginative savages painted their bodies before they thought of attracting attention by means of clothing. Dyeing may even have been practiced before anybody took the trouble to cultivate plants for food, in the jolly old days when one chased the deer and ate one's dinners from berry bushes.

But this is only a matter of surmise. The first visible evidence of dyed fabrics comes from the Egyptian mummy cerements which, while generally white, occasionally show colors which have been identified as saffron, safflower, and possibly indigo and madder. Tyrian purple there was, too, but this is derived from the beautiful molluscs of the Mediterranean which are species of Murex and Purpura.

Every land has indigenous dye plants. Northern Europe had woad, weld, madder, ling and the crottle or lichen dyes; India boasted its turmeric, cutch and indigo, while Syria and Arabia possessed saffron, safflower, madder and cutch. But the dye plants were not kept exclusively in their native haunts. They must have formed a very early article of international commerce, for the classic writings of the Mediterranean countries are full of references to and evidences of dye plants which are almost certainly natives of other lands. Somewhere in prehistoric agriculture safflower was brought to the Egyptians and Greco-Romans from the Far East, and as those forgotten travelers took it westward they may have passed others who were journeying to India with the madder of Europe and Syria.

It is no small credit to the mind of man that the excessively complicated science of dyeing was mastered by primitive men. To appreciate the magnitude of this advance in culture it is only necessary to recall what a fundamental problem in applied organic chemistry is the coloring of a fabric.

We look into a garden of flowers brilliant with blue, yellow, crimson and all the intermediate shades, and we may wonder why we cannot simply take from their petals the superb hues, as we distil from roses the attar of such famous fragrance. But when winter comes and the corollas wither to dun and ashy wisps we realize that the lovely shades were indissolubly connected with the living organism; we can no more capture the color from the flower than we can the delicate tints from living flesh. Few dyes are derived from the petals, and when this is done the petals must be picked before the sunlight commences its bleaching action. The dyes which are of economic importance are probably unexcreted waste products. They are found chiefly in the storage organs, such as roots, bulbs, fruits and, sometimes, in the stems and leaves.

A dye, if it is a true dye and not merely a stain which washes out, must approach the fabric in a soluble condition and then by one means or another be rendered insoluble after it permeates the fabric so that the color will not "run." These requirements are obviously exacting and call for chemical skill, and most of the dyes are hard to handle in the face of these conditions. In fact, very few dyes will "take," that is to say, adsorb to the molecular surface of the fabrics unless they are linked thereto with a metal. The metals enable the dyes to "bite in," hence they are called mordants. Copper, iron, chromium, arsenic, antimony, aluminum, all of which are mordants, will variously yield different colors with the same dye stuff on divers sorts of fabrics. Much of this, of course, has only been apparent in modern times, since these chemical elements have become obtainable in quantity and in a pure state. In ancient times there were seldom more than three shades which could be derived from one dye plant.

Only a few dyes are independent of mordants, and of these fewer still can be applied directly to the fiber. Cotton is especially difficult to dye directly, though it will take turmeric. Safflower and annatto belong in this class, but these are all three ephemeral dyes. The lichen dyes for wool are of this category and are fairly permanent. The rest of the dyes are vat dyes, so called because they only develop their color right in the fabric. To this splendidly permanent and interesting group belong the indigoes.

All these details, evolved in modern theoretical chemistry, were at least empirically understood by primitive man, who knew, too, what dyes were fast and what fleeting, which would dye animal fabrics and which vegetable. These problems are now all closed, and to-day the vegetable dye question is no longer one of ways or means but of the very existence of the industry. The rise to supremacy of the inexpensive and more brilliant coal-tar dyes has created such panics and epidemics of failure as were never known before in all the history of plant industry. Around the ragged edge of ruin a few of the vegetable dye industries still cling. They are those permanent dyes, or dyes which have not yet been made in the laboratory. Many others have been swallowed in failure, and these are the fleeting or too expensive vegetable coloring matters.

The world over, there are, of course, hundreds of species of plants which yield colors, but most of these are not cultivated or used outside their native localities and so have been of no importance in agriculture. Our great-grandmothers, for instance, not only did their own spinning and weaving, but they dyed their own fabrics. For this purpose they relied partly on the cargo of the ships from the Indies; but they went to the forest, too, and from walnut, hemlock, smartweed, sumac, horse sugar and wild indigo they got homemade shades of blue, yellow, red, black and brown. But the dyes which have written history for themselves are those which were cultivated and internationally exchanged. There follows an outline of their dramatic stories up to the middle of the last century.

The beautiful rose-colored dyes of ancient times were generally derived from safflower,[1] which takes its colors from the florets of a splendid thistle. This is a plant without a country; at least its native land is unknown, but it has wandered in exile through the fields of India, Spain, Germany, Hungary, Italy, Persia, China, Egypt and the Sunda Islands. All the classic ancients cultivated it. Because its cultivation in pure stands does not pay in these times, this expensive dye is grown in waste ground or sown between the rows in fields of opium, barley and tobacco. Unfortunately it is soluble in alkalies and for this reason it will fade yellow if washed in soap. Could safflower but be "fixed," it might return to a place of preëminence among the dyes.[2]

Saffron, that splendid orange yellow of ancient times is derived from the bulb of a crocus.[3]

The Romans, who probably brought it first to Britain, were particularly fond of it, and after the end of the Roman Empire it is said that saffron

---

[1] *Carthamus tinctorius.*

[2] If mixed with the fruit of *Garcinia pedunculata* (allied to the plant that yields gamboge) safflower is believed by some to be made fast. Also the Indian method of adding pearl ash and lime juice to fix this dye is said by the natives to be satisfactory. If this is true it is probably explained by the fact that the color is amphoterically precipitated, that is, in the presence of the alkaline pearl ash and the acid lime.

[3] *Crocus sativus.*

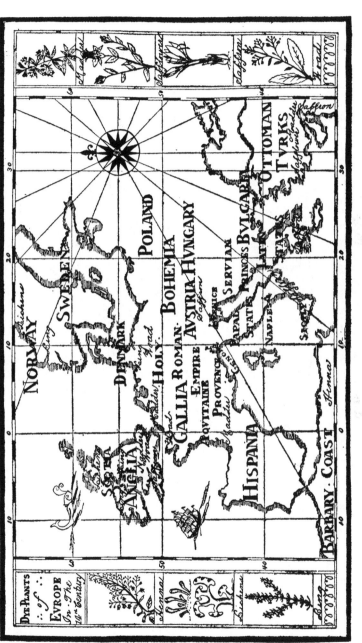

THE DYE PLANTS OF EUROPE IN THE FOURTEENTH CENTURY

continued to bloom in the cloisters of the Benedictine monks. Its culture, like that of madder, was favored by the splendidly attired Saracens, who took it to Spain, where it lingered long after the Faithful of Allah had departed. A legend has it that a pilgrim under Edward III of England concealed some of the bulbs secured in the Holy Land in his hollow palmer's staff and planted them in far-away windy Cornwall. Certain it is that saffron was once a great crop in England. To-day in that country there is still a town called Saffron-Walden, famous for its crocus fields in the Middle Ages.

> " 'Pare saffron betweene the two S. Maries daies
> Or set or go shift it, that knowest the waies.
> What yeare shall I doo it, more profit to yield?
> The fourth in the garden, the third in the feeld."

This is a sixteenth century direction for saffron culture which tells us that at that time saffron was still a common crop in England. But as a fabric dye it has long fallen into disuse because it costs much and fades easily. In India to-day, where it is chiefly grown and used, it is employed in the coloring of ceremonial cakes and bridal veils.

With the opening of the sea trade with the Far East in the fifteenth century, came a sudden influx of new dyes to Europe. The good old stand-bys like the yellow weld,[4] the blue woad[5] and saffron and madder and all the wild and cultivated dyes of Europe, were suddenly confronted with formidable

---

[4] Derived from *Reseda luteola*, a relative of mignonette.
[5] Which comes from a crucifier, *Isatis tinctoria*.

rivals. From the East came turmeric [6] root, which is also a spice. And from the island of Timor, whose location they kept a secret from other sailors, the Portuguese brought the precious sandalwood, which is not only an aromatic cabinet wood but also yields a dye.

The red and yellow gamboges,[7] the cutches, elsewhere discussed, and fustic, a yellow dye,[8] all came in the hulls of the Dutch, English and Portuguese galleons from the Indian seas. And with them, of course, came indigo, so important that its story shall be given a place by itself.

The discovery of America, no less than the opening of the East, flooded old Europe with the dyes of the New World. A superb crimson could now be had in the form of annatto,[9] while the leguminous trees of tropical America furnished a brilliant assortment of colors, chief among which were the various redwoods [10] and logwood of which the most common use to-day is in the dyeing of the black silk hats which appear at weddings, funerals and Presidential functions.

In the face of this inundation of new dyes, the old-fashioned dye workers found themselves on the verge of ruin. It was through their influence that an attempt was made to keep out the invading colors by force. In the time of Queen Elizabeth we read of ''An act for the abolishing of certain deceitful

---

[6] *Curcuma longa*, a relative of ginger, which it resembles.

[7] *Garcinia Morella*.

[8] From *Rhus Cotinus*, the smoke-tree.

[9] Or arnato, derived from *Bixa orellana* of the West Indies.

[10] Mainly species of Cæsalpinia.

stuffes used in the dyeing of clothes. Whereas there hath been brought from beyond the seas a certaine kind of stuffe called logwood, alias blackwood, wherein divers dyers,'' etc., and ''whereas the clothes therewith dyed are not only solde and uttered to the great deceit of the Queene's loved subjects but beyond the seas to the great discredit and sclaunder of the dyers of this realm: For the reformation whereof be it enacted by the Queene our Soveraygne Ladie that all such logwood in whose hands soever founde, shall be openly burned by the authoritie of the maior.''

But when the processing of logwood became better known it found its way back into English markets. During the World War, when the German synthetic dye production ceased, millions of feet of logwood were to be seen in the harbors of Europe and America, and it continues to thrive, for logwood black is a dye which sets a standard for others.

For thousands of years the finest of crimson dyes known to civilization was madder.[11] Carried to the extremes of the earth by the Arabs, the English and other great exploring peoples, it long held sway as king of the red dyes. But in England a ruinous system of tithing taxed the industry to death. A particularly blundering phase of the law was that which required that the young roots could not be set out until the tithe collector had counted them. Before he got around to it, the roots usually died.

---

[11] Or "maddar," obtained from the root of *Rubia tinctoria*, of Asia Minor.

To France, in the middle of the eighteenth century, there came a Johann Altzen or Jean Althen, a Christian Armenian of Ispahan, who had just escaped from a life as a slave in the famous Turkish madder fields. He settled in Marseilles, married a French wife of some wealth, and her money having been lost in some horticultural ventures, decided to try his hand at his old trade of madder growing. He believed that Turkish madder far excelled all other, but it was a capital offense to export living madder plants from the realms of the Sultan, for that prudent monarch was minded to keep the rich madder trade for himself. At last, however, after many failures, the madder plants were secured from a friend in Syria. Altzen then went to court and procured an audience with Louis XV himself. With royal aid he was then able to establish a large madder plantation in the south of France. Every year the culture of the root expanded, and every year the soils of Provence, never given the benefit of a rotation, grew poorer under the excessive demands of the madder plant, which gives back to the soil little of what it takes away. The craze for money blinded all but a few farseeing prophets to this danger to the soil; those who warned were no more heeded than Cassandra.

Altzen himself died poor and forgotten in the midst of the prosperity for which he himself was responsible. A petition was sent to the king requesting aid for his daughter Margaret who was ill and without a sou. In the course of time the affairs of state revolved around to granting the petition, and the royal purse arrived the day after her death.

As a dye substance the property of indigo is found in plants of a variety of families, though chiefly in the leguminous genus Indigofera of which hundreds of species are scattered all over the world. The Egyptians, the Hindus, the Peruvians, the negroes of Central Africa all had their indigoes in prehistoric times. But in Europe their place was taken for thousands of years by woad. The preparation of a blue dye from woad is far more difficult than from the true indigo plants, and gives poorer results. Yet at first, when indigo reached Europe in the sixteenth century, the woad dyers could not handle it properly, and stuck tenaciously to the rustic plant. In order to save themselves they created a public sentiment against indigo as something "foreign" and hence inferior. At their instigation Henry IV of France prohibited it, and the Emperor Rudolph banished it from Germany and Austria as "a prejudicial, cheating, corrosive, devouring and diabolical substance." The penalty for possessing it was death, dishonor and confiscation of property. In Nuremburg and elsewhere the guild dyers were required to appear once a year before the magistrate and take oath to use no indigo. It was forbidden entry to the Papal States. But perhaps because Queen Elizabeth did not wish to follow the Pope in any regard, or perhaps because, as legend has it, the royal nostrils were offended by the stench of the woad vats, indigo found its way into England when the doors of the continent were barred against it. In the reign of good Queen Bess it was generally called *indico* because it came from India. But in India, where from antiquity it had been grown, it was known as *anil*, a word which forms the root of "aniline." Indigo growing was only a flourishing native industry at the time that the Portuguese arrived in India, but soon the stately galleons were returning home with cargoes of the precious dye. On the docks at Lisbon one could see hagglers and buyers of every guild in the great textile centers of northern Europe, purchasing indigo from the shipowners.

The Dutch followed the Portuguese and then came the English. But just at this time the West Indies, too, had commenced to grow Sumatra indigo. The West Indian growers complained that if the East Indian indigo got into Europe, the West Indian would be nipped in the bud. Let India, with her hundreds of exports, do business in something else, the West Indians insisted, and let our incipient indigo trade have a show. After long controversy, the East India Company gave in and refused to buy any more indigo of the natives. The collapse, of course, was ruinous. The West Indian trade, however, lasted scarcely more than a century. Then the East India Company revived indigo in the Orient, and by the latter half of the nineteenth century it took rank as one of the chief exports of the Indian Empire.

In the New World indigo struggled for footing. There were some palmy days of indigo growing in the Bahamas, Jamaica, Antigua and other West

Indian islands. But the English at home made the same mistake that they had with madder. By 1747 they had taxed it to death.

It was the initiative of a young girl which made possible the introduction of indigo into our own country. Her name was Eliza Lucas, and she later married Charles Pinckney, Chief Justice of South Carolina, and became the mother of two revolutionary heroes. Her father, the Governor of Antigua, had removed to Charleston on account of the illness of his wife. The young girl was interested in economic botany and devoted her time to experimenting with cotton, guinea-corn, ginger and alfalfa. Not very successful in these, she tried indigo and after some failures she was able to grow just a little crop in her garden. Impressed by this, her encouraging father imported for her assistance a West Indian expert indigo grower named Cromwell. But fearful that a successful indigo crop in South Carolina would rob the prosperity of his native islands, this man purposely mishandled the plants. The undaunted Eliza, however, detected his villainy and by herself the following year worked out the proper culture of the plants and the preparation of the dye.

At her hands other planters received indigo seeds, and by 1744 her indigo was exhibited in Parliament at London. An Act established in 1748 a bounty of sixpence per pound on American colonial indigo, and with this encouragement the business soon spread up and down the coast from Charleston. At best, however, indigo paid only half as well as rice.

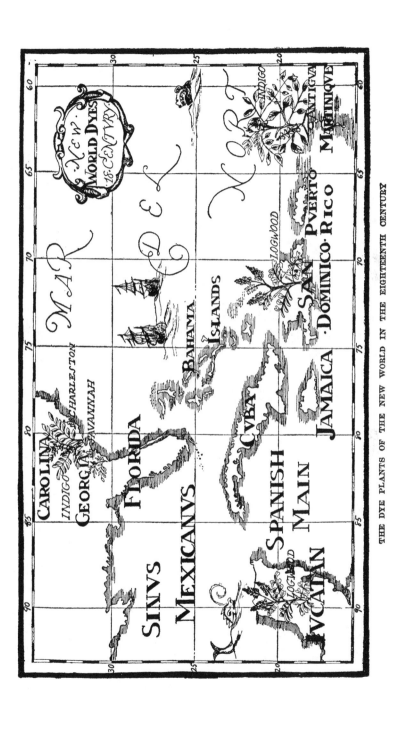

THE DYE PLANTS OF THE NEW WORLD IN THE EIGHTEENTH CENTURY

It was grown chiefly because it tolerated the dry coastal sands where rice could not be cultivated.

But then came the stirring days of '76. Indigo, without a market in England and deprived of the bounty, could not profitably be grown. At the same time the fifteen hundred Minorcans, who had been brought over to New Smyrna, Florida, by Andrew Turnbull to raise indigo, revolted in a body, refusing any longer to cultivate the uncertain crop. After the war there were straggling attempts to keep the crop alive; the business was struggling along in the face of the British embargo on American goods, when the Sea Island cotton came to the fore. The immense profits which could be realized from this cotton, which was raised on the same soil as indigo, could not leave the struggle long in doubt. Cotton encroached, acre by acre, on the old indigo plantations until to-day in the wide fields about Charleston and Savannah not a plant remains to bear witness to the great days of indigo growing in the South.

The history of the vegetable dyes, sketched above in outline, came to a climax in the middle of the nineteenth century. At this time they contributed jointly a very considerable proportion of the world's agricultural interests; there were no other dyes in the world except a few animal and mineral ones of minor importance. And then came the cataclysm.

In 1856 a boy of eighteen, William Henry Perkin, like the alchemists of old, was experimenting in Hoffman's laboratory trying to transmute various base substances into the precious one, quinine. Working alone one night in the great silent laboratory, he suddenly discovered that the adding of caustic potash to anile sulphate (which is oil derived from indigo, combined with sulphur) resulted in a deep purple-staining precipitate.

It was already known that one of the products of the distillation of coal tar was a certain "useless" blue substance. Later Hoffman had shown this to be identical with the aniline which is derived from the indigo plant. What Perkin had now hit upon was the fact that the crude substance aniline, whether derived from the indigo plant or from coal tar, could be changed by caustic potash to a substance giving a particularly powerful blue dye. The secret of the indigo plant was out at last. It only remained to be seen whether the plant or the chemist would win in the race for supremacy.

Pullar's Dye Works at Perth did not think the chemist had much show, although they praised the new dye. But Perkin took out a patent and persuaded his father and brother to set up a factory for him near Manchester. The recognition of the value of the new dye stuff was slow in getting started. One of the initial difficulties about artificial indigo was that it was at first very expensive of manufacture. And before it really got the upper hand many other synthetic hues had triumphed. But it was artificial indigo that pointed the way to the other successes. The chemical principle of madder was also synthesized, saffron and safflower followed its fate and in the space of a few years the dyer's vats were running with a bewildering multiplicity of colors.

The world went on a riot of coal-tar dyes. Waking up at last, a body of Manchester business men recognized that Perkin had a money-making enterprise, and they offered to buy his works, retain him at a liberal salary, take over the financial responsibilities and leave him to his laboratory work. Perkin was a scientist but hardly a business man, they said, and what the synthetic dye business needed was just the hard-headed sort of ability they could furnish. The deal having been struck these sagacious business men proceeded to cut down the cost of production by lowering the quality of the dye, and at the same time raising the price. And, by way of cutting down unnecessary overhead, they calmly eliminated Perkin's salary.

At the moment German dye factories had all closed down during the Franco-Prussian War. As a consequence the Manchester synthetic dye works had practically no rivals in the field. But the Germans came home from the war and their factories reopened. They knew that they could sell dyes at a dollar a pound where the English were profiteering at five dollars a pound. And in a short time Germany was once again in the market at her old prices. The hard-headed business men of Manchester, who were somewhat muddle-headed as well, strove manfully to understand how it was that the Germans could manufacture so cheaply. But the superfluous scientist who could have told them was no longer on their pay rolls. There were some large failures in Manchester that year.

In the meantime Perkin was constantly pouring

forth new and skillful patents from his private laboratory. At first the French chemists were keen rivals, but they respected his patent rights. The chief trouble was with the Germans. Whenever he tried to take out a patent in Germany the Imperial Government would send back word requiring more details; this it did until every detail of the process was known in Berlin. Perkin's patent application would then be rejected and shortly afterward the Germans proudly put forth one of their "new" dyes. Before long the artificial dye business was a German business, and it remained so until the World War.

Perkin was not without his honors. He was knighted for his discoveries and on his visit to New York just fifty years after his first discovery a coal-tar jubilee was held in his honor. The Germans, however, were content to waive the honors, for they were getting all the money, and though the world might still have contested their supremacy it lacked the initiative to try.

And what, meantime, was happening to the dye plants? They were laid low as if by a scythe. Safflower and saffron, being very expensive dyes, went at once. In France madder vanished. To-day the only place where it is grown commercially is a little in England. Up to a short time ago, at least, there was still in force a parliamentary regulation requiring the scarlet of the English soldier's dress parade uniform to be made from the root of madder. An act of Parliament is not to be lightly set aside nor loosely interpreted; if it prescribes that scarlet uniforms shall be made from the root of madder, then from the root of madder they shall be made, no matter if all the rest of the world procures scarlet from coal-tar dyes, or from the sun or moon.

At first it was thought that indigo, too, would vanish from the face of the earth. But contrary to the expectations of the Germans, the indigo growers did not tamely give up and go into bankruptcy. India, the land where indigo had been sacrificed for the sake of the West Indian trade, was now the country which, alone in the world, prepared to keep alive the imperiled industry. Here the growers are fighting competition along scientific lines and they may yet hold their own or better.

Perhaps one reason why indigo persists so strongly in India is the fact that the prejudice of the natives favors the ancestral vegetable dyes. In religious ceremonials particularly, the coal-tar products are abhorred. For similar reasons the growing of turmeric continues. Every autumn the vale of Kashmir still glows purple with the blossoms of the saffron crocus, and the splendid thistly heads of safflower are yet to be seen, sown among grain fields and around the edges of paddies.

And there are numerous dyes of which the essential compounds have never yet been synthesized. Among these are many of the New World dyes, such as quercitron, redwood and logwood. The exceedingly fast brown dyes, the cutches, are not by any means displaced. There is mangrove cutch and Bombay cutch obtained from the betel palm, and Bengal cutch which we find in an acacia, and all of them are used with incomparable success on cotton, which is difficult to dye, and are fast to light, acid, alkali and bleaching powders.

These dyes remain in the market because they are wild products and are not treated as crops but as mines. As the growth and reproduction of the trees is left entirely to nature (unless we except the betel palm), there is no expense involved in exploiting them except the expense of felling, hauling, rasping and extracting, all done with cheap tropical labor. Of course time will deplete these reserves. When they become scarce the price will rise and then they will no longer be able to compete with the coal-tar dyes approximating them, which being themselves derived from a waste product will remain inexpensive.

The situation being what it is at present, it would appear as though it were merely a matter of years before the natural dyes would die a natural death. However, there are some signs that point to a preservation of certain dye industries. After the synthetic dyes had gained the ascendancy there occurred a reaction against them in æsthetic circles. Ruskin even said that we have made no progress in dyeing since the time of Greece and Rome. The only significance in his remark lies in the voicing of a spirit among the finer craftsmen which is opposed to mechanistic art and civilization. This point of view we generally associate with the pre-Raphaelite movement, but the same spirit continues to-day. It is often asserted that synthetic dyes are garish and fleeting and fade to a different color from the original, while a vegetable dye merely becomes paler and softer as it fades. The fact that vegetable dyes never color twice exactly alike is also pointed out in their favor as giving an artistic rather than a mechanically perfect product. This is the secret of the inimitable charm of Persian rugs.

Inasmuch as many vegetable dyes are faster than synthetic ones, it is not too much to hope that the taste of the age may yet turn from the craze for cheap and temporary colors. With the scores of available mordants, the vegetable dyes might in some cases now be brought back on a footing with the synthetic ones. Perhaps on lands not now yielding profitable return it may be possible to grow plants giving the cheaper, the more light-fast and finer vegetable dyes. There is a chance, just a fighting chance, that a few dyes like indigo, cutch, logwood, and the lichen dyes, will keep their heads above the rising tide of coal-tar colors. To one who has traced their fortunes the names of the vanishing vegetable dyes will ever ring in a storied chime—saffron and safflower, woad and weld, henna and alkanet, logwood and indigo, ling and crottle, madder and turmeric—a company whose colors brightened the pageant of days long ago.

SUGGESTED READING

BAKER, SARAH M., *The Exploitation of Plants,* ed. by F. W. Oliver, 1917. Chap. VIII, "Vegetable Dyes." The most informative and pithy of all the references, and one absolutely up to date.

PELLEW, CHARLES ERNEST, *Dyes and Dyeing*, 1918. Contains an excellent account of the discovery of coal-tar dyes, and the life of W. H. Perkin. The point of view is distinctly that of the chemist *v.* the plant.

MAIRET, ETHEL, *A Book on Vegetable Dyes*, 1917. Somewhat rare, and couched in antique form, but delightful reading, with many recipes for old-fashioned vegetable dyes; those interested in home dyeing will value it.

WISE, LOUISE, "The Twilight of the Natural Dyes," *Am. For. & For. Life*, Vol. 30, pp. 235–238, 1924. An excellent popular article dealing not with all dyes as its title might suggest, but with the tropical timbers, such as logwood.

WATT, SIR GEORGE, *Commercial Products of India*, 1908, see under "Crocus sativus" (saffron), "Carthamnus tinctoria" (safflower), "Indigofera" (indigo), "Rubia tinctoria" (madder). Concise and informative yet suggestive of the colorful side of dye histories.

PHILLIPS, ULRIC B., *American Negro Slavery*, 1918. See excerpt on indigo in the United States, pp. 91–94, which vividly recounts the story of Eliza Lucas and Colonial indigo.

BOWLES, E. A., *Handbook of Crocus and Colchicum*, 1924. The botany and lore of the saffron crocus are delightfully set forth in Chap. VI.

NORTHCOTE, LADY ROSALIND, *The Book of Herbs*, 1904. The folklore of saffron is recounted (pp. 981–984).

KRONFELD, M., *Geschichte des Saffrans*, 1892. Much of interest contained in this brochure; couched in none too easy German.

HEUZE, GUSTAVE, *Les Plantes industrielles*, 1893, Vol. 2, pp. 188–383. An excellent two-volume work dealing with all the dye plants of Europe. It gives in full the story of Altzen.

JAUBERT, G. F., *La Garance et l'indigo*, 190?. Easy reading and full of facts. Rather rare.

GOODWIN, PROF. W. L., "Madder and Indigo," reprint. in *Indian Plant. & Gard.*, Vol. 7, pp. 203–204, 227–228, 1903. Setting forth the tragic story of the debacles of two great dyes.

MILLER, PHILLIP, *The Method of Cultivating Madder*, 1768. A rare work but a source book, full of significant matters.

LASTEYRIE, C. P. DE, *A Treatise on the Culture, Preparation, History and Analysis of Pastel or Wood*, 1811; Engl. tr. by A. S. Dearborn, 1816. An old book but an important one on a subject now difficult to pursue.

WILCOX, EARLEY V., *Tropical Agriculture*, 1916. Chap. XV, "Tans and Dyes." Identification of the tropical trees and plants employed, the processes and uses accurately given.

CHAPTER VII

CAMPHOR—THE STRATEGIC CROP

IT is a long way from Verdun and the Marne to distant and tranquil Formosa, but the victorious advance of our artillery was made possible only by a passive ally in that tropic island—the camphor tree. From camphor is derived celluloid,[1] which combined with nitric acid produces the modern high explosives. No other substance now known will take the place of camphor in this manufacture. What it is about camphor that contributes to celluloid its peculiar properties can only be described by the chemist in a series of abstruse formulas. But persons skilled in deciphering these puzzles admit that their elaborate structural formulas describe rather than explain the phenomenon. Camphors as a class may be empirically stated to be alcohols and ketones of the hydrocarbons known as terpenes; in other words, they are distant relatives of the familiar substance turpentine, out of which, in fact, camphor may be synthesized.

---

[1] Celluloid was first made by Hyatt, of Newark, New Jersey, by adding guncotton to melted camphor. Any form of vegetable fiber may be dipped for about twenty-five minutes in a mixture of two parts nitric acid and five parts sulphuric acid at 30° C., after which the nitrated cellulose is thoroughly washed with water and then mixed with camphor.

Camphors occur in various plants of the mint family,[2] and in certain Compositæ.[3] They are found, too, in that rare and fascinating tropical family, the Dipterocarps,[4] producing the Borneo camphor which is used to the exclusion of all others in China where it commands extravagant prices for embalming purposes. Camphor is even secreted by an animal though in extremely small amounts; Dr. O. F. Cooke of the U. S. Department of Agriculture discovered in a pond in New York State about 1890 that a small Diplopod,[5] exuded a substance which is presumably camphor.

But the camphor of camphors is that derived from the tree *Cinnamomum camphora,* one of the laurel family to which belong sassafras, spice bush, bay, avocado and many other plants with oily-aromatic properties. The camphor tree, a magnificent evergreen ornamental, is native to Formosa, southern China and possibly the southernmost archipelago of Japan. The crystalline substance camphor, which most of us know from seeing the old "rock camphor," and the more familiar camphor oil may be derived from almost any part of the tree, though the base and roots contain the most and the leaves and twigs the least. The commercial products are evolved by a process of distillation and condensation. The chips of camphor wood are steamed and the

---

[2] Such as Thymus, Monarda and Mentha.

[3] Such as *Chrysanthemum Parthenium* of Europe and *Blumea balsamifera* of China.

[4] In at least one member, *Dryobalanops aromatica* of Java, Sumatra and Borneo.

[5] *Polyzonium rosalbum.*

steam condensed on cool surfaces. The mechanical contrivances vary from the crude stoves which the Chinaman can rig up with a few stones, boxes and a little sand, to the most elaborate modern metal ovens and condensers.

In times of peace camphor finds a use in the preparation of celluloid articles, soap perfumes, solvents for varnish, diluents for lacquer, insect repellents, tanning antiseptics, disinfectants, germicides and heart stimulants. In the Middle Ages doctors thought it an infallible panacea and administered it freely and internally with very harmful results.

But though the industry is now such a flourishing one and though the odor of camphor is so marked in the tree, the properties of camphor were probably not known in antiquity. Ancient Chinese writings reveal an interest in the tree, but there is nothing to show that it was highly regarded for anything but its handsome timber. A knowledge of the oily and crystalline forms has been claimed by India for a period of one thousand two hundred years and it is certainly true that the Arabs in the Middle Ages traded in the crystalline product and that it was deemed worthy as a gift to a prince. In the arts and medicine were its only uses; it was, however, valued not for these, but like the spices because of its rarity, the distance from which it came, its curious appearance and properties, above all, that of its penetrating odor —a feature which seems to have appealed powerfully to the medieval mind and to have constituted a large part of luxurious display. There were certainly no uses for camphor so important as greatly to affect domestic or national economy. But camphor was a fascinating curiosity and its costliness made it appropriate to royal exchange. In 1350 the Great Khan of Tartary sent camphor, silks and gems to the Pope, and Marco Polo saw camphor sold for its weight in gold.

From Arabia the Venetians carried it to Europe where they practiced its refining with great skill. This was a commercial secret, and fell into the hands of no one else until the scepter of mercantile power, too, fell from the hands of Venice. Holland thereupon became heir to the camphor refining business and continued to invest the process with secrecy.

The island of Formosa, which has always had more available camphor forests than any other part of the world, was not smelled out by European merchantmen until Portuguese vessels driven from their course in the treacherous China Seas sighted the island and named it *Ilha Formosa,* or "beautiful island." Only in 1620 did any Europeans land in Formosa, when a Dutchman, having lost his vessel on the reefs, made an unwilling visit to the island. When he arrived he found it inhabited by a medley of men—adventurers, pirates, farmers, fishermen, outlaws and savages. There were the wild Malayan aboriginals, a fierce, hardy and primitive race of invaders from the south, probably of several Malaysian strains. There were the Chinese, most of whom were pirates or outlaws; a few were colonists. The Japanese in this mixture were colonists with only a few rogues among them. Japanese power did not extend far from the tip of the island but where it

CAMPHOR FORESTS OF THE WORLD

held any sway it held it firmly; and its spirit was opposed to foreigners.

However, the Dutch captain at once threw himself on the mercies of the Japanese, for the shipwrecked sailor held the same relation to the Malays and Chinese pirates that a fish washed up on the beach holds to the gulls. The wily captain, who had evidently read his Virgil, requested only so much land for a little fitting-out station as could be covered with the hide of an ox. Granted this, he cut the hide into strips and surrounded a vast plot of ground, while the Japanese fishermen watched him with open mouths.

Three years later, the Dutch having ineffectually tried to get a toe hold on the shores of China, for their old enemies the Portuguese had poisoned their reputation in the inner courts of the governors' palaces at Canton and Amoy, gladly accepted the offer by the Chinese of the island of Formosa as a trading station. As the Chinese did not own Formosa, had never owned it in fact, it probably did not make their hearts very heavy to part with it. They left it to the Dutch to take if they could.

The camphor, tea, silk, rice and sugar which the Dutch found upon their arrival astonished and delighted them, and as a hiding place for their privateersmen Formosa offered strategic advantages, for it commanded the Spanish traffic from Manila and the Portuguese from Macao. The Dutch, as was their way, were at first friendly, particularly to the Malays. In a short time, however, they had angered the Chinese and Japanese by placing taxes upon the necessities of life, such as rice and sugar, and in general comporting themselves as though they were the owners on the island and the others the interlopers.

The stout Hollanders were zealous in forwarding Protestant Christianity, and for a time all went well. But before long the morals of the savages began to worry the orthodox Dutchmen, and penalties of the most horrible nature were imposed upon any native guilty of idolatry. The elaborate system of taboo, especially sex taboos, and curious habits of intermarriage, accorded poorly with the moral notions of Peter Nuits, the governor. For everything that was the path of narrow rectitude for the savage under tribal guidance the Dutch had a prohibition with a cat-o'-nine-tails attached to it. In a short time the whole island was in a hubbub.

In the midst of this a daring Japanese adventurer called Yahei essayed a *coup d'état*. Arriving with an armed ship he applied to the Governor for permission to land. The suspicious Governor detained Yahei and a half dozen of his companions in his office while the ship was searched and a perfect arsenal of weapons discovered. But the cool Yahei and his fellows arose from their seats, bound the Governor, dashed with him from the palace shooting every one on sight and got him aboard their vessel. They promised the Dutch forts to send them the Governor's head if the ship was fired upon, and having levied a heavy tax in silk, sailed away, leaving the Governor his liberty if not his military reputation. Perhaps it was as a result of this that the

Japanese soon after thought it prudent entirely to withdraw from Formosa.

The Dutch now overspread the coast of the island. But in 1650 or thereabouts there rose to power in China one Cheng Kung, or Koxinga, a child of a Chinese emigrant to Formosa and of a Japanese woman. He had gathered about him the last of the Mings in their struggles against the barbarian invaders from the north and for years he kept the Manchu high councils in continual distress. But having at last lost his footing on Chinese soil and having become no better than a pirate he bethought himself of Formosa the beautiful, home of his fathers. The story of Koxinga's campaign is too long to tell, though it was marked by a series of dime-thriller events. In the end the Dutch were driven precipitately from the island with the slaughter of most of their men. Koxinga seems to have had a fondness for Dutch girls, however, for he set up a seraglio of the daughters of the stout burghers, his vanquished enemies.

In a short time nothing but some massive ruins remained to mark the great days of the Dutch in the isle of camphor. The sole institution which survived for about a hundred and fifty years was the use of the Roman characters among the natives, though the symbols stood for Malayan words.

For a while Formosa became "the port of missing men." Outlaws of all sorts sought it. But in the late eighteenth century and the early nineteenth, the Chinese came again, and this time laid all the coastal plains under their sway. They grew rice, sugar and tea and went to the woods for rattan, but camphor, above all, was their object. They made it a government monopoly, the abrogation of which was punishable by decapitation. All the Chinese evils of officialdom came to play on the vexed camphor question—grafting, squeeze and bribery; the merchants cheated each other; tariff officers blinked at smugglers and confiscated the wares of honest dealers; everybody kicked everybody on the step below him. The man on the bottom step was the Malayan savage. Driven from the plains he took refuge in the hills, and there for a time he was safe. But the camphor trees on the plain having all been cut down, the Chinese had to go to the hill jungles, and there they practiced every sort of deception upon the natives to get access to the trees. They swindled them out of their land, or—a favorite custom—invited the native chiefs to a parley and then decapitated them. Where a Chinese official did deal honestly with the natives he only aroused their trust to have it abused by some other Chinaman.

The natives who dwelt in savage simplicity beneath the shade of the camphor tree cannot, however, be cast in the rôle of helpless and pathetic victims. They were an intensely brave and cunning race with a marked proclivity for head-hunting. The importance and rank of a man was measured by the number of skulls he could hang before his door, and some men had to construct tiers of stone shelves to hold all their cranial trophies. In the days when the natives had nobody but each other to fight they must have suffered from race suicide, especially if it was true, as has been said, that all babies born before the mother's thirty-seventh year were killed. But with the coming of the Chinese there was "glory enough for all." In bands they continually raided the Chinese camps, and Celestials died like rats in the wake of the bloody camphor trade. Even commoner than death by organized raid was the fate of the solitary Chinese workman. Leaving his family in their jungle hut he would proceed in the morning to his camphor still. The camphor trees are generally only a few to the acre. The woodcutter had therefore to wander far from his still among the shadows of the tropic forest. He would be shuffling along, ax over shoulder unsuspecting through the jungle when suddenly he would fall on his face with a spear in his back. His assailant might well be some Malay who had suffered a personal injury from the same Chinaman. Cheated of his rental of the camphor groves, perhaps, or his sons murdered or his daughters stolen, is it any wonder that the incensed savage sought out the camphor cutter or rattan gatherer, slid like a shade behind him, hurled his spear and ended the job with the knife, dropping the head into a bag and slipping, a wordless but triumphant shadow, back to his mountain home?

The two races had declared upon each other a war of extinction. Among the glittering leaves of the camphor trees sparkled the siren lure of wealth, and the Chinese went further yearly into the hill lands. Massacres and miscegenations were killing off the original races and breeding one of mongrels.

A more unhealthy, hot, dangerous, sordid and blighted spot than Formosa could not have been found this side of Hades.

The island was the terror of every merchantman. The typhoons frequent in that neighborhood took yearly their pitiful toll of wrecks. Few shipwrecked sailors ever again saw home, for the savages promptly beheaded them for the sake of their clothing and weapons. The maritime powers made remonstrance at Peking, but the Chinese claimed exemption from responsibility in the acts of savages as they would in the acts of wild animals of the jungle. Americans particularly suffered on the Formosan coast, in as much as their ships from China left for the Horn and sailed past Formosa, while European ships heading for the Cape of Good Hope turned in the other direction. However, the Formosan camphor trade had wafted its spicy odor around the world even to the coast of America. In 1855 an American named W. M. Robinet, engaged in Chinese traffic, came in the bark *Louisiana* to pick up a rich cargo of camphor. The *Santiago* followed her; before long Nye brothers, and Williams, Anthon & Co., American firms, entered into an agreement with Mr. Robinet and soon the Americans had established a trading factory at Takow. A complete monopoly of the foreign camphor trade was granted by the Chinese, who in return were given one hundred dollars for every company ship clearing the port, as well as the assistance against pirates. Storehouses were set up in the compound which was marked off with a wall, and the American flag flew over this bit of Formosan soil. Ten thousand piculs of camphor were obtained yearly by the company at a cost of about eight dollars a picul.

In 1861 interested persons urged the United States to occupy the island and so solve the shipwreck problem. At that moment, however, we were engaged in the Civil War. Even the necessary assistance to our private enterprise in camphor had to be withheld, so that the monopoly rights were knocked off to the highest bidder, an English firm, and the American factory was closed.

The years that followed were full of vexations. The local Chinese merchants tried their best to exclude the foreigners from any share in the camphor trade; every restriction, duty or squeeze brought an angry protest from the foreign dealers which was echoed by the ambassadors at Peking. According as the Celestial Court felt amicable or hostile to foreign interests it changed its policy, and this policy in turn was interpreted in any way the Formosan officials saw fit. As a matter of fact, the more freedom trade was allowed, the greater were the number of Chinese employed in camphor production. But this fact did not matter to the loud-voiced middlemen who were more interested in keeping the camphor scarce than in producing quantities of it.

In 1874 the Japanese were resolved to punish a tribe of Formosan savages, and perhaps, too, with thoughts of aggrandizement they came to Formosa in force. The suspicious Chinese viewed the Japanese approach as nothing more than an attempt to seize the camphor and other rich trades of the island.

However, the Japanese having accomplished their announced purpose went no further. They may have felt the task of reducing the whole of the wild island too great; the cost of their punitive expeditions had been enormous. At any rate they departed, having done the world a service in cleaning up one of the nastiest spots in it.

But in the Chino-Japanese war of 1895 they returned again, this time resolute and equipped to conquer. With precision and skill they soon had in their power as much territory as was not in the hands of Malays. From that day to this the administration of Formosa has been carried on along lines intended to be profitable to Japan, but, it must be said, with intelligence and on the whole with fairness. Japanese sanitary engineers, agricultural experts, botanists and other officers and learned men have explored, improved and exploited the province in a sane and masterful way.

Immediately upon occupation the Japanese took up the plan of government monopoly of camphor, permitting growers to sell their produce only to the government officials who issued checks on the Taiwan bank. At first they introduced Japanese laborers. But no less than the white men, the Japanese are ill-adapted to tropical labor. Disease, exhaustion and homesickness decimated the labor camps, and the plan was given up. Chinese coolies are now used with Japanese overseers, and the Japanese improved still has come to replace the crude stove.

The plan of the Japanese Government in the camphor monopoly was to regulate the output so as to keep the prices high, declining to buy, or laying off the coolies whenever the production was too great. They watched the foreign market keenly, and at the least sign of a shift in demand they changed the price of camphor to their interests. In order not to lose money by change in prices, Japan refused to make contracts on camphor shipments for more than three months in advance.

This state of things kept European and American camphor importers continually on pins and needles. They at their end and the coolies at the other had to bear any losses and inconveniences, while Japan in the middle reaped safe profit. Thus, when the Chinese trees available near transportation lines were exhausted and the Japanese were holding an iron-handed monopoly over the Formosan trees, it looked as if our yellow brethren could put the price of camphor at any figure they wished. That is, in fact, exactly what they did, or at least they placed it at all the market would stand. To persons who viewed the progress of Japanese arms with suspicion it appeared as one of the most alarming aspects of the case that an essential ingredient of certain high explosives was all in Japanese hands.

But it was probably not the cries of the alarmists which brought on the struggle to break the hold of Japan upon this commodity, but the nimble wits of European and American business men who were ill-content to be tied to the chariot wheels of the Japanese Government monopolies or to be grateful for small favors in the way of camphor export business. Combining forces with chemists and agriculturalists a silent and bloodless war has been waged by occidental merchants, against camphor monopoly.

Other nations began to grow camphor. Ceylon, Java, Brazil and Argentina all became interested, and in Ceylon, the Federated Malay States, and the Dutch East Indies, a crop was raised sufficiently large to inundate the market and to cool the ardor of Japanese extremists in their camphor policy.

The Chinese, too, have entered the field of camphor production and in this way have helped to loosen the grip of Japan upon the monopoly. It was, however, a Japanese, Jiro Shirakawa, who first set the axes felling the camphor tree of the new forests. Chinese camphor consumption in this country has steadily increased, chiefly in the preparation of celluloid for motion picture films.

But the camphor crop reached its high point of importance with the outbreak of the Great War. It then became a matter of life and death, victory or defeat. The world's supply of synthetic camphor was locked up in Germany; the vegetable camphor was in the hands of Japan. In 1916 she alone harvested ten million pounds, and tens of thousands of trees were felled. This was the largest crop in the world's history, and the most wholesale destruction of trees. Of this crop in the following year the United States bought over six million pounds to celebrate her entry into the conflict.

But the United States Department of Agriculture had already investigated the question of camphor production. For perhaps half a century Americans had been growing the camphor trees as ornamentals so familiar in the picturesque old ports of the Gulf coast. California, too, had its camphor trees, and the gardens of Charleston knew its glossy leaves. For the brief duration of the War we were able to sell our Government a creditable amount of camphor derived from native trees.

Our home-grown war camphor was cultivated under a particularly efficient method. In the first place, the seeds are planted with the pulp left on, which apparently assists germination. Then the young trees are cut back to form hedges, so that only the branches are taken and the tree lives on, while in Formosa the tree must be allowed to grow fifty years or more, and then at the blow of an ax it is sacrificed forever. By the American system it is possible that less camphor is produced per weight of wood, but the rapid returns and the fact that the tree is not killed convince us that these methods yield superior net results. The Japanese have not been slow to realize this and are imitating us.

But when the War was over down went the demand for camphor. And down, too, went the price. The high cost of American farm labor precluded American production in the face of slack demand, and there, for the moment, our camphor enterprise rests. German synthetic camphor is back in the market, and we are its biggest buyers. Will we too make camphor synthetically, as for a while during the War we did? Will we ever get American vegetable camphor on a paying basis? Will synthetic camphor drive vegetable camphor from the field? Will camphor oil, up to the present time never synthesized, be made artificially? Will the Japanese lose their grip and abandon the government monopoly to the competition of private firms of all nations, Japan included? No one knows the answer to these questions. The camphor industry remains what it long has been, the enigmatic, the strategic crop.

SUGGESTED READING

DAVIDSON, JAMES W., *The Island of Formosa*, 1903. A long, absorbing book, concerned with much beside camphor. Practically the authority on Formosa in English. Easy reading and a vivid narrative.

HOOD, S. C., and TRUE, R. H., "Camphor Cultivation in the U. S. A.," *Department of Agriculture Year Book*, 1910, pp. 449–461.

LE WALL, CHARLES H., "The Romance of Drugs," *Am. Journ. Pharm.*, Vol. 96, pp. 246–247, 1924. A brief but colorful sketch of some of the outstanding facts about camphor.

COOKE, ORATOR F., "Camphor Secreted by an Animal," *Science n. s.*, Vol. 12, pp. 516–520, 1900. This brief article is only a bypath in the curious chemistry of camphor, but is worth reading, especially for those interested in general natural history.

Further references, some of them chiefly statistical, others in foreign languages or in publications rare in this country are:

DUBOSC, A., "Le Camphre synthétique aux Etats-Unis," *Caoutch, et gutta-percha*, Vol. 16, p. 9937, 1919.

DJEINEM, A., "Le Crise du Camphre," *ibid.*, Vol. 16, pp. 9937–9940, 1919.

PERROT, E., and MME. V. GATIN, "Le Camphrier et ses produits," *Travaux d'Office National des Matiéres Premières Végétales*, No. 4, 1920.

COBLENTZ, V., "History and Uses of Camphor," *Journ. Soc. Chem. Indust. London*, Vol. 26, p. 382, 1907.

WILCOX, EARLY V., *Tropical Agriculture*, 1916, Chap. XIII, "Rubbers and Gums." See brief, scientific explanation of camphor.

CHAPTER VIII

THE POTATO—THE POOR MAN'S FRIEND

OUR daily bread seems our most important food, but a greater harvest wins the crown of laurel for the humble potato. Figures since the War are incomplete, but it was established that from 1909 to 1913 the potato led the world's food crops with almost five and a half billion bushels yearly, followed in turn by oats, corn, wheat, rice, rye, and barley. The food value of potatoes, of course, is surpassed by the great cereals, but at least among white races potatoes are second only to wheat in the amount of their bulk consumed per capita.

Not only as human food but in the preparation of starch, flour, dextrine, sago, sirup, caramel sugar, industrial alcohol, amyl alcohol or fusil oil, bran, fodder meal, flakes, and a host of minor by-products, the potato stands revealed as the Jack-of-all-trades in the plant world—Jack-of-all-trades yet master of many.

No wonder that the potato has been the cause of hundreds of thousands of humans leaving their homes to dare the ocean and a strange land, that a queen once wore potato flowers in her hair, that a whole host of legends and superstitions has grown up around this tuber that came from the New World to the Old, altering the agricultural basis of every civilized country.

The Irish potato, it is called, but it is Irish only by enthusiastic adoption into the green isle of Erin where, indeed, it might well vie with the shamrock as the national plant. It was on far Andean slopes that red men tended the first cultivated potato. A traveler, Pedro de Cieza de Leon, in the upper Cauca Valley of Peru in 1538 relates in the tale of his journeying that the two principal foods of the Indians there were quinoa [1] and the potato which he describes as "a kind of groundnut which when boiled becomes as soft as a cooked chestnut but which has no thicker skin than a truffle." [2] Some twenty years

[1] Quinoa, the seeds of *Chenopodium quinoa*, a sort of pigweed, came recently to the popular notice in America through the indefatigable work of Luther Burbank, that prestidigitator of plant breeding. In 1913 an article appeared in a Los Angeles paper to the effect that in that city in a deposit vault lay for safety a half ounce of the most precious seed in the world, a cereal which would soon feed the whole human race, taking the place of wheat, rye, rice, corn, oats, barley and all other cereals. It had been created, the newspaper said, after eleven years of patient and difficult labor. It was so carefully guarded because it was the only half ounce of that seed in the world.

Fortunately for posterity there were then, beyond the half ounce in the Los Angeles bank, two hundred pounds of quinoa in a warehouse of the Department of Agriculture. That quinoa, which is nothing new, but was a sort of breakfast food known to the Incas, has not yet appeared on the American table is obvious and tends to disprove a sensational newspaper report. Some tests have shown that the plant is so susceptible to plant lice as to be wholly impractical for many parts of this country, depriving us of a curiosity on our menu.

[2] The comparison to a truffle is interesting as tracing the origin of the chief German word for potato, *Kartoffel* (other vernacular names are *Erdapfel, Erdbirne, Grundbirne*), which is varied only slightly in the Scandinavian languages. *Kartoffel* is but a form of *Tartuffle*, meaning truffle. Obviously when potatoes first came

later came another pilgrim to Peru, José de Acosta, who leaves us further word of the potato as it was used in those remote mountains:

"In the elevated regions of the Sierra of Peru and the provinces which they call Callao . . . where the climate is so cold and dry that it will not permit the cultivation of wheat or maize, the Indians use another kind of roots which they call *pappas.* . . . These *pappas* they collect and leave in the sun to dry well, and baking them they make what they call *chunyo* which will keep for food in that form many days and serves them for bread. And of this *chunyo* there is great commerce in that kingdom with the mines of Potosi. *Pappas* are also eaten fresh, either boiled or roasted, and from one of the mildest varieties, which also grows in warm situations, they make a certain ragout or *cazeuela* which they call *locrox.* Indeed these roots are the only wealth of the land, and when the season is favorable for the crop the Indians are glad, for many years the roots are spoiled and frozen in the grounds." [3]

Dr. Francis McBride of the Field Museum has described the smell of the chunyo as worse than rotting flesh. His recent explorations in South America make us realize that chunyo, despite its odor which is probably only excelled by the stench of rotting breadfruit in the pits of Polynesia, has not been exiled by the advance of civilization. It is still a fact

to Europe there was no name awaiting them, and owing to their subterranean habits they were likened to the edible fungi which dogs are trained to hunt.

[3] Dr. Safford's translation; see reference under "Suggested Reading."

that Indians of the Andean region have often little else to eat. One of the advantages of chunyo which doubtless gives it favor with the Indians, is that after being trampled and desiccated, it becomes as light as cork and consequently easy to store and transport.

But the red men's staple was all unknown in Europe until in 1598 there was put into the hands of the interested Clusius, a learned botanist of Vienna, a strange tuber for which medieval science knew no name. The Papal legate who gave it to Clusius called it "Tartoufli" (truffle) and said that it had come to him in Italy by way of Spain. Unfortunately there is no record of the name of the conquistador who did so much for posterity by first introducing to Europe the gnarled and homely thing grubbed from the earth that was to prove more than a gold mine to the hungry generations of men.

Yet how the spud reached welcoming Ireland is a matter so clouded by popular fancy that only a variety of legends are distinguishable. There is the tale that Sir Walter Raleigh, having brought the potato from Virginia gave it to his gardener to plant on his estate near Cork. We must regretfully recall that Sir Walter was never in Virginia, that the potato does not grow there in the wild, nor has it ever been found among Virginian relics of Indian life. Undaunted by fact, popular fancy has transferred the good deed to Sir Francis Drake who also, it would seem, gave the potato to his gardener to plant on his estate near Cork. In Baden, Germany, there even stands a statue to Drake, holding the potato, in grateful tribute from the honest farmers. However, it is not established that the brave admiral had any Cork estate, and though he did meet the potato in Chile, he makes no mention of bringing it home. Moreover, we are told by the grandson of Sir Robert Southwell that his illustrious grandfather brought home potatoes and gave them to his gardener to plant on his Irish estate, and when it is added that Southwell received those potatoes from the hand of Sir Walter Raleigh we return to our false start and come to the conclusion that these potato-growing estates in Ireland are but castles in Spain.

A slightly more credible legend is that a ship, wrecked on the coast of Lancashire, bore a crop of potatoes which floated ashore and that thus the potato became naturalized in England. But perhaps this is nothing more than an attempt to account for the fact that early in the English history of the potato Lancashire became famous for that crop.

And one must always remember that historical references to "potatoes" may mean either sweet [4] potatoes or white potatoes. When Falstaff talks of its raining potatoes, he means sweet ones, which were known in England some time before the white.

---

[4] Sweet potatoes (*Ipomoea batatas*) belong to the morning-glory family. Originally they were *the* potatoes, so that Safford has said the "Irish potato" is Irish by adoption and potato by analogy. To deprive *Solanum tuberosum* of the appellative of potato leaves it without a common name and is probably pedantic since the name has such wide acceptance. Sweet potatoes are often called yams, yet the real yams are species of Dioscorea, a principal food of many peoples of Asia and Oceania. In this chapter when speaking simply of "the potato" we shall mean the white potato, *Solanum tuberosum.*

It is probable that Sir John Hawkins was responsible for this introduction of the sweet potato. In Venezuela, he relates, "naked Indians brought me hennes, potatoes, and pines." The "hennes" were native pheasants, the pines were pineapples, and the potatoes were sweet potatoes, indigenous on that coast. But to the daring mariner's door has been laid, again, the credit of the first white potato introduction, even though he did not possess the indispensable estate near Cork.

But the honest potato, though at first regarded in Europe with interest as a curiosity, had a hard fight to win its way to popular acceptance. It was met with suspicion, with the silliest of prejudices, with those blind and angry denunciations that confront anything new. It was denounced from the Scotch pulpit on two counts, first, that it was not mentioned in the Bible and was therefore not fit food for Christians, and second, that it was the forbidden fruit spoken of in Genesis and had caused Adam's fall. Like its cousin the tomato it was thought to be poisonous and every conceivable disease was attributed to it. Also it was declared that it would exhaust the soil.

But Frederick the Great Elector, first among the monarchs, favored the potato. It had been brought to Prussia by Laurentius Scholtz at Breslau, and in

---

NOTE to Map on Page 157.—The original home of the potato, the Andean highlands, whence also came some of the most famous parent-potatoes of modern times, is of practically negligible importance in commercial production. The New-World potato is largely become an Old-World crop just as coffee, which originated in Africa, is to-day enthroned in Brazil.

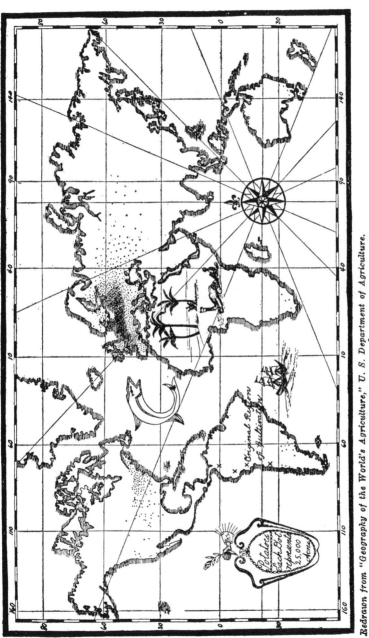

Redrawn from "Geography of the World's Agriculture," U. S. Department of Agriculture.

THE REGIONS OF THE WORLD WHICH PRODUCE POTATOES

1651 the Elector caused it to be planted in the Lust-garten at Berlin. His grandson, Frederick William I, so enthusiastically sponsored the new tuber that he threatened to cut off the noses and ears of all who refused to plant potatoes, and Frederick the Great in 1744 also compelled the peasants to cultivate the crop. He put out bulletins on the planting and use of potatoes, adding his own cooking recipes, and gave away potato seed—foreshadowing the Congressional free seed distribution and the Farmer's Bulletins from our Department of Agriculture. A dash of superstition colored the great soldier's science, however, when he ordered potatoes to be planted in the dark of the moon and to be dug at Michaelmas.

It was from the Germans that Dr. Antoine Auguste Parmentier learned the incomparable nutritive value of potatoes when, during the Seven Years' War, he was captured and made prisoner at Hamburg. Returned to France where he took up practice in Paris as a doctor and chemist, he was grieved by the terrible cereal failures of 1760 and wrote a book on potatoes and what they might mean to the farmer and the city consumer. His work was greeted with ridicule, except that a society of arts and sciences gave him some encouragement, but at last he interested Louis XVI in his plans. He sent a tub of potato plants to the King, who wore their flower in his buttonhole, and Marie Antoinette appeared at a ball with a wreath of potato blossoms in her hair.

With the King's aid Parmentier secured a plot of land near Paris in which to grow potatoes experimentally. The King even provided a cordon of soldiers to guard this potato garden. When the people saw this they began to think something pretty good must be buried in a field that needed the protection of the military. The result was that at night people came and stole the potatoes, ate them, liked them, planted them, and so fell victim to the kindly trap which Parmentier had set for them. To this day potato flowers bloom upon his grave.

To Lavoissier and Benjamin Franklin, Parmentier had given a dinner at which only potatoes were served, in a variety of ways. How the great economist Franklin may have been impressed by this dinner we can only imagine. It is possible that he brought potatoes back to America with him. But the potato was already established to some extent in our country. Contrary to a belief general at that time, potatoes were not native to the thirteen colonies, but were actually brought there from England. By earliest record it was the sturdy Scotch-Irish settlers of Rockingham County, New Hampshire, who in 1751 planted our first potatoes in their new home. From there the crop has spread all over our country, where the leading potato states are now New York, Michigan, Wisconsin, Maine, Pennsylvania and Minnesota.

By the middle of the seventeenth century the potato had become common in the British Isles, and it is said that ten thousand men with families in England and Wales who had been practically paupers before the precious tuber came, were made self-supporting by it. The population of Ireland—

a poor country for growing the cereal foods—increased after the potato became common, from two million in 1785 to more than five million in eighteen years, and by 1845 it had passed eight million. And then came the crash.

As early as 1810 the leaf curl of potatoes had been noted, the first of the potato diseases to receive general recognition. But so little was the fungoid nature of plant disease understood then (even the bacterial nature of human disease being undreamed of before Pasteur's time) that any sickening of the potato crop was laid to weather, bad cultivation, dung, alkali, drought, too much rain, or whatever fancy suggested. Diseases were simply called "fail" or "taint," just as human consumption was called "a decline." Then in 1839 the black rust hit New England, and by 1841 stem rot and scab ravaged the potato fields of Germany.

Unwarned by these signs of the times, however, the overcrowding population of Ireland continued to depend wholly on potatoes. The rising birth rate of the Irish was a sort of human stock market speculation, a speculation without "margin." For potatoes are the cheapest of the highly nutritive foods of the temperate zone, that is, they furnish a larger amount of food in proportion to the land used than any other crop. Obviously a population subsisting on potatoes can easily be crowded densely on a small farm acreage, if all goes well with their crop.

For peoples subsisting chiefly on grains and meat, more expensive and acreage-consuming crops, a cheap food like potatoes furnishes a margin in case of grain failures or meat shortage. But the Irish were already living on the cheapest possible food. When the potato murrain hit Ireland in 1845, causing a total failure of the crop, famine came inevitably. The number of persons who died as a direct or indirect result of starvation has been placed at three hundred thousand souls, some say even six hundred thousand.

And so began the flight of the Irish to America, initiating the first of those tidal waves of immigration that have repeatedly washed our shores. In the year when "all the praties had black hearts," when the priests came out to bless the potato fields in vain, when the "laughing potato," the "flowery potato," as the Irish called it, died of the "gangrene," every one who could buy a steerage ticket saved himself and his wife and children by terrified flight.

Dreadful now beyond realization were the conditions of the steerage vessels with their crowding and bad food, their typhus epidemics, called "ship fever," their unburied bodies. The port of New York had to take over an old fortress later known as Castle Garden, now the Aquarium, to meet the immigrant problem and to save the poor refugees from the evil designs of the "runners" who preyed upon the ignorance of the newcomers. This was the era of the tenement growth in New York, this era of potato failure, when the country estates along the Bowery gave way to the interminable ugly rows of five-storied, many-familied shoddy erections.

To stem the helpless tide, anti-immigration societies were formed, like "The Supreme Order of the

Star Spangled Banner'' which indulged in riots and mob violence. Its members were forbidden to say anything about the name or purpose of the organization and usually replied to questions ''I don't know,'' whence they became known as the ''Know-Nothing Party,'' which actually ran a candidate for President.

But the Irish had come to stay and when the first fury of the potato disease had spent itself and with it the wave of Irish immigration and its undertow of enmity had ebbed, the potato passed through an uneventful few decades except that active work of selection and breeding commenced in 1850. For the subterranean tuber has indeed been a mine from which skilled horticulturalists have brought forth unparalleled yields. If statues are erected to Raleigh and Drake, whose connections with the potato are but mythical, it is strange that the labors of men like Goodrich, Bresee, Brownell, Pringle, Gleason, Heffron, Carman, Craine, Bovee and Van Orman should not be heralded and gratefully commemorated. Yet the only name that is popularly known among those of potato breeders is that of Luther Burbank. Perhaps because men of science are modest and discourage sensational publicity about their work and personalities, the great potato breeders have all lived and died in practical oblivion. For it is only recently that a general interest in the subject of plant breeding has been aroused.

Yet there remains a great deal of superstition prevalent regarding plant breeding, exemplified in the ''plant wizardry'' myth that has grown up

around Mr. Burbank's California farm. The truth
is that there is nothing magical about plant breeding
though much is marvelous. We need to remember
that there are two ways of creating something new
in plant life. The commonest method is by selection
—that is, by growing plants in quantity and watch-
ing for all the especially fine variants that will inevitably spring up in, for instance, a large field of
potatoes grown from seed.[5] For seeds seldom come
true to type and consequently can be relied upon to
produce something extraordinary in the way of variants, whether better or worse than the parent type.

If from such a patch of potatoes the finest variants
be selected and then reproduced asexually, that is,
not by fertilization and seed, but by division of
tubers, the new and promising variants will usually
be perpetuated true to type and can be multiplied in
a short time in large quantities. If only the best of
these selected strains be preserved there will obviously be a gradual racial improvement, even
though the individuals may at times revert to type
so that freshly selected strains have to be substituted.

And secondly, there is plant breeding proper,
which consists primarily in the mingling of the finest
strains. If, for instance, we have a race of potatoes

---

[5] Potatoes grown from seed and seed potatoes are not the same
thing. Seed potatoes are pedigreed tubers grown and distributed
for planting out new potato fields, and tend to perpetuate a race
of potatoes more or less true to type. Real seeds of potatoes are
in some varieties, at least, rather rare and are seldom resorted
to as a method of propagating potatoes except for the production
of new variants.

resistant to disease but poor in taste, and another with fine flavor but a tendency toward disease, by cross-pollinating the flowers and growing the seeds of them, we may hope for profitable results. In a bunch of such hybrids we may obtain some plants that will have both disease resistance and good flavor.

The technique of hybridization, which depends primarily on preventing the pollen of any but the desired male flowers from reaching the female flowers, is one of the nicest arts in horticulture. It has come late in the history of gardening, for it is only in the last few centuries that it was realized that plants had sex. On the other hand, the simpler art of selection dates back, of course, to we know not what prehistoric men who bred our cereals and fruits.

The great development of the potato came just at the moment when horticulture was becoming a science as well as an art, when hybridization was combining with selection. As an example of the selection method pure and simple, take the work of Luther Burbank. His famous potato, which he named for himself, first appeared in 1873 in his father's potato patch at Lancaster, Massachusetts. From a berry of a particularly fine potato young Burbank grew twenty-three seedlings and these in turn proving promising, he interested the celebrated nurseryman Gregory of Marblehead, who put the Burbank potato on the market. Migrating some years later to California, the struggling young pioneer took his potato with him. It was at that time the good man's sole asset, but for his fertile brain. On the Pacific coast the Burbank proved a surprising success, rapidly spread all over the western states and for some years set something of a standard of excellence. It is perhaps not so much grown as formerly, though many potatoes are being raised that are called Burbank which have in reality a sketchy ancestry.

A recent work on potatoes is dedicated to Luther Burbank, "greatest potato breeder in the world." By comparison, consider the selection work of that pioneer in his field, Rev. Chauncey Goodrich of Utica, New York, who selected eight thousand varieties of potato. This man's heart had been grieved by the sufferings in the potato famine of the Forties, and he looked about him for the cause of the sudden ravages of disease in the crop. He came to the conclusion that potatoes were being weakened by continual propagation without sexual reproduction. He believed that the division of tubers, making thousands of plants descendants from one parent instead of two, resulted in a degeneration similar to that sometimes following close inbreeding of humans.[6] As a result they fell prey to disease. It was Goodrich's idea, therefore, to grow potatoes from seeds.

But it chances that not a few of the varieties of

---

[6] In this connection compare the apparent degeneration of the Lombardy poplar, which is a sport or freak of the common Italian black poplar. Only a single tree is the parent of all the Lombardies in the world, and as this was a male tree no seed could be procured from it. Apparently after several hundred generations of reproduction asexually, from cuttings of the wood, signs of degeneration are appearing. The life of many Lombardies is now short. Beside a natural tendency to die young, beginning at the top, there is extreme susceptibility to fungi and insect pests.

potato do not or do but rarely flower or set seed. Perhaps this is a natural tendency of the potato in the wild. It is often so with plants that can also reproduce by tubers or other asexual means.

So Goodrich sent to the American Consul at Panama and asked him to secure some South American potatoes, hoping to get from the homeland of the potato some fresh blood. In the consignment which the obliging Consul sent in 1851 were some which had a rough purple skin, an unfamiliar type promising the very infusion of new vigor for which Goodrich was looking. From these he grew a few flowers and carefully saved the seeds. These, of course, proved a highly variable lot, not all coming true to type. In fact between 1849 and 1854 he discovered and selected 5,400 varieties, of which he saved only 33. In the year 1855-6 he made 3,000 varieties. His final product, the Garnet Chile, made his reputation and drew the praise of Henry Ward Beecher who said of Goodrich, "He was so busy with experiments he had no time to make money."

A chance sport of the Garnet Chile produced the famous Early Rose. Few potato varieties have kept a high reputation so long as this one, and when we consider the number of fine varieties that have spontaneously appeared from it, the Early Rose may well be called the mother of potatoes. The origin of the Burbank potato is not a matter of record kept at the time, and the stories circulated about it are a bit conflicting. The concensus of opinion has it, however, that it was a chance sport of Early Rose.

In that case the genealogy of Mr. Burbank's celebrated tuber would be:

Unknown Rough Purple Potato from South America
↓
Goodrich's Garnet Chile
↓
Bresee's Early Rose
↓
The Burbank

The work of really hybridizing strains of potatoes began, so far as America is concerned, with the work of C. G. Pringle, noted botanist and explorer, whose creations were so valuabe that he could get one thousand dollars a pound for his seed. Many others have followed his work.

And what is it that makes a good potato variety? Good flavor? Something more than that. Old Goodrich laid down the first rules formulated for standards of potato excellence—that a potato should have good shape, white flesh, strong growth, hardiness, fine flavor and early ripening. To-day that list of requirements has been somewhat amplified. Good cooking qualities are essential. It must not be soggy when cooked, nor yet too lumpy. The yield must be heavy, and resistant to disease, and a popular fancy demands of the finest grades that they shall be round or oval and flattish. Also convention has outlawed the red-skinned potato, except in the southern states. A tendency in the plants to second growth is also desirable, and seed tubers must come true to type. No potato, perhaps, wins 100 per cent merit on all these counts, but a census of the favorite commercial varieties all over the country shows that some at least are close to perfection. Of the early varieties North, Bliss, Triumph and Early Ohio have proved their superiority through the years, whilst Green Mountain, Carman, Rural New Yorker and Sir Walter Raleigh have led among the "lates."

To test the cooking and eating qualities of a potato ordered from your grocer, cut a raw tuber and examine the cell structure with your magnifying glass. The pith should be small and the cells of approximately uniform size and color. A roughish purple skin is also a sign of many of the finest grades. After cooking, the potato should stay white when cold, glisten, crumble easily and contain no lumps.

To-day Europe produces almost 90 per cent of the world's potato crop and North America only about 8 per cent, while the remaining 2 per cent is divided among the other continents in negligible amounts. And so when the Great War broke out in Europe, potatoes came very naturally to the front rank of national policies. By June in the year 1914 it was apparent to German agricultural experts that there would be a bumper crop of potatoes in Germany. By the last of July German troops were on the march. Too much stress must not be laid on such inferences, of course; still it is as unlikely that Germany would have made war without a fine crop of her most important food staple as that she would have challenged the world with a low supply of ammunition.

In the story of rubber it has been told how the Germans used potatoes as a culture medium in which to grow bacteria to manufacture acetone both for the big guns and for synthetic rubber. The project had to be abandoned because the bacterial action was too irregular and because potatoes were so sorely needed for human food. The same crying need led England to issue a Potatoes Order in 1917, following the potato failure in Ireland in 1916. The price of potatoes had risen to £20 a ton, and threatened to soar higher till the Government fixed the price at £6 per ton.

Since the potato laid down its arms, as it were, in the years of peace since 1918 the chief interest in it has centered about the renewed search for the original wild potato. Darwin on his South American travels had commenced this work, and he brought home what he believed to be the wild potato, though it appears that it was what is really another species. The difficulties of determining what is really the wild ancestor of a cultivated plant become apparent when we realize that in all probability selection of advantageous variation through the ages of cultivation has bred the potato, like other crops, more or less away from the type of the original stock. Further, when a potato plant is found growing in the wild it is difficult to prove that it is not merely an escape from cultivation. Obviously the plant is a "wild" potato, but it has run wild, and was not "born" wild. From the point of view of infusing fresh blood into the cultivated strains, a mere wild escape from cultivation would probably not prove useful.

The ever increasing list of ills to which the potato

is heir have constantly intensified the need of obtaining wild strains in the hope of repeating the experiment that has so often been tried successfully with other plants, of getting healthy blood into over-civilized, weakling garden strains. Whether or not recent agricultural explorations have brought forth the genuine wild potato from its Andean home or not might still be questioned. But on plants believed to be the ancestral wild potato have been found in mild form some of the diseases now widespread and virulent.

Despite the onslaughts of the potatoes' enemies, however, the great tuber's future rests assured, a future bright with the promise of eternal usefulness. Humble the potato may be, plebeian even, but it is fraught with the destiny of common humanity the world over—the greatest public servant in the world.

SUGGESTED READING

SAFFORD, WM. E., "The Potato of Romance and of Reality," *Journ. Heredity,* Vol. 26, pp. 113–126, 175–184, 217–230, 1925. By far the most entertaining account of the potato, with detailed discussion of the Raleigh and Drake legends and long quotations from interesting source books on the archæology of the potato.

STUART, WM., *The Potato,* 1923. Excellent statistical information about potatoes as a world crop, also most entertaining accounts of potato breeding and breeders.

GILBERT, ARTHUR W., *The Potato,* 1917. Much good historical information on the introduction of the potato into Europe, on the potato famine, and Parmentier.

FRASER, SAMUEL, *The Potato*, 1905. On the horticultural side this work, while not exactly recent, remains authentic, and is easy reading.

SANDERS, T. W. (ed.), *The Book of the Potato*, 1905. Good on both the historical and horticultural sides and contains some information not found in any other references.

CHAPTER IX

BREADFRUIT AND A MUTINY

LIEUTENANT WILLIAM BLIGH, of H. M. S. *Bounty,* was sleeping peacefully in the dark hour before the dawn when the door of his cabin was burst open. Rudely awakened, he met the threatening faces of Mr. Christian, the first mate, and three others. They warned him of instant death if he made the least noise and in a trice had bound him securely.

Surrounded by bayonets and cutlasses and urged forward by curses, the master of the ship was forced on deck. Here in the chill and windy dawn he made out the forms of Mr. Nelson, botanist, Mr. Peckover, gunner, and Mr. Ledward, surgeon, bound like himself and but half-clad and shivering. The furious Bligh demanded to know the meaning of such revolt. But for threats upon his life, no one paid him the least attention, save one or two of the seamen plainly not of the mutinous party.

These were so few in number that they were powerless to resist the mutineers, who, cursing, forced them over the side into a small boat. The mate, ringleader of the conspiracy, was only with difficulty prevailed upon by the merciful to put the

Lieutenant and his adherents into the larger of the two ship's boats, the smaller being so worm-eaten that even Christian had to acknowledge it unable to stay afloat for a mile.

Into the boat went also one hundred and fifty pounds of bread, thirty-two pounds of pork, six quarts of rum, six bottles of wine and twenty-eight gallons of water. Besides these provisions were four cutlasses, a tool chest and a few nautical instruments. These last were allowed Bligh not without some misgivings upon the part of the mutineers.

"I'll be damned," one of them swore, "if he does not find his way home if he gets anything with him." And said another, "Damn my eyes, he will have a vessel built in a month." But most of the men who leaned jeering over the rail while the little craft was pushed off could imagine nothing but destruction as the fate of the occupants of the shallow boat so low in the water that even in calm weather its gunwales rode close to the waves' edge.

The distance grew wider and wider between the *Bounty* and the eighteen men adrift in mid-Pacific, and the last that Captain Bligh heard of the mutineers was a faint shout borne down the breeze, "Huzza for Otaheite!"

And thus disastrously ended the hopeful expedition which in 1788 had set out by order of His Majesty King George III in search of the almost fabulous breadfruit tree. Ever since the voyage of Captain Cook, eighteen years before, the tales about the marvels of this tree had been growing. The West India Committee of planters had repeatedly formulated resolves for its introduction from the South Sea Isles into their own islands, where it was hoped its many uses would turn to an idyll the life of the negro population.

The breadfruit and the coconut, the only two large trees which can support existence on the tiny and entirely coral islands of the Pacific, furnish jointly every necessity for existence. Before the more modern uses for copra were developed, the breadfruit had perhaps a slight preponderance of importance to Polynesians. The bast fibers of breadfruit furnish cloth, the seeds yield oil, the wood is light, strong, elastic and useful for the framework of houses; the roots yield an astringent decoction useful in dysentery and cutaneous troubles, while the fruit is the very staff of life in the lands where it is best known.

The name breadfruit is no such misnomer as grapefruit or alligator pear. The flesh when cooked has distinctly the taste of the finest white breadcrumbs, though richer and with a peculiar additional flavor which is described in as many ways as there are people to eat it. To some it tastes like "roasted chestnuts," to others it is peachlike; Lyon considers it to be "gummy" if at all overripe, and the most unfavorable opinion is that of the traveler Elmendorf, who says "it tastes like a wet dishrag!" The shape and size and markings of the fruit are various and the weight may be as little as a pound or as much as ten pounds. The best varieties are the seedless, which have been selected from Nature and propagated by man.

The appearance of the fruit is not unlike that of the familiar Osage-orange, a relative of breadfruit found in our country. That is to say, it is a large globose or pear-shaped compound fruit composed of many united carpels ripening into a joint, segmented and often nubbly head. The tree itself is fine to look upon, handsome in shape, with large, shining, somewhat fernlike or cut-lobed leaves. The big fruits hang on stout stalks from the leaf axils and are as striking in their way as growing grapefruit.

Dampier, that splendid old seaman, as far back as 1688 had been the first to tell the English-speaking world of breadfruit when he said, "It grows on a large tree, as big and high as our largest apple trees; it hath a spreading head, full of branches and dark leaves. The fruit grows on the boughs like apples; it is as big as a penny loaf when wheat is at five shillings the bushel; it is of a round shape and hath a thick, tough rind; when the fruit is ripe it is yellow and soft and the taste is sweet and pleasant. The natives of Guam use it for bread. They gather it, when full grown, while it is green and hard; then they bake it in an oven, which scorcheth the rind and makes it black, but they scrape off the outside black crust, and there remains a tender, thin crust; and the inside is soft, tender and white like the crumb of a penny loaf. There is neither seed nor stone in the inside, but all is of a pure substance like bread. It must be eaten new; for if it is kept above twenty-four hours it grows harsh and choaky; but it is very pleasant before it is too stale. This fruit lasts in season eight months in the year, during which the natives eat no other food of bread kind.''

On his first voyage around the world, Captain Cook met with breadfruit and was so delighted with it that he described it in such glowing terms as these: ''Of the many vegetables that have been mentioned already as serving them (the Polynesians) for food, the principal is the breadfruit, to procure which costs them no trouble or labour but climbing a tree. The tree which produces it does not indeed shoot up spontaneously, but if a man plants ten of them in his lifetime, which he may do in about an hour, he will as completely fulfill his duty to his own future generations as the native of our less temperate climate can do by ploughing in the cold of winter and reaping in the summer's heat, as often as these seasons return; even if, after he has procured bread for his present household, he should convert a surplus into money and lay it up for his children.''

This sounded very much like the material foundation for one of those Utopian societies desired ever since the days of the lotus eaters. Obviously the dweller beneath the breadfruit's grateful shade was under the necessity of no exertion but reaching forth a hand to provide himself with food, clothing and shelter. Still more glowing accounts of this tree were returned on Captain Cook's second voyage by the two Forsters, the botanists who accompanied him. Even Byron, who had no first-hand acquaintance with breadfruit, was led to celebrate it in atrocious poetry—

"The bread-tree, which, without the ploughshare yields
The unreaped harvest of unfurrowed fields
And bakes its unadulterated loaves
Without a furnace in unpurchased groves,
And flings off famine from its fertile breast
A priceless market for the gathering guest—"

The line about loaves baked without a furnace is a reference to the habit of some Polynesians of baking the fruit in the sun. Breadfruit was, as a matter of fact, more often cooked over a fire, or not infrequently, fermented in pits. Frederick O'Brien in his much-read book of South Sea travel dilates on the horrors of smelling the breadfruit pits of the Marquesas. In fact, a whole complex of culinary practice was evolved by the South Sea islanders in the varied preparations of what may be called their national dish.

A belief among the West Indian planters that breadfruit was the solution of all the negro's troubles was the stimulus prompting the West India Committee at last to offer £100 to any one who would bring in living condition plants certified to be the best varieties for plantation in the West Indies. This prize, offered year after year through the Society of Arts, Manufactures and Commerce in London, kept up the popular interest in the fruit. In 1787, under the auspices of Sir Joseph Banks, President of the Society, an expedition was fitted

out to go in search of the fabulous manna. The
botanist Nelson was selected to discover the fruits
and care for their transplanting, and Lieutenant
Bligh, who had served with Cook on the second trip
around the world, and knew many chiefs of Oceania
personally, was given command of the ship
Bounty. She sailed from Spithead on a stormy
December day and scudded under a furious wind
towards South America. The ship's leaks and the
resulting damage to the food stores were not only
auguries of doom, but were indications that she was
an old and unseaworthy vessel. She had to put in
at Teneriffe, off the coast of Africa, for refitting
and provisioning, and then under the gentler trade
winds she sailed for the equator. In the Doldrums
dreadful mildew attacked the food, the bedding and
the very clothing of the men and made life miserable
for all, especially the common seamen whose bunks
were far down in the boat where sunlight and fresh
air did not readily penetrate. But farther on in
the southern hemisphere chill came upon them, and
off the Horn terrific seas and icy cold were encountered. For thirty days the hapless ship tried to
batter its way around that angry promontory, until
at last the attempt was abandoned, and sailing with
the wind, the *Bounty* turned toward the Cape of
Good Hope. Once more time had to be granted to
refitting and resting, on this occasion at Cape Town,
and not until October 25 was the island of Tahiti
sighted, ten months after the departure from England. The natives welcomed Bligh as an old acquaintance, eagerly asked after Captain Cook, and

proudly showed Nelson the two shaddock or grape-fruit trees which he himself had planted there before. The description of that land before the days of white aggression pictures a sailor's fairyland. Languorous, soothing weather, rustling palms, rich foods, plenty of wild game to shoot and a people as unaffected and genial as ever dwelt in unspoiled innocence of heart. As for the ladies, as Bligh calls them, every one is agreed that they were in their deportment modest, innocent and gentle. These virtues seem not, however, to have been incompatible with a merry promiscuity of relations among the sailors; in fact, their very ingenuousness and un-awareness of all sentiments of wrong or shame doubtless made possible the rollicking good time enjoyed by most of the *Bounty's* crew. Bligh sup-presses all mention of this in his book and journal, but in veiled terms attributes to these revels the real cause of the mutiny. If he may be believed, the sailors after six months of care-free life with the Tahitians were unfitted for anything but lotus-eating among the cordial and beautiful daughters of the island. Further particulars of the story in-dicate that the implication in Bligh's narrative was the merest hint at the reality. Of course, Bligh was certainly responsible for this state of affairs. He did not need to spend six months at the island to get wood and water and collect breadfruit plants. One suspects that not only did he neglect discipline (notoriously necessary for sailors on shore), but that he himself was mightily enjoying his stay. He delighted, if not in some of the fair ones of the island, in the easy and pleasant rôle of white god, showered with hibiscus blossoms, loaded with gifts by the chiefs and enjoying, on the whole, a halcyon vacation.

In the obtainment of breadfruit plants the Lieutenant and the botanist were not, however, negligent. With the greatest ceremony Bligh presented to the chief gifts from King George in return for the kindness shown by the old man to Captain Cook. "And will you not send something in return to King George?" Bligh asked. "I will give him everything I own," said Tinah. And he proceeded to enumerate his possessions, including breadfruit trees. At this point his offer was eagerly taken up. King George would be overwhelmed with delight to see breadfruit trees at his great house in London. Suitable arrangements were made, and when at last the *Bounty* weighed anchor she carried seven hundred and seventy-four pots, thirty-nine tubs and twenty-four boxes of the long-sought tree. This amounted in all to a thousand and fifteen plants. There were also on board plants of "the *avee*, the *ayyah*, the *rattah* and the *orai-ab*, all delicious oceanic fruits." The hold was loaded with breadfruit for provision on the voyage. From the deck the crew witnessed affecting scenes of grief, as the natives, with tears coursing down their cheeks, waved a melancholy farewell to the white men's great proa.

On the twentieth of April, 1788, soon after leaving Tahiti, and while in the neighborhood of Tofoa, one of the Friendly Islands, the mutiny broke out. If Bligh is to be believed, he had taken every pre-

caution for the health and comfort of his crew. He
was, he says, just congratulating himself on a particularly successful and uneventful voyage when he
was without warning seized upon, denied every re-
quest for explanations, and cast adrift in a small
boat on the vast of the seas. At least that is the
story he tells in his journal published at the time
of the trial of the mutineers and intended for the
general public. He did not, however, allow any one
to see his original journal, kept from day to day,
where he makes mention of his accusations of theft
against the crew, of several chastisements, and of
threatening one sailor with a cutlass. These incidents, to which Bligh barely alludes, are substantiated, with corresponding dates, by members of
the crew, who interpret them quite differently and
also refer to further incidents of the same sort not
disclosed by the captain.

Quite contradictory to Bligh's account is the journal kept by Morrison, one of the mutineers, a man
of more than ordinary education and intelligence.
This relates how Bligh was haunted by a constant
obsession that the crew were stealing bread, coco-
nuts and other provisions. He held to the accusa-
tion, though unable to discover the offenders and
though the crew vowed the stores were untouched,
and continually ordered cuts in the mess. During
the voyage several floggings were administered, and
Bligh quarreled constantly with his officers, whom
he calls disobedient and impudent, but whom Morrison declares the victims of the captain's irascible
temper and abusive language and of the forgetful-

ness which caused him repeatedly to countermand and confuse his orders. Even the admirers of Bligh and his fellow officers, in later years, admit his testy temper and autocratic command. His curses at the mate are said to have particularly infuriated Christian, a man of good family and gentle upbringing. Morrison cites, for instance, the occasion when Christian was sent ashore to get water, under orders not to fire on any natives. Attacked with clubs and poisoned arrows, Christian and his men retreated without the water. For this he was abused by the captain as a damned coward. Of this incident Bligh makes no mention; indeed, he suppresses knowledge of practically all friction. He wrote, "Had the mutiny been occasioned by any grievances, real or imaginary, I must have discovered symptoms of their discontent, which would have put me on my guard, but the case was far otherwise." Yet Morrison relates that complaint was once formally made by the crew in respectful manner, according to the fashion prescribed by the articles of navigation.

But whether the crew rebelled with good cause or none no one can now tell, nor can any one say what were the plans of the mutineers as they watched Bligh's little boat fade to a speck on the blue horizon. The encumbrance of breadfruit trees was thrown overboard and Fletcher Christian took command. His first objective was Tahiti. But when the graceful palms of that island were seen once more waving in the breeze, varying sentiments attacked the mutineers. Of the twenty-five, all but nine de-

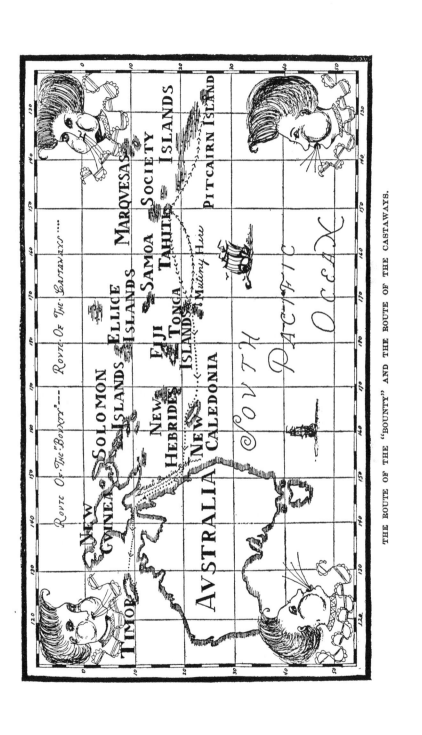

THE ROUTE OF THE "BOUNTY" AND THE ROUTE OF THE CASTAWAYS.

cided to stay at Tahiti. The adventurous nine set sail for parts unknown, and for a quarter of a century nothing more was heard of them. All believed that the *Bounty* and her occupants had gone to the bottom.

Meanwhile Bligh and his eighteen companions in their frail craft had determined with splendid courage to try to reach the nearest civilized settlement. They measured out the rations for each day —a wineglassful of water, a few ounces of salt pork, a teaspoon of rum and a couple of biscuits a day. A brief experience while trying to gather supplies at Tofoa convinced them that in their defenseless condition they dared not land at any islands until they reached the Dutch settlement at Timor, the isle of sandalwood, twelve hundred leagues away. They might well have shrunk before the impossibility of this feat, in the face of the weakness of their craft and the scarcity of provisions. But they dared to imagine its accomplishment. And with incredible sufferings from starvation and bad food, and in constant danger from the seas that half swamped the boat, the little band actually sailed and rowed that immense distance. They arrived at the palace of the Dutch Governor of Coupang looking like ghosts, nearly naked, reduced to skin and bones, and almost unable to stand. A boat conveyed them to England, all except the botanist Nelson, who died of rheumatic fever in Timor.

The pitiful and heroic story of Bligh and his associates was quick to fire public anger against the men who had with inhuman feeling cast them upon the waters of the Pacific. In the following year the frigate *Pandora* with twenty-four guns and one hundred and sixty men was dispatched under the command of Captain Edward Edwards to punish the mutineers. Arrived at Tahiti, the ship had no sooner anchored than there boarded it one of the mutineers, Phillip Heywood, who at the time of the mutiny had been but a promising lad of fifteen. When Bligh had returned to England, Heywood's mother had written inquiring for her son. Bligh replied with abusive language about him, and the hope that Mrs. Heywood might easily console herself for the loss of such a wicked boy. Heywood maintained throughout his life that he and Morrison had been forcibly detained on board the *Bounty* and not allowed to get into Bligh's boat as they wished. What substantiates his claim to good intentions is the readiness with which he boarded the *Pandora* and answered all questions regarding the mutiny.

The capture of fourteen members of the rebellious crew of the *Bounty* was soon after speedily affected. All were thrown into irons with hands and feet manacled, and placed in a cage on the deck, known as "Pandora's box." Sailor's superstitions might account these unhappy men Jonahs, for the *Pandora* met with disaster and wreck. Amid the storm the terrified prisoners, says Morrison, besought the Captain to open the scuttle and free them from their chains. No heed did he pay to their entreaties,[1] but one of the crew, as if by accident, let the keys for their release fall through the scuttle.

---

[1] Captain Edwards omits any mention of this in his account.

Nevertheless several of the mutineers were drowned. Morrison got his feet out of irons, though not his hands, and kept afloat until he was picked up. In a small boat the survivors had to traverse one thousand miles of sea, until, like the party of Bligh, they reached Timor.

But the load of breadfruit which Captain Edwards had also taken on at Tahiti, like its ill-fated predecessor went down to the bottom of the Pacific.

The trial of the mutineers in London caused the intensest excitement. Christian, the ringleader, had, to be sure, disappeared into the unknown with the *Bounty*, but the rage of Bligh and the indignation of the public turned savagely upon the captured men. On board H. M. S. *Duke*, in September, 1792, the court-martial assembled, Vice Admiral Lord Hood presiding. Morrison and Heywood were the only men who offered any strong defense except the few whom Bligh pointed out as having been unwillingly kept on the ship. Heywood's defense was marked by great manliness and courage, convincing evidence and considerable eloquence. The court acquitted four men of any voluntary participation in the crime and six were condemned to die by hanging, among whom were Heywood and Morrison. The court, however, recommended that these two be shown mercy. The king's warrant carried out the suggestions of the court in full, and on the whole it must be said that with the pardon of Heywood and Morrison, who were probably never guilty at all, justice was served.

The excited echoes of the *Bounty* mutiny had died

away when twenty years later Captain Folger in the U. S. S. *Topaz* reported to an astonished world that he had discovered on Pitcairn Island, in the South Seas, the descendants of Christian and the others who sailed away in the *Bounty*. The island, previous to the expedition of the *Bounty*, had not been inhabited. Its very location on the charts of the time was shown by Folger to be many leagues out of its true latitude and longitude. Then, two years after, in 1814, Captain Pipon of the *Tagus* was cruising in the Pacific when he sighted an unexpected island. Upon drawing near a small settlement he was surprised to hear a brown-skinned naked boy hail him in perfect English, "Won't you heave us a rope now?" This lad, Thursday October Christian, came on board and explained that he was the son of Fletcher Christian, now dead, and a Tahitian mother. He related the story of the *Bounty's* career in his father's hands as well as he knew it, but he was so excited by the sight of a cow and a dog on the boat, neither of which he had ever beheld before, that he had little interest for the telling of old tales. When the English landed they found that there lived on the island about ten native women, who had been Tahitian girls enticed or smuggled on board the *Bounty* when it sailed away under Christian, a host of children and unmarried boys and girls, and one old man who had been Alexander Smith of the *Bounty's* crew, and had now appropriately changed his name to John Adam, as he was the only man on the island and as, no doubt, he boasted the paternity of many of the handsome,

half-brown lads and maids who clustered about him.
It was perhaps the duty of Captain Pipon to hail
Adam back to court-martial. Actually he was as
guilty as any of mutiny and piracy. But by this
time almost every one else connected with the mutiny
was dead, except Heywood, who had risen to high
rank in the navy. The old man was the religious
leader of the island community, adored and looked
to for guidance by every one. With rare humanity
the captain put the past out of his mind, and no
one has ever suggested that he was wrong in so
doing.

Pitcairn Island at that time was a peaceable little
paradise in the midst of the most trackless part of
the Pacific. But when the mutineers and their
begged, borrowed and stolen Polynesian girls had
first arrived it had for a while been a hell. Some
Polynesian men had accompanied them; these the
whites enslaved and treated so brutally that they
had at last risen and slain half the tyrants. In
retaliation the mutineers pursued the Polynesians
into the interior, where ambush and counter-ambush
ended in the death of all but old Adam himself.
Since then gentleness, peace and joy had reigned in
a land that belonged, but for the old patriarch, entirely to women and children. As for Christian,
who had beached the *Bounty* and dismantled her, he
had been killed in a quarrel that came about when
he took a Polynesian girl away from a young native.

Such was the Utopian state of affairs in the early
part of the first century on Pitcairn Island—a Utopia
founded, one observes, on a sort of matriarchal rule

rather than breadfruit, but none the less quite a
heaven. The population of Pitcairn Island soon
after the visits of Pipon and Folger began to increase by reason of the marriages which ensued as
the boys and girls grew older. These budding ro-
mances would be all very sweet and innocent if it
were not for the fact that in the course of some
generations the few original strains became closely
intermingled. The young people, of course, were
not to blame for this state of affairs, nor, unedu-
cated in eugenics, for getting completely, and some
say dangerously, entangled the strands of their kin-
dredship. Attempts to solve the problem of consan-
guinity on Pitcairn have been made several times.
The inhabitants were vainly urged to disperse or to
procure fresh strains. Then the British Government
removed them *en masse,* in the hope they would gain
new blood, to Norfolk Island—whence they returned
in a body, for paradise is paradise, though inhabited
entirely by one's relations. A number of eugenicists
have sought out the island to study its problem, and
some have reported that degeneracy set in as a result of so much intermarriage, while others have
seen no ill effects.

And what of breadfruit, the Golden Fleece of this
unhappy Argosy? Captain Bligh, who, whatever
his faults, was certainly persevering, set out once
more on his quest. This time success attended him,
and breadfruit was brought to Jamaica and other
islands of the West Indies. In awarding him the
prize for the first introduction of breadfruit into the
West Indies, the West India Committee had for-

gotten an old record of its introduction in a French vessel which had been captured in the Caribbean by the British and brought to Spanish Town, Jamaica. From it some breadfruit trees had been removed and planted.[2] These were of the seedy variety, while Bligh's introduction had been seedless. It is said that the two strains can be traced to-day in the breadfruit trees of Jamaica.

But, after all, the much-lauded breadfruit was a bitter disappointment to the West Indian planters. Perhaps the glowing praise of Cook and others had set a mark impossible of attainment. Certain it is that it was never able to compete with the banana which was already established in the favor of the negroes as well as of the whites. The breadfruit trees fruit shyly in the West Indies, and as they are nearly all of the same variety they bear all at the same season; while in the East Indies the many varieties have different fruiting dates, furnishing food to the natives practically the year around. Moreover, breadfruit has no popularity in the markets of the United States. Its shipping qualities have proved poor, so that it does not arrive here in good condition. As a result breadfruit orchards are often cleared away to make room for the money-making banana.

Of late years, however, the Department of Agriculture has secured the best seedless varieties of the breadfruit as well as of the Jak, a close relative of southeastern Asia, and tried them out in tropical

---

[2] Also the Number Eleven Mango, forefather of one of our finest strains.

Florida. Breadfruit has been grown as far north as Manatee, on the West Coast. At present it is too rare in this country to be accounted an important fruit. But in view of modern refrigerated shipping facilities and the propagation of improved varieties, the breadfruit stands a chance of becoming better known and liked in northern markets.

One of the latest developments in the interest which has so long attached to breadfruit is the work of P. J. Wester, of Manila. He has devised an especially advantageous method of propagating the tree vegetatively and he now proposes to apply this to the selection of the finest varieties. He declares that in the various Polynesian islands a host of horticultural varieties have been evolved. As the Polynesians carried the tree from one island to another they acclimatized it to the different conditions of the countless isles and atolls of the Pacific. The result was the production of numerous local and often excellent varieties. These, he proposes, should now receive what they have never had before —scientific study and comparison. The best races should be propagated, hybridized and disseminated. From these experiments might result a race of breadfruit which would make for itself a place as important in the food supply of the world as it has a rôle fascinating in the annals of the Pacific.

SUGGESTED READING

BLIGH, WILLIAM, *A Narrative of the Mutiny on Board the Bounty*, 1790. A first-hand, terse, exciting account.

BARROW, SIR JOHN, *A Description of Pitcairn's Island and Its Inhabitants, with an Authentic Account of the Mutiny of the Ship* Bounty *and the Subsequent Fortunes of the Mutineers*, 1832. Practically a source book of the history of Pitcairn Island. Presents the mutineers' side of the case, and an account of the *Pandora* and the trial.

BAUM, H. E., "The Breadfruit," *Plant World*, Vol. 6, pp. 197–202, 225–231, 273–278. An entertaining account of the romantic history of breadfruit, with much about its economic botany.

WESTER, P. J., "The Breadfruit; a plea for the preservation of varieties," *Journ. Heredity*, Vol. 13, pp. 129–135. The outlook for breadfruit. Dr. Wester is the foremost horticultural authority on this matter in our day.

WASHBURN, F. L., "Breadfruit in the Marquesas," *Science*, Vol. 59, pp. 359–360, 1924. A recent, hopeful view of breadfruit in the South Seas.

WILCOX, EARLEY V., *Tropical Agriculture*, 1916, Chap. X, "Starchy Foods." Information on the character of the breadfruit tree, its culture, and the variety of uses for the fruit.

CHAPTER X

THE POPPY—BLESSING AND CURSE

O N one side of the balance blessed sleep, relief from pain for millions of sufferers. On the other side a hideous drowsiness and sloth and the degrading of millions of souls. Thus do curse and blessing counterbalance each other in her scales when impartial Justice weighs opium.

To-day there is probably more land under the opium poppy than ever before, and, if report speak true, more addicts of opium and its derivatives morphine, heroin, laudanum and codeine. How did such a degrading and pernicious state of things come about, and how is it to be put to rights?

During the centuries that the poppy was grown in Asia Minor in ancient times, the hydra had not assumed its shape. In the days of the classic medicobotanists, Theophrastus, Hippocrates and Dioscorides, the stems, leaves, and capsules of the lavender-flowered poppy of Persia were employed for preparing an extract called *meconium*. This soporific drug was a mild sleeping potion and soothing beverage which might have been administered to children in those far-away days, just as, until recent years, mothers gave teething children soothing syrups containing opium. Later in the history of

Greek medicine came the knowledge that the juice or *opion* of the seed-pods of poppy was powerful as a nerve-benumbing drug. With this discovery the value of the poppy was enhanced many fold and its fame among the herbalists and doctors spread far and wide. Those clever physicians, the Arabs, took with them in their conquering era seeds of the sleeping poppy—*Papaver somniferum* as botanists call it—and sowed it in the fields of India, whence it spread to China and throughout southeastern Asia.

There is no mention among Greek texts of the abusive employment of opium. By the high-minded doctors of Athens and Alexandria it was regarded in the same light as in professional circles of Europe to-day. Apparently it was rarely used except by order of a physician, and it is probable, too, that the classic extracts and tinctures were not nearly so powerful as the modern ones, and almost certainly not so heavily charged with morphine.

But when the poppy reached the Orient it fell into hands that turned its kindly power to evil. Its excessive use probably originated among the luxury-loving, sensation-jaded princes, for at first it was a monopoly of the moguls. Those who wished to excite themselves in love, especially persons exhausted by excess, swallowed little pellets of opium wrapped in rare, tasty spices; if they got from this dose the sensations they looked for it was probably only mentally. Opium is not really an aphrodisiac except that it weakens the will and induces roseate trances. But in such guise was it consumed by the great princes.

From the palaces down to the hovels the use of
the poppy spread. As a cure for malaria, dysentery
and cholera—diseases endemic in the unhealthy lowlands of India—opium gained immense popular
repute. There was no doubt about its ability to
relieve the sufferings from those maladies, and in
the cases of dysentery and cholera the astringent
effect upon the intestines certainly gave relief in
the gravest phases of those dreaded plagues.

But whether really or apparently a cure, the use
of opium as a medicine is distinctly dangerous. The
patient's nervous system, once thoroughly drugged,
becomes hypersensitive. Presently the victim dis-
covers that his usual dose does not suffice him; to
numb the pain he must increase the potion. Even
if perfectly recovered from the original disease, he
now feels sick and shattered without the drug. This
is the beginning of the end for the opium addict.
Business affairs go to the wind, the moral fiber
softens, physical prostration follows and death
comes at last in the rôle of mercy.

When once opium had fastened its tentacles upon
India, princes forgot the affairs of state and allowed
their power to crumble, merchants failed to open
their shops, laborers let their fields grow up with
weeds. Of all those who took the poppy only those
in the initial stages of the habit showed any signs
of energy—and this was that feverish, stimulated
energy that comes while the nervous system is yet
new to the narcotic.

A graphic sketch of a case of opium poisoning has
been given by Garcia da Orta, the Portuguese phy-

sician who lived and practiced in India five hundred years ago. In the form of a dialogue he describes the excited entrance of a girl who states that her mistress has been poisoned. The doctor hurries to her house and sees the woman lying on the floor in delirium. He notes the feeble pulse, the pin-point pupils, the clammy hands, the incoherent speech. The physician then sends the girl for antidotes and discourses learnedly upon the ancient and contemporary uses of the drug.

When the Portuguese came to southern India they were quick to grasp the idea that opium, a rare and precious drug in Europe, could be exploited for enormous gain. With the spices and the dyes, it made up part of those colorful cargoes which the mariners of Lisbon brought home. From Portugal the drug sold to all parts of the world—not only in Europe but in the Americas as well. And now it was not only the physicians bringing relief from suffering who bought the drug. The opium habit practically for the first time fastened its grip upon the West. Literature reflects that a small, a very small, but an ominous proportion of Europe was yielding to the temptation of the narcotic. The cloud was then no bigger than a man's hand.

After the Portuguese, the Dutch, and after them, the English. So goes the sovereignty of oriental trade. When the Honorable British East India Company inherited Indian commerce, it received also from its predecessors the legacy of the opium trade and its monopolies. The Dutch had discovered in opium a goose which laid golden eggs and they fat-

tened the prolific fowl in Java. When they withdrew from India they presented to their conquerors
a Pandora's box. The English opened the lid of the
opium chest, and out flew the evil spirits.

Whether in the hot lowlands of Bengal, or the dry
uplands of Rajputana, travelers have marveled to
see the irrigated acres of the poppy, splendid and
ephemeral with its gorgeous and fragile petals of
lavender, red or white. But it is a sight to be caught
only at certain times. For after the petals have
been four days expanded, they are removed and carefully stored, for they are the "flower leaves" in
which the opium is wrapped. When, therefore, the
brief Indian winter is over and the January spring-
time has arrived, the collection of opium begins.
From then until March the great harvest proceeds.
Later in the season there may be a second or even a
third sowing, but from these no such yields of opium
may be expected, even on the rich black "cotton
soils" where it is generally raised. In the first and
principal harvest the native planter expects the big
green seed pods or capsules to ripen about nine days
after the petals are plucked, and if he is so lucky as
to have gentle showers at this time his labors will
be more swiftly rewarded. When at last the capsules
are adjudged mature, and the farmer assures himself of this by testing to see that they yield to the
pressure of the fingers, and notices that they have
that soft bluish bloom which easily rubs off, then it
is time to tap. A diagonal slice is cut in the wall of
the capsule. After each incision, the collector draws
the knife through his mouth so that by wetting the

blade with saliva he can prevent any juice from being lost by adhering to the iron. Working after the heat of the day, he thus moves swiftly down the rows, tapping hundreds of plants until darkness stops his labors. In the morning he returns to collect the juice which has exuded from the incisions. With a *setwah,* a small trowel-shaped scoop of thin iron, the half-coagulated sap is scraped off into a poppy leaf held in the hand, or into an earthen vessel, and when the vessel is full it is conveyed to the farmer's house. Standard amounts of opium are then wrapped in steamed and cohering "flower leaves" or poppy petals, so that the finished opium packet looks like a Dutch cheese.

In this work whole farm communities take part. The children hoe and harrow the fields, the women, schooled in just the right caressing, deft motion by which the petals are pulled off, delicately do their part; the young men tap the capsules and finally, one and all sit in the shade with little brass molding cups, rolling the cakes. Sometimes, too, there are still others who engage in the wily craft of adulteration, adding to the juice linseed oil, or including in the cakes "trash opium" (rejected scraps) and such a shameless miscellany of substances as *ghur* or date sugar, cow-dung, sand, clay, mud, soot, tobacco juice, stramonium the trance-inducing drug, and gums of every sort.

But picturesque as is all this, and there is no doubt that it has the appearance of a wholesome family industry, the great areas under the poppy in India constituted in the early days of the English su-

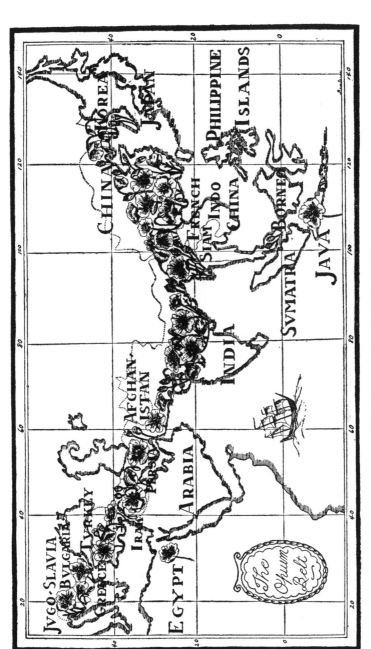

THE OPIUM BELT OF THE WORLD

premacy just such an evil as they do to-day. National and international were the complications, the tyrannies, the financial ruin, and the crimes, which opium caused. The British East India Company, "finding that the opium trade was growing inordinately" established a monopoly upon it as early as 1797. It was not only the inordinate growth of the trade but the dangerous fluctuation of price which induced them to try to control opium.

Sir George Watt has retold the narrative of Ram Chand Pandit, an Indian dealer of those days: "There was a body of native merchants then resident at Patna, known as opium dealers, who made advances to the cultivators and received in return the opium produced, took it to their houses, and made it up in the form required by the exporters. After the growers had delivered as much as liquidated the advances received" (the farmers regularly borrowed money in advance on their crops), "they disposed of the surplus as they thought fit, and the price rose accordingly. In October the opium being prepared in the required form, the merchants used to offer it for sale first to the Dutch, having previously agreed among themselves as to the rate they would accept. . . . After such preliminary sales the dealers would then go to the English merchants and offer a further quantity at a higher rate and finally they would go to the French and dispose of some more at a still higher rate. Thereafter, say in November, the Dutch would make a second contract with the opium merchants, but at a higher price than their first agreement, and usually by this time the *pykars*

or small traders who had picked up here and there
small odd parcels, brought their much adulterated
article to market and thus lowered the price of the
closing sales."

Such a system was plainly more profitable to the
native vendors than to the English. Warren Hast-
ings, Governor of the Company's province of Bengal, in 1773 sought to knit together discordant
elements by a fresh state monopoly. A fixed amount
of opium was promised to the Danes, Dutch and
French. The Company reserved to itself the exclusive right of manufacture, and made contracts
with foreign buyers on four-year agreements. It
had, on the other hand, to make some corresponding
agreement with the native middlemen who were
regular contractors and these in turn, lending money
to the peasant farmers, could, especially if they were
skilful in keeping the farmers in debt, force thousands of landowners to raise the poppy when they
really did not wish to do so. As the demand for
opium steadily increased abroad, especially in China,
the poppy every year widened its areas. If there
were slaves of the opium habit there were also many
more involuntary slaves of poppy culture, who had to
raise the plant in order to pay their indebtedness
to the contractors or else give up their land to make
room for those who were willing to produce opium.

There was also a law framed which prevented the
cultivator from holding back any of his produce, and
so, under pretext of a poor yield, defraud the middlemen who had advanced money on the crop. Dealing
in opium contrary to the regulations of the monopoly

was a criminal offense. The severity of the law fell most heavily upon the cultivator, and the compulsory growing of the poppy could not be escaped.

The contract system having proved pernicious, direct government control was substituted, intended to eliminate the meddlesome native middlemen. By this arrangement, which is still practically in force, any native may grow the poppy, and may even receive an advance from the Government banks. He disposes of his crop directly to the Government, and by law may sell to no one else. In this way the British Government attempts to prevent "leakage" of the drug from the collector to unauthorized buyers. But the Government, after selling regulated amounts of opium to European wholesale drug firms accredited to import it, disposes of the surplus at public auction. What the native buyers at this sale subsequently do with the immense amounts of opium so distributed every year appears to be no concern of the Government.

But it is in the Flowery Kingdom that the history of the poppy has been the darkest. Even before the Portuguese came to India, the Chinese had learned of the use of opium from the Arab traders. When the English gained control in India a thriving trade in opium was going on between that country and China. To be sure, the last of the Ming emperors issued an edict against opium just about the time that King James I in his *Counterblaste to Tobacco* tried to stem the tide in favor of the more innocent smoke. Previously opium had only been swallowed; the effects of taking it this way, sensuously made attractive by spicing it, were bad enough. But the idea of burning it and inhaling the fumes only came to the Orient after the spread of tobacco smoking had pointed the way. When Sir Walter Raleigh popularized the pipe he brought a mild solace to the world, but at the same time he unconsciously did humanity a great harm. Tobacco smoking having become prevalent in the Spanish colonies, it spread from the Philippines to Canton, where instead of "the weed," the poppy was smoked. The physician tells us that in this way much more morphine is obtained and absorbed by the system. The morphine habit is many fold more terrible than that of swallowing opium, and is, relatively speaking, a new evil. Pure morphine is a product of the present day rather than of the past. But as early as 1620 the morphine habit had begun its ravages in South China in the form of opium smoking.

After the end of the Ming dynasty a new and more barbaric line of rulers came to the throne. It was in these years that, with the connivance of many officials, opium smoking spread prodigiously. Not for a hundred years did another ruler try to stop the nefarious traffic. Then came His Celestial Majesty, Yung Cheng, a man of strong moral courage, with the welfare of his people at heart, who prohibited with death the smoking of the poppy. But not until seventy years later was the importation of opium forbidden. Previously Portuguese ships had been allowed to bring it to their treaty port at Macao and sell it up river in Canton. When the British trade came to supersede that of Portugal, it found that opium was one of the few products which its ships could profitably carry on the voyage from Calcutta to Hongkong. Great was the indignation of the English when an imperial edict forbade them to land their drug. They howled about the "ruin of the trade," and the Indian Government, which drew from the opium revenue vast fortunes, complained that it could not carry on the duties of administration if the export of the narcotic were curtailed. To the remonstrances of the court at Peking the British were deaf. Their trading ships merely anchored off the mouth of the river and waited for the Cantonese merchants to come out in their junks. Merchant and captain then haggled the price, and finally, in midwater, the chests were transferred. Of course the merchants were forbidden to bring the opium into the city, but they usually bribed the customs officers. Sometimes the mandarins themselves were engaged in the smuggling business. More than likely they were opium addicts and had no moral scruples about admitting the drug; they may even have been too stupefied to notice what went through their hands.

Again and again the Emperor requested the British to withdraw the ships which hung about the entrance to the corrupted city of Canton as flies hover around carrion. Receiving no answer the Celestial Court dallied no longer. Nothing could be done with the corrupt local officials, so the Emperor dispatched to the scene Lin, an imperial commissioner. This man appears to have been unusually active for a mandarin. Arrived in Canton, he cleared out all grafting officers and proceeded to issue his edict of 1839 in which he threatened violence to the opium ships. He knew very well that there were more than sixteen thousand opium chests a year imported into China, and no equivocal answers could alter these figures. As the smuggling continued, Commissioner Lin decided on drastic action. Quite without warning he entered the British compound at Canton, ignored the British flag, seized twenty thousand two hundred and ninety-one chests of the drug and burned them before the traders' eyes. Then what a clamor of protest arose! The British merchant traders clamored for war. They had lost two million pounds' worth of opium— the Indian revenues would be ruined—the Chinese had violated the English flag.

The conflict which followed has always been called, even by the English, the First Opium War. A great deal has been said in condemnation of Lin and in defense of the English. It is undeniable that the Commissioner violated the British flag and that he burned British property. The British, however, were breaking the laws of his country; they knew it and refused to rectify matters. Their attitude in fact said: "Well, what can you do about it?" Lin's reply when he violated the flag was not according to the Marquis of Queensbury's rules. From his point of view, however, the British flag represented only a barbarian country, for the British whom he knew were all smugglers and incorrigible lawbreakers. He had his orders from his Emperor and he did what he had been sent to do—he stopped the opium traffic.

The British have argued that the Chinese could have adjusted the whole matter with the Indian Government and so saved themselves the war that followed. They explained in this wise: "Had the Chinese Government taken the course open to it, and that too, without arbitrary injury to a trade of large proportions (the growth of several centuries), namely, to impose a gradually increasing taxation on imported opium; had it exercised also the power which it should have possessed if it did not do so, of restricting or prohibiting the cultivation of the poppy within its own territory, little would have been heard of the perplexing Opium Question to-day."

Sir George Watt's ingenious, litigatory argument, above quoted, has done much to becloud the now almost forgotten issues of that war. In reality this line of thought answers nothing to the justly indignant contentions of the Chinese. From the point of view of Tao Kwang, Son of Heaven, a seducing evil beyond the limits of the individual's self-control was demoralizing his people. One half the land in the province of Yunnan was under the poppy. Everything that could be done to terminate this cultivation was tried, but officials sent out to stop it became themselves opium addicts, or saw a chance to grow rich in the business, and failed to carry out orders. The talk about taxing imported opium was folly, because it merely meant that smuggling would increase. With a long seacoast and no strong navy,

China could not possibly stop smuggling when half
the officials were interested in opium importation
and while the English stationed their opium ships
off the coast and defended themselves with superior
guns. The Emperor had negotiated politely to the
end of his patience. He got no results, and so
ordered Lin to take any measures to see that the
law was carried out. Sir George Watt, and every
one else who has tried to explain the British case,
has been careful to avoid trying to answer the
Chinese arguments. The reason is simple; there is
no answer.

But might triumphed over right. The war ended
inconclusively in the Treaty of Nanking by which
the British forced China to open five treaty ports
for British trade and to cede to them the island
of Hongkong, close to Canton. Ever since Hongkong has been the chief strategic center of British
trade and naval strength in China waters. Its
growth involved the ruin of the near-by ancient
Portuguese trading city of Macao.

The opium question itself was not mentioned in
the treaty; but the English had not forgotten it and
they approached the Emperor on the matter. That
unfortunate monarch was wrestling with the suppression of poppy culture in his own land; province
after province had taken it up. Acres needed to
grow food for the millions of his people were given
over to the crop that brought only woe. The smuggling from India was more rife than ever. He replied that he certainly did not intend on top of these
difficulties in trying to save a people bent on their

own destruction, to hasten their end by legalizing foreign imports. The British, rebuffed by the Government they had just defeated, were bellicosely disposed. They and the French had a long list of grievances against the Chinese Government, and it is quite true that many of them were real, for the Chinese officials were a haughty and dishonest lot obstinately bent on obstructing European trade. But for the Chinese it must be said that the British were registering the smuggling junks as British boats at Hongkong, and that they kidnaped Chinese coolies and impressed them as seamen. When the Chinese stopped a ship flying British colors and removed from it three Chinamen said to be pirates, the Second Opium War began. It ended in the Treaty of Tientsin, by which the importation of opium was legalized. Beside this England, France, Russia and the United States obtained the right to maintain ministries close to the Sacred City, and were given leave to trade in the interior.

Now the last dam of resistance was broken down and the lethal waters rushed over China. The apathy and lack of decision displayed by the whole nation in subsequent years shows only too plainly the ravages of the drug habit. To-day every province in China grows opium. In Shansi they have a saying that nine out of every eight persons smokes opium. And recently morphine imported from Europe and America has come to add a worse menace to the situation

More than once persons in England have sought to undo the work of the Opium Wars. Commissions have been appointed by the House of Commons to investigate the evil, both in China and in India. But, as a recent writer has put it, the commissions have generally shown more interest in seeing that the opium revenues of India were not diminished than in finding ways to stop the evil. In 1906 Lord Morley said: ''I do not wish to speak in disparagement of the Commission, but somehow or other its findings have failed to satisfy public opinion in Great Britain and to ease the consciences of those who have taken up the matter. What was the value of medical views as to whether opium was a good thing or not when we had the evidence of nations who knew opium at close quarters? The Philippine Opium Committee in a passage of their report, which I hope the House of Commons will take to heart, declared the United States so recognized the use of opium as an evil, for which no financial gain can compensate, that she would not allow her citizens to encourage it even passively.''

The report of the Royal Commission in 1904 had suppressed further discussion of the opium problem. But Lord Morley's plea two years later was instrumental in reopening the whole matter, to the satisfaction of China. In good faith India and China agreed on measures to suppress the traffic by a gradual curtailing of imports. India was to reduce the amount of opium exported to China by one-tenth annually; in this way in ten years no opium at all would be exported. On her side, China agreed to suppress the cultivation of the poppy within her borders. This was to satisfy the Indian growers that China was not merely trying to localize the culture of the poppy at home, to her own profit. By tapering off the exports gradually India was saved from ruining her opium growers. It meant an annual loss in her revenue of thirty million rupees for the administration of the Indian Government, but to her credit be it said that she undertook this sacrifice without complaint.

Both parties were carrying out their agreements in good faith when there came the years of the world's upheavel. Strong government in China gave place to rule by armed bands; law and order melted away, and the poppy, like an evil growth cut back, sprouted again.

Now famine hovers over China. The land is yielding to the seductions of the poppy. It is from three to twenty-three times as profitable to grow opium as it is to grow wheat or most other foods; as a result few farmers in Yunnan, for instance, raise any food crops. Since there are so few railroads in China such a condition of affairs means that though the farmers may grow rich off opium they will have nothing to eat. Money cannot buy food if there is no food, and men with their belts lined with gold have been known to starve to death.

To-day all countries have their opium and morphine problems. The poppy, grown from Turkey to Manchuria, is used to poison and stupefy, to degrade and kill, in every land on the earth. Despite the splendid work of private and official organizations for the suppression of the drug evil, the situation seems scarcely better. In our own country startling revelations are continually coming to light; officials employed for the suppression of opium smuggling have been found to be the worst smugglers of all; sanitariums are exposed as factories from which drug addicts are turned out. The worst alarmists have much reason on their side. Where does the "dope" come from? In part by the underground railway, from ill-regulated Mexico and from Canada. Our neighbor on the north has her own anti-opium legislation, and conscientious Canadians are as anxious as we to stop the evil. But somehow the drug gets in, smuggled probably from other British possessions, in the East, and it seems to be easier to whisk it over our border from Canada than it is to get it into this country directly.

For this problem there appears to be no ready solution. However active our customs officials, they are up against long odds while Turkey, Persia, India and China continue to grow opium without restriction. Could all the nations which grow the poppy be induced or forced to stop its cultivation, the evil would be at an end.

Yet at the International Opium Convention at The Hague in 1914 only five nations would sign the protocol. The recent conference in Geneva faithfully imitated its predecessor. India and the Dutch East Indies found it impossible to regard the interest of humanity as greater than their own. Only China and the United States took a clear-cut stand for international morals and withdrew from a conference to the narrow sentiments of which they could not subscribe.

Suppose for a moment even a fraction of possible pressure were brought to bear upon the question of opium production. Suppose that some nation could be found so intelligent as to protest against the poisoning of its citizens by foreign drugs as forcibly as it would were its national honor to be insulted. Might not some good results follow? But it is doubtful if this will happen.

Diplomats rush to war over an affair of national vanity, but they hedge and evade over the drug question. The only exception to this was the war to force the Chinese to permit the importation of opium. Has it occurred to any nation to force the Chinese or any one else to stop exporting opium?

But if the poppy should no longer be cultivated, where would we obtain opium for reputable use? It should be made plain that all the opium legitimately prescribed by conscientious doctors the world over could be produced on very little land. Each of the opium-consuming countries, for instance, might be allowed to raise a certain prescribed amount on officially supervised farms. In such case there would be no dangerous surplus, almost no chance that the growers would secretly dispose of the crops to dishonest dealers. No excuse could be offered for importing any opium whatever, as each nation would have its own supply measured out by its government in such small quantities as medical use actually demands. The thousands upon thousands of acres now devoted to the poppy could be used for growing wheat, cotton and other useful plants.

The opium poppy is a legacy from the ancients. To it we owe what is undeniably an immense benefit. But that benefit can be overrated; there are other soporifics and anæsthetics as efficacious as opium and its derivatives, and some of them are not nearly so menacing. If these were increasingly used there would be less and less excuse for growing opium. It is time that the poppy should reverse its history. Up to the present it has emerged from a rôle merely ornamental through the stage of use as a mild sedative, moderately and locally grown, to a place of vast importance, a crop from which cities like Singapore derive over half their revenue, one occupying many thousands of acres, driving out more useful crops, causing wars, degrading nations, ever intensifying its grip on land and on man. Now one would like to see the drama played backwards, see the poppy recede from its present high-water mark, see even its legitimate use confined to that of a carefully administered soporific, see it give back to wheat and cotton the precious soil which it usurps, until at last the poppy comes to the end of its story, where it started, as a gay, beautiful denizen of our gardens.

When that day comes we may all honestly grow the poppy; the art of opium extraction will be forgotten—known only to a small class of pharmacists and special cultivators, and as we look on the splendid flower we can regard it with that curiosity and interest which one feels when seeing the effigy of some general of long ago—one who has moved nations, made wars, brought terror, brought peace.

SUGGESTED READING

La Motte, Ellen M., *The Opium Monopoly*, 1920. A trenchant view of the opium evil in the British Orient to-day.

Wright, Elizabeth W., "The Trail of Opium," *Asia*, Vol. 24, pp. 667–672, 1924. A vivid account of modern opium smuggling and the Opium Wars.

Watt, Sir George, *Economic Products of India*, 1908, see *Papaver somniferum*. The story of the Indian opium trade in encyclopedic style. Sir George champions England's crime.

Encyclopædia Britannica. See "Opium." Much historical and agricultural detail.

Wilcox, Earley V., *Tropical Agriculture*, 1916, Chap. XIV, "Drugs." Methods of opium growing and producing explained simply.

CHAPTER XI

TOBACCO—THE COMPANIONABLE WEED

The Frenchman sips his minnikin roll;
The Dutchman loves his porcelain bowl;
The woodsman lights his cob with a coal;
The Scotsman puffs it brawly.
Then here's to the good old Indian chief
Who sowed the seed, who gathered the leaf,
And gave the pipe that banishes grief
To brave Sir Walter Raleigh!

ARTHUR GUITERMAN.

DID your school history have a picture of a servant throwing a pail of water over Sir Walter Raleigh as that great gentleman sat a-puffing on his pipe? The scene smacks a bit of the cherry tree story about George Washington, and there is nothing in Raleigh's own writings to support it. In fact, the historian, always unmerciful toward our favorite legends, does not grant Sir Walter even the honor of being the first to bring tobacco into England or to smoke it there, though he permits us the gallant picture of Sir Walter smoking before his execution.[1]

---

[1] There is no reason to think that Raleigh was either the first grower or smoker of tobacco except for the statement of Howe, chronicler of Queen Elizabeth's reign, that "Apricocks, Mellycatons, Musk-millions and Tobacco came into England about the second

215

Columbus himself was the first white man who ever saw tobacco, though he did nothing towards introducing it into Europe, just as he was the first to note rubber and yet foresaw none of its possibilities. At the time of the Discovery tobacco and corn were the two most widely grown crops of the Indians, both in North and South America. Tobacco was grown from southern Canada to northern Patagonia except on the deserts and high mountains of the Pacific coast. To regions too cold for tobacco's culture the leaf was carried and bartered for among the tribes of those districts, except among the Indians of Tierra del Fuego, who knew nothing of its use, and those of arctic North America.[2]

The smoke that is now the common man's everyday solace was to the ancient Indian a significant reverence. For tobacco was well-nigh a sacred plant, and its smoke was analogous to incense. Its

---

yeare of Queene Elizabeth" (1577), and the marginal note, "Sir Walter Raleigh was the first that brought Tobacco into use, when all men wondered what it meant." As Howe was historically unreliable in many ways, it is impossible to give weight to his claim for Raleigh.

[2] About the early introductions of the weed into Europe controversy has centered for years, and a great deal of misunderstanding prevails. Confusion arises from the fact that two chief kinds of tobacco were in use among the Indians (beside many minor local species) and were separately brought to Europe. The first species to reach Europe was *Nicotiana rustica*, which was grown by the Indians of the United States east of the Rockies, and in the West Indies, and still persists in some states in old fields, as a relic of Indian cultivation. It is commercially grown now only in the Near East and often enters into cheap grades of Egyptian and Turkish cigarettes. A far superior species, *Nicotiana tabacum*, reached Europe later. It is the real tobacco, in the modern sense of the word, and is the chief commercial kind the world over. It was a native of the Caribbean region.

use in ritual was varied; it was cast into the air, or buried, or left as an offering by pilgrims to a shrine. The angry gods might still the waves if tobacco were thrown on the troubled waters. But to abuse tobacco would have been to the Indian as impious as it would seem to us to get drunk on communion wine. Such bestialities remained for his European conquerors to commit.

Thus when the white man learned to smoke he adopted an art already developed. It was in 1565 that Admiral Sir John Hawkins brought from the West Indies the first tobacco (*Nicotiana rustica*) to reach England. It was only in 1753 that Sir Francis Drake exhibited the first samples of modern tobacco (*Nicotiana tabacum*), and only then did smoking commence in earnest.

The smoke of tobacco encircled the globe, penetrating every cranny, stealing through the barriers of race, language and prejudice. The speed of its spread may have been due in part to the increased transportation facilities of the sixteenth century, when the Portuguese and Spanish ships crossed and recrossed the seven seas, exchanging the hitherto local products of all nations. Cotton of the New World was taken to the Old in the same bottoms that brought tobacco, and corn invaded the East from the West at the same time.

But though corn and cotton are now widespread they got their foothold only slowly. Tobacco spread faster from the New World than the discovery of the western hemisphere itself—not in enlightened circles of Europe, of course, but among the people of Asia,

Africa and Oceania. A little more than a century after the Discovery, brown men, black men, yellow men, who were puffing their tobacco as though their ancestors had done it from antiquity, would, if told that a new hemisphere had been found, only have removed their carven pipes from their lips in a gesture of mild interest.

Tobacco spread faster than news, faster than cholera and smallpox. In fact, in a short time the tobacco habit was so firmly established in the Orient that did we know nothing of its American antiquity, it might be supposed that the habit originated in the East. The pipe has reached its most elaborate development east of Suez in the form of the water pipe or hookah. Made of gold, ivory, jade and every precious substance, decorated with all the minute skill of the Oriental painter, sculptor and metal worker, the water pipe, with all it stands for of a reflective indolence and a large hospitality, is what the Asiatic has made of the religious ritual of his far-away red brother.

Yet the attempt has often been made to show that smoking originated in the East, and that early Portuguese sailors took the custom to Europe and America. But every evidence is against this. No smoking instruments of any antiquity can be produced in the Old World, and the custom has never entered into the religious life of the East. There are, further, no native species of Nicotiana in Eurasia. The genus is indigenous in Polynesia and a small tribe of Australian natives chewed the leaf of a species of their own. Culturally these people

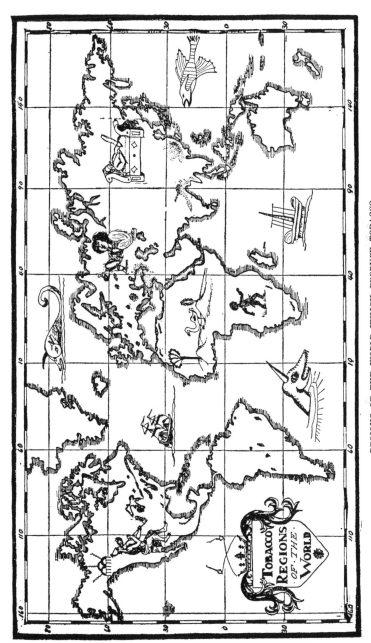

REGIONS OF THE WORLD WHICH PRODUCE TOBACCO

were, however, quite out of contact with the rest of the world and their custom, in all events, bears no relation to smoking. In fact it had not even occurred to the Asiatics that opium might be smoked instead of swallowed until tobacco smoking reached China from the Philippines.

Nothing in the spread of tobacco around the world is so remarkable as the zonation of the various uses to which it is put. The tobacco habit was clearly divided into geographical zones among the Indians. In South America and the West Indies, especially Cuba, the cigar was the dominant smoke, and as these lands were nearly all conquered by the Spanish, it is but natural that the cigar became and still is the national smoke of Spain. The juxtaposition of the United States and Cuba has also given the cigar strong hold in this country. The Spanish dominion of the Philippines has made Manila cigars famous, and to such extent as Asia has taken up the use of the cigar it was by borrowing it from the Philippines.

The cigarette, on the other hand, is primarily the smoke of Mexico and Central America—in Aztec times as to-day. The Spanish took the cigarette to the mother country, where it vies with the cigar for popularity but scarcely outdistances it. Spreading eastward through the Mediterranean countries, however, the cigarette came into its own. It seems to make an especial appeal to the Italian, Greek, Algerian, Egyptian, Arab and Turk. The religious or commercial influences of Greece and Turkey, by way of the Black Sea, are probably responsible for the dominance of the cigarette in Russia and it was by way of Russia that the cigarette, like snuff, reached Siberia, Mongolia and finally, having completed the circuit of the world, got into Alaska among the Indians, who were largely ignorant of its use and smoked only pipes. Now, throughout civilization, the cigarette is the smoke of to-morrow; the rate of its production increase excels that of any other form of tobacco using.

The pipe is, primarily, the invention of the Indians of the United States. There were, to be sure, some pipes among the Mexican Indians—pipes indeed of more diverse and elaborate form and more beautiful workmanship than the cruder Indians of the United States could boast.[3] There were pipes, too, in South America, some of good workmanship, but there the cigar was ever dominant.

Thus it was that the English conquerors of the Indians of the United States were the men who spread the pipe through Europe. The fame of the English pipe is securely supreme. In elaboration the jewel-encrusted water pipes of the Orient are surpassing, but to the Anglo-Saxon his simple, useful, comradely pipe is completely satisfying. The pipe was long in establishing itself in France, where it was considered a loathsome object and where snuff was the only gentlemanly use of tobacco, but it ap-

---

[3] But this was due to the higher level of culture to which the Mexican Indians attained; it does not mean that pipes were really common in Mexico. In fact, it is often asserted that they were used only by one Mexican people, the Toltecs, who preceded the Aztecs and were conquered by them, when the pipe gave way to the cigarette.

pealed at once to the Dutchman. He had perforce
to make his pipe of clay, and therefore drew out the
stem that the smoke might be pleasantly cooled.
The true "Dutch pipe" is elephantine, its bowl
so large that it must rest on the ground, its
stem long enough to reach the mouth of a seated
man.

The pipe appealed to all the Teutonic peoples. It
spread through Germany and Scandinavia. The
great Swedish botanist, Linnæus, who gave tobacco
its scientific name, *Nicotiana tabacum,* was himself
an inveterate pipe smoker, and would sit for hours
with his long pipe resting on his knees, his apple
cheeks creased in a smile of content.

And it was the pipe that first captivated the Oriental fancy. In contrast with the Dutchman's all-
day smoke, the pipe of Japan is tiny, because the
Japanese consider it indelicate to smoke much at a
time. A long bamboo stem with a tiny metal bowl is
the favorite smoking instrument of Japan and it is
said that at an evening gathering in a Japanese
house one may continually hear the tap-tap of the
bowl, emptied in a few puffs, as its owner knocks out
the ashes.

Almost every conceivable pipe is used in China,
but the long stem is universally the favorite. Chinese
tobacco boxes, snuffboxes and other smoking appli-
ances were elaborated with artistic embellishments
not dreamed of elsewhere. The Persians, who il-
luminate with every minute design and brilliant
color their "sweet-scented manuscripts," have given
to smoking an exquisite appeal to the senses. Their

coffeehouses, according to John Fryer, who traveled in Persia in 1681, "are modelled after our theatres, that every one may sit around and suck choice tobacco out of long Malabar canes, fastened to crystal bottles, like the recipients or bolt-heads of the chymists, with a narrow neck where the bowl or head of the pipe is inserted, a shorter cane reaching to the bottom, where the long pipe meets it, the vessel being filled with water; after this sort they are mightily pleased; for putting fragrant and delightful flowers into the water, upon every attempt to draw tobacco, the water bubbles, and makes them dance in various figures, which both qualifies the heat of the smoke and creates together a pretty sight."

The less lovely custom of chewing tobacco arose from independent sources. Indians did not chew tobacco, with a single exception in northwestern South America, just where the tobacco-using tribes bordered on the tribes of the West Coast who chewed coca [4] and did not know the use of tobacco until the Spanish taught it to them. Apparently tobacco chewing among other than Indian peoples was of independent growth. Pioneers of the North American English colonies conceived the idea and the custom was adopted also in England. It is probable that tobacco chewing got its start as a prophylactic

---

[4] The leaf of *Erythroxylon coca*. Tobacco did not grow naturally on the arid Ecuadorean, Peruvian, and Chilean coasts of the Pacific, and its ceremonial and popular place was taken by the leaf of coca from which cocaine is now derived, a plant sacred to the Incas. This really dangerous drug was mixed with powdered lime (a custom that also sprang up among the betel chewers of the Far East, quite independently).

during the Great Plague in 1665. Samuel Pepys in his diary, under June 7, 1665, records:

"'This day, much against my will, I did in Drury Lane, see two or three houses marked with a red cross upon the doors and 'Lord have mercy' writ there; which was a sad sight to me, being the first of the kind that, to my remembrance, I ever saw. It put me into an ill conception of myself and my smell, so that I was forced to buy some roll-tobacco to smell to and chaw, which took away the apprehension.''

It was popularly believed that the plague never touched a tobacconist nor his shop. The antiquary, Thomas Hearne, quotes an old beadle who recalled that in his Eaton school days every boy was instructed to chew tobacco against the plague and that he had never received such a whipping in his life as when he neglected to do this. When the influenza epidemic swept the United States in 1918 the superstition revived; some doctors smoked furiously on their rounds and advised men to ride in smoking cars only.

When the Great Plague subsided the custom of chewing remained fashionable in England and the perfect dandy carried a silver spittoon as an appointment necessary to an exquisite. To-day the quid belongs to the workingman since he can enjoy it without pause in his labors. During the World War it was generally revived as, kept in the cheek, it made the saliva flow and quenched the thirst on hard marches. Among the betel-nut chewers of India, Siam, Malasia, Melanesia and Arabified Africa to-

bacco chewing took root easily and maintains to-day
its greatest hold. The seed fell there on fertile soil.
But snuff was a variation probably unknown to
the North American Indians. It is said that a certain tribe did inhale through the nose the powder of
another, obscure narcotic plant, but of tobacco snuff
apparently the Indians knew nothing. So far as can
be discovered snuff started in Spain and France, for
tobacco was first introduced into these countries as
a medicinal herb in the belief that it cured headaches,
colds and toothaches. Jean Nicot, who gave Nicotiana its name, a Frenchman, saw tobacco when an
ambassador at Lisbon and brought it back with him
to France, though he was not the first introducer of
tobacco into that country, having been preceded by
André Thevet, who brought it to court in 1561. The
first to use it were Catherine de Medici and her son
Francis I, who were cured, so they said, of headaches and colds by putting tobacco powder up the
nose. From its use at court snuff became the polite
form of tobacco in France, and thence it spread, in
the reign of Queen Anne and her French influence,
to England, momentarily displacing smoking from
good society. Snuff taking became a fine art. One
could take snuff deprecatingly, sarcastically, with
boredom, with sorrow, with finality. The snuffbox
passed into the realm of hospitality, of display of
wealth and taste. It was the treasured memento
among friends, the gift between ambassadors and
kings. There was morning snuff and afternoon snuff
and evening snuff. The world was ransacked for
curious materials for snuffboxes upon which the

miniature painters lavished their skill. No grace save the minuet so marked the gentleman from the boor as the art of taking snuff.

From France the custom became prevalent in Scandinavia. Snuff is taken by the Japanese, the Tibetans, the Indian Brahmans and above all the Chinese. During the Manchu dynasty when the Jesuit missionaries were active, the Emperor K'ang-Hi received two bottles of snuff from the priests. France gave snuff to China, and so it chanced that the first bottles sent bore the three lilies as a coat of arms—a symbol adopted by the Chinese snuff dealers for their street sign, recalling thereby the wooden statue of a highlander in kilties with a snuffbox in his hand which for centuries was the English tobacconist's symbol. The American cigar-store Indian is but a variation on this badge of trade.

Characteristically the scenting of their snuffs was wondrously perfected by the Orientals. Modern snuff taking in China has, however, been debased from a gesture of polite social usage to a genuine narcotic habit. One may frequently see a Chinese laundryman with a long snuff quill stuffed in one nostril, to be left there for hours.

In fact the whole history of the spread of tobacco usage over the world illustrates the gradual change of the estimate in which it has been held. The story is ever the same—introduced first as a medicinal herb that would cure colds, pains, rheums, headaches, toothaches, dropsy, malaria, ague, gout, fever and the Great Plague, it soon passes into the stage of the social rage—the polite gesture, the idol of the court dandy, the petty, secret vice of ladies. Then it emerges to a habit upon which the lower classes of the population become pathetically dependent and in its worst forms shades off into admixture with genuine narcotics like opium or to habitual and repulsive chewing, as objectionable as the mastication of betel.

The story of tobacco using in England exhibits every one of these phases in a greater or less degree, with the pipe as the dominant smoke, and the cigarette coming in later. The pipe was the symbol of hospitality. A country inn might be known for the grade of its tobacco and pipes, and in a London tavern a man called for his pipe and his bowl with his dinner as mechanically as one orders dessert and a demi-tasse. Ben Jonson, Kit Marlowe, Ford, Drummond, Shakespeare, the glorious company of the immortals, blew rings together from the pipes of the Mermaid Tavern.

And yet the opposition to tobacco was enormous from the start in England as elsewhere. Just as the Emperor of Japan ordered the burning of the English tobacco in his dominions in 1615, so nine years before did King James publish his *Counterblaste to Tobacco* in which, as the generations have decided, "the King most Quixotically broke his lance against one of the great appetites of man." On King James's side of the question it may be said that he feared for the welfare of his subjects and that he viewed with distress the expenditure of good English money on Spanish and Portuguese tobacco.

Also he did make a distinction between a moderate and an immoderate use of the weed. Beyond that, however, his *Counterblaste* is a strange mixture of prejudice, superstition, animosity and preposterous logic. He condemned the hypocrisy of those who pretended that tobacco was medicinal, yet he was willing himself to reap an enormous revenue from the sale and production of tobacco in his colonies while piously professing to hate tobacco's ill-effects.

Spencer, Lilly, Holinshed and Marlowe early sang the praises of tobacco, but Shakespeare was silent on it, as on the other wonders of the New World. Those who wrote against tobacco were, as a rule, the pamphleteers of King James. In 1614 was published a poem, threatening with hell all smokers, under the title "Tobacco Battered; and the Pipes Shattered (About their Eares that idlely Idolize so base and barbarous a Weed; or at least-wise over-love so loathsome Vanitie): by a Volley of Holy Shot thundered from Mount Helicon." Men left their wills conditioned against smoking by the beneficiaries, whilst others made elaborate dispositions of their several pipes to friends. Young blades went to smoking teachers who taught them how to blow manly rings, and controversy about the propriety of smoking by women and girls waxed hot, then as now.

Thus was England divided in support of tobacco, though abroad tobacco itself was the support of her middle American colonies of Maryland, Virginia and North Carolina. Tobacco, in fact, was the foundation stone of the Jamestown colony. The first settlers had come over intending to raise silk and wine grapes and had even imported Italian gardeners to guide the culture. Both crops proved to be quite unsuited to the colony and the pioneers were on the point of abandoning Jamestown when the Indians showed them how to grow tobacco. The first shipment of Virginia tobacco to England came at a moment of great demand. The colony was saved.

And from that now extinct colony spread out the cultivation of tobacco as wave on wave of the incoming tide of early pioneers carried it farther. The ax cleared the forests from the coastal plain, the plow broke the land, the gun drove out the Indians, and in the span of a few decades the wilderness was transformed to a gracious and stately civilization.

It was the tobacco leaf that created the culture which produced Washington, Jefferson, Madison, Monroe, Marshall, Harry Lee and Counselor Carter. It was tobacco that built those stately old houses of Tidewater society, with their baronial masters and regal mistresses, their famous balls, their fashionable horse races, their empire of slaves. But though slave labor played its part, yet tobacco growing flourished long before slaves became common in Virginia (they were not even introduced from Africa before 1619) and since the abolition of slavery tobacco culture has not suffered, but prospered.

For there was something in the very nature and requirements of the tobacco crop that determined much of the structure of Tidewater life. Tobacco is among the most intensively grown annual crops of the world, and in its exhausting effects upon the potash of the soil it has perhaps no rivals. In colonial times imported guanos, phosphates and such fertilizers were lacking to maintain the fertility of tobacco lands. The only method then practiced to prevent the prostration of the soil's vitality was the fallowing system. The result was inevitably the maintenance of vast tracts lying idle for from five to ten years, whilst only a small proportion of a man's holdings were actually growing tobacco at any one season.

Thus, since it was easy for influential persons to secure from the Crown vast tracts of land in the New World, tobacco claimed for its masters enormous estates. A single pioneer in the Tidewater might hold a tract larger than several English shires. The nearest neighbor of one of these American barons might be another tobacco raiser who lived twenty, thirty or forty miles away. From such a circumstance developed the old-fashioned Tidewater plantation, a self-sufficient community, with tool shops, docks (for some arm of the ocean was ever close at hand), tobacco warehouses, fish houses, barns, stables, cattle sheds, slaughter and smoke houses, servants' quarters, even a separate school, and above all the Great House, built in the beautiful endemic colonial style. The pastor for such communities had to be itinerant, and received his stipend in tobacco.

And it was tobacco's claim for vast acres that

created the hospitality famous down to this day. In yellow coaches swaying over the terrible colonial roads, in little sailing yachts tacking up and down the windings and the creeks of the Tidewater rivers and Chesapeake Bay, came the planter's guests, for merrymaking that would last many days and candle-lit nights. Beauty and comfort welcomed them at the Great House, for in exchange for tobacco the planter could buy all the luxuries from Europe with which the New World could not provide him—the silks, satins, firearms, books, wines, surveying instruments, silver and glassware, rugs, mirrors, perfumes, powders, and a thousand other of the appurtenances of stately colonial life. Ships from the docks of London sailed directly to the tobacco baron's private little inlet opening off the James or York River. Some fine morning he might be roused by the excited shouts of his slaves in the low-lying tobacco fields beside the water and could look out of his window at the approaching sails and say to himself, "Oh, there, that must be my wife's lute-string gown ordered from London!"

In all these pleasant doings, these delightful importations in exchange for tobacco, there was the fundamental evil that England was too shortsighted to see—that it does not pay to export raw products only, and to import manufactured ones. The Crown thought it had done its duty by tobacco when it forbade the entrance of Spanish tobacco in order to foster that of the English colonies, and to prevent English gold from passing to the hereditary foe. It did not see that a policy of trying to hold the middle colonies exclusively to tobacco production would drive them either to ruin or independence. Nor could it recognize how galling was the restriction of tobacco to English ships. Had the Dutch or French ships been allowed to come into the American waterways and barter with the planter for his tobacco, the price would soon have gone up and no false condition of overproduction would have been created.

For the English middleman the ideal scheme was to have Virginia and her neighbors overproducing tobacco, and France and Holland hungrily clamoring for it. This strategic position the English brokers actually occupied in colonial times, and resolution after resolution petitioning relief went from the Virginia Assembly to the Crown, without result.

There were many attempts, of course, to prevent overproduction. Price fixing was tried and found wanting; limitation of acreage worked no better. As substitutes for tobacco, hemp, flax, cotton and silk were tried in Virginia. Of these only flax and hemp are suited at all to the climate, and there was never enough money in them to lure the Virginian from the lucrative if treacherous tobacco crop. Moreover, whenever Virginia curtailed her tobacco acreage by substituting other crops, Maryland merely profited by this and either increased her tobacco acreage or her price.

The Revolution, of course, put a stop to the galling restrictions of English tobacco regulations, but it also brought the American grower into active competition with the West Indies. And hardly was the

Revolution over than England commenced the blockade of Europe during the Napoleonic wars, excluding our tobacco. Then came the War of 1812, with great damage to tobacco exports again, and when at last the smoke of battle had cleared away, American tobacco was found to be safe and sound, but established in a new home, the Piedmont and Kentucky.

Gone to-day are the great Tidewater plantations. Few even of the houses remain to tell of their former greatness. The piles of the docks in the little creeks have rotted away, the warehouses have vanished, the sons of the great families are scattered. For tobacco, which made Tidewater society, also slew it. It killed the soil at last. The visitor to the Northern Neck, as the peninsula between the Rappahannock and the Potomac is called, is impressed with something that has been called desolation but is nearer to obsoleteness. The charming diary of Fithian, a Jersey schoolmaster in the Northern Neck, on the eve of the Revolution, reveals, though unconsciously, the three causes for the desertion of the Tidewater. They were malaria, slavery and tobacco. Slavery killed the class of free white laborers and small farmers; malaria killed the great lords and their families; tobacco killed the soil.

On the Piedmont of Virginia and North Carolina were discovered not only healthier sites for homes, but virgin soil for tobacco, and soil naturally richer. In those days a dark leaf was in demand (and in Europe very largely still is), and the darker Piedmont soils could produce a blacker, heavier and more aromatic tobacco than the light-colored, sandy Tide-

water soils. In the new country the free white
farmer and laborer got a fresh chance. Fertilizers
were coming in to use, reducing the necessity of vast
plantations with fallow fields, and the whole agricultural structure moved toward a small farm system
with intensive tobacco culture and even some healthy
signs of crop rotation. Conditions such as these
came close to breaking down the slave system.
Robert Carter, Fithian's employer, who owned slaves
both in Tidewater and Piedmont, and had vast estates all over Virginia, freed his slaves. Washington
and Jefferson expressed their belief that slavery
was economically unsound and morally repugnant,
and felt that Virginia was drifting toward abolition.
The importation of slaves from Africa dwindled
slowly. And then came cotton in the states to the
south, and the vexed slave question commenced its
swift and terrible growth. Virginia, unable to raise
cotton, no longer supreme in tobacco (for Kentucky
was now bidding fair to outdistance her), turned her
great estates into slave-breeding grounds that supplied the cotton states. And that was the beginning
of her woes.

During the Civil War, when production fell off in
the southern states, an impulse was given to northern tobacco production. Kentucky profited most by
this, but for the first time Indiana, Ohio and Connecticut took tobacco raising seriously. To-day
some of the finest tobacco in the world is raised in
Connecticut as a result of the lesson learned in war
times. Despite the fact that tobacco suffers heavily
from the least touch of frost, it is now grown in

southern Wisconsin and southern Massachusetts. On the other hand tobacco has spread southward to Georgia and Florida, despite the increased difficulties in the South, where excessive moisture and greater danger from insect pests and fungi make the culture precarious.

One of the fascinating results of the spread of tobacco cultivation over the country has been the gradual growth of extreme specializations in the kinds of tobacco raised. Local varieties have developed as a result of the local environment—such as the "Burley" in Ohio that blazed forth from obscurity to a star of the first magnitude and made Ohio farmers rich, or the sudden appearance of "Yellow Bright" in some of the north-central counties of North Carolina.

And with this specialization each tobacco district has acquired a reputation for its special kind. The manufacturer who wants cigar leaf tobacco knows that Connecticut, Ohio and Wisconsin are famous for this kind. The light-colored cigarette and ground pipe tobaccos come from northern Kentucky and the Carolinas, while the dark type of leaf such as Europe chiefly demands, and such as we use for sliced pipe tobacco, chewing tobacco and snuff, come from southern Kentucky, Tennessee, Virginia and Maryland. And there is the famous perique tobacco of Louisiana, soaked in wine and buried for a year, to be exhumed incredibly stronger than ever.

To-day the United States stands supreme in tobacco production, manufacture, export and consumption. A rotation system has been worked out

for tobacco that solves the soil exhaustion problem—
a plan including wheat, grass, clover, corn, tobacco
and the use of tobacco stems for restoring potash to
the soil. This scheme, practiced in Lancaster
County, Pennsylvania, has thoroughly proved its
worth. Lancaster County is still behind the rich-
soiled Connecticut valley, but Lancaster's production
per acre is rising while that of the valley under the
one crop system is falling.

This country leads the world not only in quantity
of tobacco but in quality. The English, the most
discriminating smokers in the world, esteem straight
Virginia unblended tobacco above all others. No
country in the world (and our competitors include
all central Europe, Turkey, South Africa, India,
Japan, China, Cuba, Brazil, Sumatra and Argentina)
produces so many kinds nor such fine ones.

The story of the great tobacco trust, of its relation
to child labor, the story of the elaborate marketing
machinery for tobacco, the intricate systems of
duties that nations have imposed on tobacco and
its manufacture through the centuries, of the government monopolies like those of France and Japan,
of tobacco's use as insecticide or fertilizer, are fascinating but beyond the range of this brief account.

So also is the question of the possible injury the
use of tobacco may have upon the system. At any
rate, when all the charges against smoking have been
brought forward, the voice of the majority of humanity, whether rightly or wrongly, is still raised in
a general acquittal of the red men's weed. If man
must have some solace—and it would seem he must—

the gentle brown leaf is far better than its rivals, betel, hashish, opium, coca. The sun that has looked down on so many a scene of depravity, stupefaction and ugliness brought about by the genuine and fearful narcotics, beholds to-day the triumph of tobacco, and as it sets around the world it sees continuously the trail of smoke from the millions of mankind lighting up the evening pipe. The calumet, the peace pipe, has come to stay.

SUGGESTED READING

LINTON, RALPH, "Use of Tobacco among North American Indians," *Field Museum, Anthropological Leaflet,* No 15, 1924. An excellent popular account of the pipes and pipe ceremonies of the Indians of the United States.

LAUFER, BERTHOLD, "Tobacco and Its Use in Asia," *Field Museum, Anthropological Leaflet,* No. 18, 1924. A study at once learned and popular, with much historical information.

"Introduction of Tobacco Into Europe," *Field Museum, Anthropological Leaflet,* No. 19, 1924. A very clear bit of historical research in which much that is popular and romantic is brought to light.

MASON, J. ALDEN, "Use of Tobacco in Mexico and South America," *Field Museum, Anthropological Leaflet,* No. 16, 1924. A brief and entertaining study of ancient smoking and chewing customs.

APPERSON, G. L., *The Social History of Smoking,* 1914. A book at once entertaining and precisely critical.

FAIRHOLT, F. W., *Tobacco: Its History and Associations,* 1876. Not up to date, but containing much unusual information.

SETCHELL, W. A., "Aboriginal Tobaccos," *Am. Anthrop.*, Vol. 23, No. 4, 1921. This interesting article carries one farther into the kinds and uses of tobacco plants than has been done in this chapter.

GARNER, W. W., and MOSS, E. G., YOHE, H. S., WILKERSON, F. B. STINE, O. C., "History and Status of Tobacco Culture," *U. S. Department of Agriculture Year Book*, pp. 395–468, 1922. The history referred to in this title is very largely industrial history, and as this has not been followed fully in this chapter, it is well worth while to read this reference, which is a good example of something rare, statistical information made entertaining.

YOUNG, WILLIAM W., *The Story of the Cigarette*, 1916. Records the history and remarkable development of the cigarette industry, corrects many mis-statements and superstitions, gives accurate information, and includes a frank discussion as to whether the cigarette is more harmful than any other form of smoking tobacco.

WILCOX, EARLEY V., *Tropical Agriculture*, 1916, Chap. XI, "Tobacco." An interesting account of the many different methods of raising and treating the tobacco leaf.

CHAPTER XII

THE REIGN OF COTTON

COTTON, they say, is king. And though no-body denies this now, there was a time when it was fiercely contested, and, earlier than that—and not so very long ago—when cotton had never been heard of. For in olden days, in early Greece and Rome, when men walked abroad they wore garments only of linen, unless perchance they ventured north among the barbarians, or the long arm of winter reached with cold touch into the Mediterranean balm; then they threw about their shoulders a cloak of the finest Thracian wool. For thousands of years Egyptian mummies were swathed only in white linen, for flax was a native of the great delta while cotton was unknown. It was not until late in the history of classic Egypt that there first made its appearance in the fertile lowlands a strange "tree wool" brought from the forests of upper Nubia. Seeds of this "tree" which botanists now know as *Gossypium arboreum* were brought to the delta and grown in its black soil. From the fleecy lint upon the seeds a new and pliant fiber was spun. Of this precious textile there is a mention on the Rosetta stone.

In Greece cotton was known only as one of those

hundred storied wonders of Egypt. Not till the sword of Alexander cut its way to the Orient did the Hellenes behold the wide-flung cotton fields of the Indus, or see the women and children picking the downy seeds, or the girls spinning cotton thread in the doorways. To the soldiers it seemed impossible that this fleece could be anything but wool; it must be wool growing on a shrub. And so it came about, when the veterans told their grandchildren about the great wars that there came to birth the story of the "vegetable sheep." This mythological and useful anomaly, with its hooves rooted in the ground, browsed eternally on the herbage about it and suffered the Hindus to cut the wool from its back.

Of such vague and fabulous ideas was composed the ancient knowledge of cotton. When, in the Middle Ages, the great eastern trade routes were established, with terminals at Venice, Amsterdam and such great cities, cotton goods arrived in quantity at the doors of Europe. Their progress was fiercely contested by the other textiles. Flax and wool growers and the manufacturers of these fabrics all over the continent conspired to stop the tide which was rising in favor of cotton. They had recourse to prohibition acts, to boycott; they appealed to the patriotic pride of their countrymen not to desert time-honored cloths for foreign goods. But of what avail? Cotton was cheaper. A cloth raised, picked, carded, spun, dyed and cut in the Orient could be sold more cheaply in the markets of Flanders and Italy than either woolen or linen. Thus were not only the retailers of Europe deprived of their living, but flax and sheep raising and the home industries of spinning and weaving which supported so much of the population were undermined.

But nothing seemed able to check the influx of the "callicoes," as they were called. The last country to yield to their seduction was England, ever the conservative of medieval times. But when in the fourteenth century the English people finally allowed the superiority of cotton, their acceptance of it was enthusiastic. In 1709 Daniel Defoe lamented in this vein, "The general fansie of the people runs upon East India goods to that degree that the chints and printed callicoes which before were only made use of for carpets, quilts, etc., and to clothe children become now the dress of our ladies. . . . The chints was advanced from lying upon their floors to their backs, from the footcloth to the petticoat; and even our queen herself at this time was pleased to appear in China and Japan, I mean silks and callicoes."

But this rage for cotton was no whim of fashion. Of all the world's fabrics it is the most generally useful. Its intrinsic strength lies in the peculiarity of the tiny fibers of which it is made up; each one of these consists in a long, strong, flat and twisted ribbonlike hair. The natural twist assists enormously in spinning and enables each fiber to interlock its spiral with many others, giving to cotton thread tensile strength which in proportion to its flexibility and lightness is unsurpassed.

This inherent superiority was perceived not only

by the Hindus of ancient times. In Africa, from Nubia at the Nile's headwaters all across the equatorial belt to the hot, rainy West Coast, various species of Gossypium are native, and these the negroes have long known and exploited. At the same time in far-away America other species were employed by the Indians. Inca mummies were swathed in cotton, and cotton was cultivated by the red men from Mexico to Bolivia. When Cortez came to the Aztec capital he found the people clothed in splendid cotton robes. Among the spoils which he sent to his great emperor, Charles V, were waistcoats, handkerchiefs, counterpanes, tapestries and carpets of cotton, all dyed in brilliant colors. And when that other famous *conquistador,* Pizarro, plundered Peru, he saw with amazement that cotton was growing in the fields. In his own land such a sight had not been beheld since the Moors, who had brought the cotton plant to Granada, were expelled. What particularly interested the Spaniards was the recognition by the Indians that cotton exhausts the soil. In order to maintain the crop upon the same land year after year they fertilized the fields with guano. It is as a result of the discovery of cottons in the New World by the Spanish and Portuguese that American "blood" is found in so many Old World hybrid cottons to-day. A search of early records of plant introduction by these nations has shown that astonishingly soon after the discovery of America the New World plant had been disseminated in the Old.

But three hundred years were to elapse before the

first cotton was grown in the United States. Only toward the close of the colonial period did Americans come to the realization that the southern states could raise that crop. They began with what is known as Upland cotton, that is to say, *Gossypium hirsutum,* which is a native of Mexico. But a new cotton, with much longer staple, made its appearance just after the Revolution. Where its native home was it is difficult to say. It has been supposed to come from the Barbados, and it thus received the name *Gossypium barbadense,* but this is only conjecture. From the fact that we grew it first on the islands off the coast of Georgia and the Carolinas it came to be known as Sea Island cotton. The splendid yields, and the high price it fetched, soon caused it to spread over the coastal plain of the southern states, killing in its progress the less profitable indigo culture.

At first Southern planters had much to learn about cotton culture and there were some curious experiments in it. In early times cotton was raised as far north as the eastern shore of Maryland and the Piedmont and Tidewater of Virginia, where tobacco culture was in difficulties and cotton was hailed as a deliverer. From thence the cultivation ran along the coast to Georgia. To-day a very different map presents itself. The tide of cotton growing has ebbed away from Maryland and Virginia, which were too far north; with one long arm it curves up the rich bottom lands of the Mississippi to the mouth of the Ohio, and with another it reaches to the heart of Texas. Sea Island cotton is confined to the coastal plain, while Upland cotton occupies the higher, drier and poorer soils.

The swift expansion of cotton in our country was not only due to the favorable growing conditions of the southern states but to the sudden enormous increase in demand. In the middle third of the eighteenth century there came into being a series of interactive devices for weaving and spinning cotton which altered not only the fabrication of the textile but the fabric of society. These momentous inventions were the work of two mechanic's apprentices, a barber and a man who could scarcely sign his name.

It was in 1738 that Kay invented the flying shuttle for the cotton looms. About 1764 Hargreave, a fellow mechanic of Kay, came forward with the spinning jenny. The barber, Arkwright, invented the spinning frame about 1769. In the following year the steam engine was patented by Watt, and soon after steam power was hitched to the looms. Close on the heels of these events came the birth of the safety lamp for miners' helmets. This quite literally opened up the coal mines, and scarcely had this happened when the farseeing if illiterate Brindley proposed the ship canal from Liverpool, which made Manchester a seaport. The stage was set for the industrial revolution.

In the years which followed there were many dark days for England, and suffering, death and the overcrowding of ugly cities. But the change, unlike most revolutions, went on in outward silence. No man who lived then, in the thick of things, could view the alterations as a whole; it was only after the revolution was complete that it became apparent that, whatever human distinctions had stood or fallen, the despised cotton had emerged from the struggle victorious over all other textiles. Historians have been inclined to represent the triumph of coal and steel only. But for what was the coal mined or the steel tempered? Primarily it was to serve the cotton industry, expanding to such a stature that it overtopped every other in the British Isles.

There were some aspects of the industrial revolution not to be contemplated without regret. The cottage industries, for instance, were in ruins. And of these, the first to suffer was wool. Sheep raising, while perhaps not seriously declining in absolute figures, declined relatively; that is to say, it remained stationary while the population increased by bounds. The younger generation recognized that more profitable employment lay at the cotton mills. The gold of England was spent in foreign lands for the fleecy product of the bolls instead of at home for wool from the backs of Shropshire sheep. The healthy, simple, happy days when the whole family was engaged in cleaning, carding, spinning and weaving wool at home were gone beyond hope of return.

The eclipse was shared by flax and linen of which the production receded to distant places like Ireland and Russia still untouched by the factory system, unconquered by the legions of cotton. But the revolution spread out in all directions like ripples from a stone cast in water. In Holland and Belgium it swept away the vestiges of medieval linen and woolen guilds; thence it rolled on into France, through Germany to Scandinavia, and finally to the United States.

In our country fiber flax made a last stand. In colonial times the regions which grew flax extended from New York State to South Carolina, centering in Tidewater Virginia with its strong Old World traditions. Like indigo it was a famous crop of the early settlers, and the raising of a little flax for home use was part of the economy of every plantation. The mistress herself oversaw the spinning and weaving after her husband had grown the fiber and retted it. Washington and Jefferson spoke public words of encouragement to the industry. And then came cotton. In a handful of years the fair fields of flax with their sky-blue flowers graced our land no longer. In the South cotton was raised in its stead; in the North corn and wheat supplanted it as the New England spinning wheels began to turn. To-day flax in our country has receded to the northwestern states where it is grown for linseed oil alone. The flax textile industry has vanished from the land; only in a few counties of Virginia where tradition is still strong does flax raised for the home looms linger as a picturesque relic.

Cotton as shown on the accompanying map, grows only in a warm climate, and it does not, from the present distribution on the map, appear to occupy a large area. This is partly because it can be so intensively cultivated as compared, for instance, with

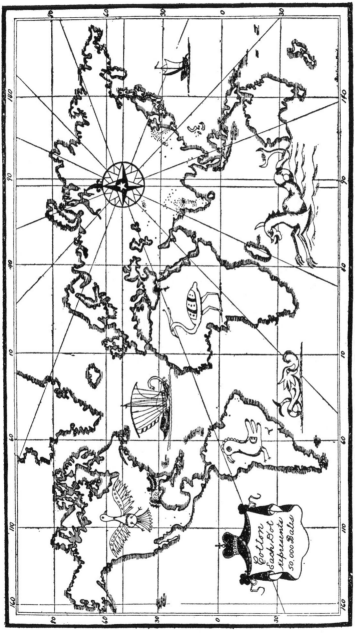

Redrawn from "Geography of the World's Agriculture," U. S. Department of Agriculture.

REGIONS OF THE WORLD WHICH PRODUCES COTTON

wool. It is also due to the fact that probably three times as much land as is now under cotton could support that crop.

If the triumph of cotton over wool (and more incidentally, over flax) meant the supremacy of the factory over the cottage, the city over the country, it meant also a pushing of pastoral civilization towards the ends of the earth, and what is more, it meant the rise of agricultural slavery. There had been rubber slavery, cacao slavery, spice slavery, but in our own country a new and different sort of enslavement came into being. Just as there was a cotton factory system in Great Britain and New England, so there grew up in our southern states a cotton slavery.

When the spinning mills of Manchester began to roar, and cotton growers in the South responded to the new demand, American negro slavery was on the point of dying out. Tobacco was fetching a low price and was exhausting the soil and Virginia and Maryland were on the verge of abandoning both the crop and the slaves who, rather inefficiently, cultivated it. Washington, Madison, Monroe, Jefferson, Virginia's greatest statesmen, planters and landowners, were selling off their slaves and openly advocating emancipation. When cotton took its sudden leap early in the last century, two prospects were revealed. First it was clear that Virginia, Maryland and much of North Carolina were not going to share in the boom, for the more southern states were able to raise more and better cotton. And the obvious deduction was that the necessary

labor would have to be negro labor. As a result
Virginia, faced with economic ruin in other quarters, went into the business of breeding slaves for
work in the cotton belt. And then began that vast
exodus of planters and slaves from the old seaboard
districts west into the new, unopened regions of
Alabama, Mississippi, Texas and Arkansas. As they
went they drove before them the red man who up
to this time had held his own against the less adventurous and more peaceful rice and cane planters
of the coast. The rich black mucks of the Mississippi
were seized with a rush and the plow was driven
through that virgin loam to make way for cotton,
the crop that year by year brought greater riches.

As a result of this new found power that lay in the
fleecy bolls, there grew up that peculiar culture now
familiar to all from poem and story. The pride and
elegance of the Southern gentry is too familiar to be
told again. But this aristocracy which defied the
Federal Government in 1861 was not wholly the
same as that which, in the seventeenth century,
founded Charleston, Jamestown, New Orleans and
Savannah. Those older gentry—adventurers, religious exiles, soldiers and cavaliers, had reached
the zenith of their influence during the Revolution.
Then came a new, a cotton aristocracy, drawn only
partly from the older families. A good eye for cotton land, an executive ability with slaves, a business
sense in the market—these were the qualities which
selected men of influence. Persons unable to compete in this new struggle for existence, were, eco-

nomically speaking, eliminated, and many of the old order had to give place to those of the new. The "small farmer," the free white of the South, unable to compete with slave labor and often without a vote, was crowded into the background; he had neither education nor political influence. The new landed aristocracy, able to command whatever it wished in Congress, grew daily in pride and independence. It trusted in negro slavery as implicitly as it trusted in a Deity. Slavery was right—the Bible said so—and it was necessary for the culture of cotton, and cotton was king.

Another powerful impetus to slavery was given by the invention of the "gin." Its inventor, Whitney, was a New England lad who had from childhood shown marked mechanical genius. Just graduated from college he was on his way to Georgia to act as schoolmaster. On the boat to Savannah he met a Mrs. Greene, widow of the American Revolutionary general, who took a fancy to him and invited him to visit her plantation on the Savannah River. There he heard some gentlemen talking about the need for a mechanical contrivance to clean the lint from the cotton seeds—at that time the most laborious and expensive operation in the whole industry. Ten days later he invented a lint-separating engine or "gin," which revolutionized the business. Friends in Georgia helped him financially until he could send a working model for a patent application. Thomas Jefferson, then Secretary of State, was the first to see it, and was instantly struck with its tremendous possibilities. He wrote at once for all details, and having been satisfied, he granted a patent. George Washington himself signed the patent order.

Shortly after this success Whitney's troubles began. He refused to sell any of his machines. He would only rent them out, demanding as his share one bale in every three of the cotton which his engines ginned. This attempt at monopoly was unbusinesslike and unfair; it aroused enmity and was not to be tolerated. Then came the lawsuit with Hogden Holmes. This Georgian had invented an improvement on the Whitney gin. The New Englander had used spikes to tear the lint from the seed, but these broke the fiber and mashed the seeds, releasing the oil, which gummed the machinery. Holmes substituted fine saw teeth, which left lint and seed intact. Instead of adopting this improvement, Whitney chose to regard it as an infringement of his patent. A Georgia court decided against him, and he could never believe that it was not the verdict of local prejudice. An impartial examination leads one to believe that Holmes had the right of the case. In justice to Georgia it should be said that a monument to Whitney has been raised in Hogden Holmes's home town.

Whitney had not said too much when he promised that the gin would do the work of fifty men without throwing anybody out of a job. When the gin came into general use the resulting increase in production was met by a corresponding expansion of demand in the English and Northern spinning mills, and a rise in price. As a consequence the acreage under cotton grew every year, and more slaves were ever in demand.

Never had the world seen such a slavery as the cotton serfdom of the South. In the number of humans it involved, and in its industrial efficiency it was unsurpassed. And it must be said in all justice, that whatever abuses it may have implied, it was the least cruel or perverted form of slavery that ever existed.

But the slave system and that gracious and polished society which rested upon it at last crashed to ruins. And with the declaration of secession cotton became more than ever a vital factor. The South had no gold to back up its paper money; it had only millions of bales of cotton standing on the seaport docks unable to get to Europe on account of the blockade. It had nothing to offer to speculators in Europe who might float bonds except the cotton crop. It could make no appeal for foreign intervention except the pertinent observation that if France and England forced the North to give in, the cotton famine in Europe would end.

During the four terrible years of the war the only Southern families that did not suffer want were those who made their fortunes in blockade running. The majority of the cotton ships which tried to dash through the Northern fleets were captured, but those that achieved success reaped a golden reward. The blockade runners drank French wine and their wives dressed in silks, while all other families, no matter how old their lineage, were pinched by poverty.

Europe hungered for food for its mills. When
Slidell went as an emissary from Jefferson Davis
to Louis Napoleon he offered that monarch as a
bait for intervention one hundred thousand bales of
cotton worth then twelve and a half million dollars.
He was able to float a cotton loan of fifteen million
dollars, which paid for the building of the infamous
privateers in Liverpool. In two days the loan was
thrice oversubscribed in London alone, so convinced
were the English speculators that a bale of cotton
was as good as gold in the bank. Even after Gettys-
burg and Vicksburg the bonds continued to sell.

But when the war came to a close and the clouds
gathered over Lee's army, the Southerners burned
what of their own cotton escaped the enemy rather
than allow it to enrich the North. They applied the
torch both in the field and on the dock. When the
day of reckoning came, such cotton as the South had
she could not afford to give to Europe, and as the
Federal Government did not assume the Confed-
eracy's debts, the foreign investors were ruined.

The mild panic which this caused was as nothing
compared to the suffering during the cotton blockade
in the Lancashire spinning mills. One half the
spindles of England were idle. What misery this
unemployment spelled for the densest industrial
population in Europe may well be imagined. The
idea that if the North raised the cotton blockade or
gave up the struggle their sufferings would end, was
naturally clear to the textile workers of Manchester.
Against the hostility of England three Americans

fought with splendid courage. Our ambassador, Charles Francis Adams, not only sought to prevent the escape of Southern privateers from English ports, but manfully strove to stem the angry tide of the workingmen's hatred of the Northern blockade. And then came that courageous minister, Henry Ward Beecher, who dared to rise in Manchester Hall and face the mob in an anti-Southern speech. He was not allowed to open his mouth for three quarters of an hour and stood silent while he was booed and pelted with missiles. But when at last voices were too hoarse to yell, he spoke, and when he had done, a sobered and thoughtful audience filed out. And lastly, Abraham Lincoln wrote a public letter to the English cotton spinners—one of his Christlike messages of sympathy, appeal, tolerance, patience and firmness. He told them how deeply he sympathized with the sufferings consequent on the cotton famine; he assured them that it was the doing not of the North but of the South, whose blow at union and liberty was a blow at the very principle which all Anglo-Saxons prized above all others. Were the South allowed to export her cotton to England she would almost certainly triumph in her cause of disunion and slavery. Surely no Englishman could wish that.

These noble efforts had their effect, and before the close of the war the English workingmen endured their hardships in silence, sure that they were suffering for a cause that was essentially their own. English statesmen throughout the conflict sought other sources of cotton. Over thirty nations sent cotton samples to an exhibition in London. But ten years later almost none of them could show any cotton production. Failures resulted everywhere, and the English mills were almost as dependent as ever upon our southern states.

In the South our cotton culture recovered its equilibrium with amazing rapidity. Instead of suffering from abolition, the Southern population in the end profited by it, for the huge, almost feudal and monopolistic plantations worked by gangs of slaves, broke up and gave place to the profitable farms of white landowners—in antebellum days in a hopeless situation. The small farmers who could not have bought slaves at a thousand dollars apiece, could, however, afford to hire free negroes for a few dollars a week. And to-day Southern prosperity is on a firmer footing than ever. Cotton is second only to corn in this, the greatest agricultural country in the world. Southern cotton constitutes over three-fifths of the world's supply. And the world's richest industrial crop is cotton.

The South, of course, is not without its competitors. In Egypt a splendid staple is grown on the light dry soils of that land. India, too, grows excellent cotton, and for the newly planted cottons of British West Africa claims are advanced of superiority over all others. Brazil's cotton production is considerable, and there is no doubt that it will increase many fold in the future. Two countries which now produce almost no cotton, Mexico and Argentina, are capable of tremendous output.

A rival has even appeared in our own country, in the Imperial Valley of California. This land is below the level of the sea; it is almost rainless, hence the cotton runs no risk of staining from water, and it is irrigated from the Colorado River, so that water is applied only when it is wanted and in the desired amounts. The Durango cottons which have been produced in the Imperial Valley are of especially long staple and command a high price. Once only did disaster threaten this promising valley, when the Colorado River broke its banks and flooded a great portion of the valley, forming the Salton Sea. The brilliance of engineering achievement has removed this danger and now the cotton cultivator can till in safety that marvelous black loam.

What further developments the future holds for cotton it is hard to prophesy. Only a short time ago cotton seeds were regarded as useless after being linted, and were even thought to be poisonous to stock. To-day about seventy-five uses are known for the products of cotton seed. The most interesting of these from the agricultural standpoint are the cakes for stock and the fertilizers by which nourishment is returned to the soils from which cotton robs so much.

Whatever other countries may come to compete with us for this master crop, whatever dangers we run from the boll weevil or from soil exhaustion, the United States may look forward with confidence to the long and prosperous reign of that goodly old monarch, King Cotton,

SUGGESTED READING

CRAWFORD, M. D. C., *The Heritage of Cotton*, 1924. A résumé of cotton history and the influence of cotton in the modern social and political fabric.

SCHERER, J. A. B., *Cotton as a World Power; a Study of the Economic Interpretation of History*, 1916. An excellent panoramic view in readable form.

BROOKS, EUGENE C., *The Story of Cotton and the Development of the Cotton States*, 1911. A colorful account, and easy reading.

DODD, WILLIAM E., *The Cotton Kingdom; a Chronicle of the Old South*, 1919. The agricultural-social interpretation of history. The viewpoint, while anything but narrow or prejudiced, might be described as Southern.

DODGE, CHARLES R., "Flax Culture for Fiber in the United States," *Fiber Investigations*, Report No. 4, U. S. Department of Agriculture, 1892. Contains notes on flax here and in other countries and a valuable chapter on the survival of colonial flax culture in Virginia.

HUBBARD, W. HUSTACE, *Cotton and the Cotton Market*, 1923. Complete information on the subject of raw cotton written by an authority and in a style that makes the book attractive reading.

WILCOX, EARLEY V., *Tropical Agriculure*, 1916, Chap. XI, "Fiber Plants." Something of the botany, agriculture and uses of cotton and other fiber plants.

There has been a great library of books written on all phases of cotton, and they cannot be cited here. The references above are merely some of the recent works which give facts in untechnical language with interpretative viewpoints.

CHAPTER XIII

THE TREE OF THE LEPER

"UNCLEAN! Unclean!" Down city streets in the days of Christ, heralding his approach, came the cry of the leper.

More ancient than the Bible is the dread disease of leprosy. Prescriptions for its treatment are known from Egyptian records as far back as 1500 B.C. Leprosy defies the student of epidemics to discover its origin. But among the dark-skinned races inhabiting the Mediterranean basin, India and intermediate lands, the hideous disease was certainly early endemic—that is to say, it did not expand and contract in the fashion of epidemics but dwelt in the land as a native disease with which some proportion of the population was always infected.

So little was understood about the organic causes of disease in classic times and so few were the precautions taken against contagion that it is a wonder that this hitherto incurable malady did not carry off most of the population. But perhaps certain persons or even families had inherent immunity. Men of the Middle Ages, keenly alive to the possibilities of leprosy infection, exercised at least the safeguard of ostracism. One of the parochial duties of every medieval priest was to cast out lepers, which is to

say that the unfortunate sufferers were merely ousted from that parish and went to another. No one was permitted to give them food or shelter and if the people of that time had been accused of inhumanity they would have replied that they were hastening the termination of incurable suffering.

From those far-away days there rings still in our ears an echo of the terror which leprosy inspired and the horror which its visible signs awoke in its beholders. Even in the United States, where leprosy is rare, hysteric fear is exhibited concerning this not very readily transmitted disease, in marked contrast to the careless regard in which we hold endemic diseases quite as menacing.

Modern specialists are convinced that a number of skin diseases of the past have been confused with leprosy in the popular conception—diseases which resemble it only in symptoms. From a study of bacteriology doctors have come to believe that leprosy is not a relative of most other skin diseases, but rather a kin of the organism which causes tuberculosis.

The etiology of the disease may follow several courses. It may be rather swift in its action with hideous disfigurements, or perhaps chronic, in which case, with care, the patient may live for twenty or thirty years. In the first stages of this form there is to be noticed only a certain porcelainlike whiteness of the skin. Whatever the forms of the disease, however, it was admitted for thousands of years that the proposed cures were nothing more than quackery.

With no measure to check it, leprosy spread far from its original habitat. By the Middle Ages it had reached Norway, and even in Iceland and China and Japan it was known by that time, if indeed not earlier. In western Europe, every considerable town had its leper house. There exists a picture by Holbein in Munich of St. Elizabeth giving bread to lepers that shows pitifully the ravages of the disease; it is generally believed that the painter had drawn from the life in a visit to the leper house of Augsburg in 1516.

Then in the middle of the sixteenth century the dread pestilence suddenly disappeared from northern Europe. No similar recession occurred at the same time anywhere else, and there seems to be no assignable cause for this great relief. Except in some Mediterranean countries it is steadily declining among Europeans and Americans. But elsewhere this scourge popularly regarded as something belonging to antiquity and almost extinct is on the increase. In South Africa it has spread among the Dutch as well as the natives, and leper establishments have now been organized on islands near Cape Town. In Australia the Chinese have spread infection to the Europeans there, and in New Zealand the Maoris are affected by it. The most striking and pathetic case is that of the Hawaiian Islands. Before 1848 the Hawaiians knew nothing of this plague, as indeed they were free of most of the other dreadful cosmopolitan diseases, and happily ignorant of drink, drugs and the rest of the white man's blessings. Then Chinese labor was imported to work the Hawaiian fields. With it came leprosy, whose ravages among the natives have now become proverbial. The leper settlement at Molokai is perhaps the most famous of its kind. Stevenson has vividly described its strangely beautiful surroundings, the courage and pathos of its doomed inhabitants—an island of the living dead, a pest house and charnel house in one. The work of Father Damien at Molokai and his tragic death by the nightmare disease is now one with the stories of martyrs.

In different times and countries has perennially sprung the hope that a cure for leprosy was found. These panaceas, however, never gained acceptance in reputable medical circles because the cures which they seemed to effect were so few that they might be accounted for by the fact that a certain small proportion of lepers do throw off the disease naturally. But in the middle of the last century British doctors in India became aware that some native peoples, especially the Burmese and the Bengalese, were using in the treatment of leprosy the seeds of an unknown tree. So great was their efficacy that there was no denying their specific value. But only in the opening of our century was there any medical investigation of the seeds. At the Wellcome Research Laboratory in London, some brilliant work was done upon the oils and acids of the seeds by Frederick Power, now of the United States Department of Agriculture. The treatment of lepers with these oils was conducted by Dr. Dean and his associates at the leper receiving stations in Honolulu and Molokai, with remarkable results. And now, after centuries of exile ending only in an incredible misery of degradation and slow decay the accursed beheld hope shining from the far forests of Burma.

But what one of the thousands of jungle trees bore these strange and healing seeds? To this question the vendors in the markets of Benares or Rangoon replied that they bought what they called *chaulmoogra* or *kalaw* seeds from wild tribes who inhabited the jungles of the upper Chindwin district in northeastern Burma. The journey to this country was a hard one, and the natives when approached could not give a recognizable description of the tree. The seeds, to be sure, were matched with named specimens of an obscure species preserved in the Indian herbaria, but misinformed botanists had so thoroughly confused the source and identity of the seeds and had buried them in such a maze of Latin synonyms that the finding of the chaulmoogra tree appeared a Herculean task.

When at last the knots had been unraveled by persevering druggists and botanists, the time had come to search for the living tree. The Office of Foreign Seed and Plant Introduction was the first to take up the quest. On this mission they sent out in 1920 the agricultural explorer Joseph F. Rock. This dynamic and magnetic scientist whose adventures have led him through such perils as tigers, Chinese bandits and treacherous native servants, was well qualified for this new enterprise.

In Bangkok, the capital of Siam, Mr. Rock found an avenue of trees related to the true chaulmoogra and containing the same essential oils, or closely

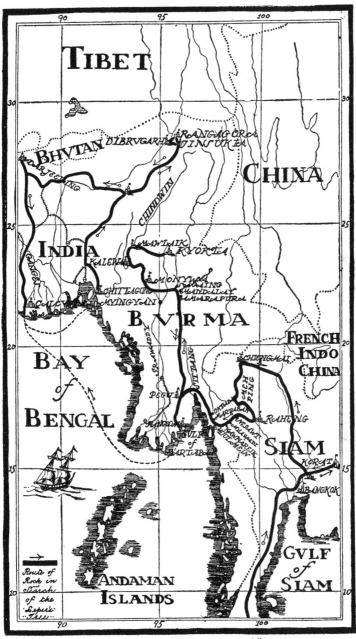

TIBET

CHINA

BHVTAN DIBRVGARH ROANGAGOROA NYINSUKEA

Darjeeling

CHINDWIN

INDIA

MAWLAIK KYORKA

KALEWA

MONYWA SAGAING MANDALAY AMARAPVRA

CHITTAGONG MYINGYAN

CALCVTTA

BVRMA

FRENCH INDO CHINA

BAY

of

BENGAL

PEGU

CHIENGMAI

MEPING

RAHENG

RANGOON

GVLF of MARTABAN

ATTARAN THAUNGYEN MEPAWN MEGAMAT

SIAM

KORAT

BANGKOK

Route of Rock in Search of the Leper's Tree

ANDAMAN ISLANDS

GVLF of SIAM

Redrawn from "Inventory of Seeds and Plants Imported," by Courtesy of the Office of Foreign Seed and Plant Introduction, U. S. Department of Agriculture.

ROUTE OF ROCK IN SEARCH OF THE LEPER'S TREE

similar ones. These were the Hydnocarpus trees, or as the natives call them, *maikrabao*. Seeds were sent to Honolulu by Mr. Rock, and from this consignment several thousand have grown. In northern Siam Mr. Rock learned from her serene highness, Princess Bovaradej, with whom he was dining, that maikrabao trees grew plentifully in eastern Siam, near Korat. Thither, through bamboo groves and rice fields, went the explorer, accompanied by a Siamese forester, and there indeed found Hydnocarpus; but only half ripe seeds could be obtained at that season.

It was not until the end of 1920 that Mr. Rock, after many attempts quite literally fruitless, succeeded in procuring near Moulmein, in Burma, heavy-fruiting specimens of maikrabao or Hydnocarpus. The following are Rock's own words of description:

From Paung the party proceeded by bullock cart to Oktada, a small village at the foot of the Kalama Range. The same evening the writer followed the steep dry creekbed, strewn and lined with enormous boulders of quartz rock, to the Mondo Range. In the crevices between these enormous boulders, of ten feet high or more, there grew in great abundance a tree which was loaded with young fruits, then the size of a tennis ball and covered with a fawn-colored tomentum. The trees observed had a height of about 80 to 90 feet and their size was much greater in every respect than that accredited to *Taraktagenos Kurzii* (the true chaulmoogra tree). . . . The approach to the *kalaw* forests (*Hydnocarpus castanea*) led through a jungle of peculiar, broad-leaved procumbent bamboo, called *wanue*. . . . The bamboo covers the lower hillside in dense stands, through which the natives make regular tunnels.

It was here that fresh tiger tracks were encountered which led through this dense bamboo jungle and the kalaw forest to the top of the ridge. . . . The seeds of the kalaw trees are collected by the natives, who take out licenses from the forest office in Moulmein for that purpose. None of the seeds of this region are sold to Europeans, but are immediately disposed of to native vendors in the bazaars. Much of the seed, however, is lost, as the collectors do not take the fruits from the trees when ripe, but wait till they drop, a much less troublesome way to collect them. Moreover, monkeys are fond of the fruit flesh and attack the fruits on the trees, dropping the seeds to the ground; and many seeds are lost in crevices between the innumerable rocks and boulders. Porcupines also devour the seeds, and the result is that in all probability about 50 per cent of the crop is lost.

Rock goes on to tell that the fruiting of the maikrabao tree is irregular, particularly under forest conditions, while trees standing free in the sunlight bear regular heavy crops. This would indicate the value of plantation culture. He tells, too, how the bark is stripped by children sent to the forest for the purpose. From this is decocted a drink for use in skin affections. Decortication is followed by the ravages of the termite or white ant thus given access to the tender part of the stem.

At last Rock found the true chaulmoogra tree. In the Chindwin district, near Kyokta, he came upon the stately slender-trunked straight trees, with their shining broad leaves and fawn-colored fruits the size of an orange. In this case, too, the trees were shy fruiters. The natives, they said, came only once in three years to gather the seeds, as in the other seasons there were not enough seeds to make collection profitable. At that, only about half the seeds of the fat season could be secured, because of the fondness of monkeys, boars and bears for the chaulmoogra fruits. The natives, having no firearms, are afraid to encounter the hordes of browsing bears, and so wait till near the end of the season, glad for what is left of the spoils.

It was winter, and Rock found the dark, forbidding jungles pleasantly cool, but winter is the mating season of the larger animals, and perils abounded. Fierce with hunger and the mating instinct, elephants and tigers roam the forests. A tiger at some distance followed Rock's party all of one day. The next morning a little boy came running into the village of Kyokta, Rock's headquarters, with a ghastly tale. He reported that his hut had been entered by a tiger, and all the occupants killed except himself. Five long claw scratches marked his face. He was followed to the hut, where were found two dead women, another with her cheek bitten out, scarcely living, and of a small girl nothing remained but a trail of blood leading into the jungle. Pandemonium prevailed in the village. A bamboo trap was set for the tiger, into which the body of one of the dead women was set as bait. During the night a terrific storm arose. Amidst the thunder crashes a louder crash was heard, and screams. A herd of wild elephants running in panic from the storm had entered the village and in five minutes had demolished part of it more thoroughly than could a cyclone. In the morning when the storm had ceased the trap was visited. The tiger was caught. The next morning Rock started away to convey to a hospital the one woman still living. She was borne gently by carriers and everything possible was done to save her, but she died before the cortege had gone far on the jungle path.

On his return from India Rock brought a large consignment of chaulmoogra seeds and with them a legend about the origin of the leprosy cure. Long ago, before the time of Buddha, runs the tale, there dwelt in India King Oksagarit. He had five sons and five daughters by his first wife, but he passed on his throne to the son of a second wife, younger than all the rest. Angered by this, the other young princes and their sisters went into an exile of protest and dwelt together in the forest. The eldest girl, Piya, became afflicted with leprosy. Her brothers and sisters took her to a cave, and telling her that they were going farther in the jungle, there forsook her. They had left her provisions, at least, and had chosen a cave with so narrow an entrance that wild beasts could not get in.

At the same time there fell ill of leprosy, Rama, King of Benares. The splendor of his palace, his silken robes, his flattering courtiers, his superstitious physicians, all were but the hollow mockery of an outward royalty and power in the face of the implacable malady consuming his body. Driven to despair, he left the throne to his son and fled away into the jungle. Here, he kept life alight with the wild fruits of the jungle, among them the seeds of the chaulmoogra tree, and after a time he found that by eating these he had become cured of leprosy. Dwelling in a hollow tree, and with the healing seeds for food, he was a far happier monarch than when he had dined on pheasants and lived in a palace of marble and malachite.

One day a tiger, smelling human flesh, came prowling near Piya's cave. He tried to break his way in, and poor lost Piya screamed in terror. Rama, whose hollow tree was not far off, heard the cry, and went forth to find whence came the sound of a woman's voice. Discovering the hiding place he called out, "Who lives in this cave?" Piya replied, and told her plight. He called on her to come out, but Piya, being a modest maiden, only ran into the back of the cave. Then Rama entered it and took her out in his arms and carried her to his hollow tree. He cured her of her leprosy by means of the chaulmoogra seeds, and having restored her to her health and beauty, he took her as his wife. She bore him twins sixteen times, making in all thirty-two little princelings.

A hunter from Benares straying that way one day recognized Rama. He returned to the reigning monarch, who was Rama's son, and told the whole story. The king then came with a great retinue and invited Rama to return with Piya and mount the throne. Rama replied that he would found a new capital where he stood. Accordingly, the city was built and called Kalanagara, and Rama's son returned to Benares and ruled in that place.

If all this be true, and there is nothing incredible in the story unless it be the number of Piya's babies, then it is to the ancient King of Benares that the modern leper owes his chance of salvation. In two years two hundred lepers were discharged from the Honolulu receiving station and from Molokai, cured or practically cured. Chaulmoogra is injected intravenously. The chief difficulties have proved to be the fact that in the initial stages chaulmoogra does not act so efficaciously as in the older courses of the disease, and also that some patients react anaphylactically, that is instead of receiving good effects they develop inflammation, sores and swellings. It has also been asserted that patients apparently cured by chaulmoogra do not stay cured, but have to return for further care. This, however, has been denied by some of those most qualified to speak. The consensus of able opinion is that chaulmoogra is a genuine and on the whole efficacious cure for leprosy—the one treatment, in fact, which offers real hope of arresting this ancient and still formidable disease.

It has been reported from the Philippine Islands that chaulmoogra yields results in the killing of tubercular bacilli grown in cultures. Considering the similar reactions, both chemical and physical, of the leprosy and tubercular bacilli, this may well be so. The belief awaits a wide acceptance; it is to be hoped it will be substantiated by successful experiments with human patients. It has been claimed also that castor oil and cod liver oil will alleviate leprosy and tuberculosis. This is doubted by Dr. Power, the discoverer of chaulmoogric and hydnocarpic acids in their pure state. The whole matter remains to be critically reviewed by competent judges.

In our own country are growing at present chaulmoogra and Hydnocarpus trees. They are to be found in the greenhouses of the Office of the Foreign Seed and Plant Introduction, located in Maryland. It is the chaulmoogra trees that foreign botanists and physicians who visit this experiment station ask most often to see. The desirability of growing chaulmoogra under plantation conditions becomes obvious when one considers the unsatisfactory conditions of the wild crop. Not only are the natives wasteful in their harvesting, but at present monkeys, bears and porcupines are getting half the world's supply! The trees under forest conditions fruit shyly and irregularly, and are inaccessible to satisfactory exploitation. The seeds on their long journey from forest to bazaar get rancid and lose their properties, and lastly, the price is higher at present than it will be when chaulmoogra plantations come to bearing. Americans, too, will feel a pride, since there are so many lepers under our flag in our island possessions, in knowing that we are growing our own chaulmoogra and are not dependent on Burmese hill tribes for our supply.

But continental United States does not offer a great future for these strictly tropical trees. It is in our Pacific island possessions that plantations have been started, and there surely they are most needed. From Hawaii and the Philippine Islands, after they are able to supply their own demands for the precious seeds, will in future flow to other parts of the world the human boon, ten times more precious than its weight in gold.

SUGGESTED READING

Rock, Joseph, and Power, Frederick B., "The Chaulmoogra Tree and Some Related Species," *U. S. Department of Agriculture Bulletin,* No. 1057, 1922. Gives a good account of the botany and chemistry of chaulmoogra-yielding plants, with some of the picturesque phases. Summarizes the treatment of the lepers in Hawaii.

Rock, Joseph, "Hunting the Chaulmoogra Tree," *Nat. Geogr. Mag.,* Vol. 41, pp. 242-276, 1922. A popular account, concerned as much with travel in Burma and Siam and adventures with animals as with chaulmoogra itself.

Schoble, Otto, "Chemotherapeutic Experiments with Chaulmoogra and Allied Preparations," *Philipp. Journ. Sci.,* Vol. 23, pp. 533-560, 1923. The medical aspects of chaulmoogra, with a hint at its possibilities in the treatment of tuberculosis.

Wilcox, Earley V., *Tropical Agriculture,* 1916, Chap. XVIII, "Oils." See concise account of chaulmoogra oil.

Encyclopædia Britannica. See Leprosy.

CHAPTER XIV

OUR INHERITED CROPS

AT breakfast no oranges or grapefruit, no oatmeal, no cream of wheat, no grapenuts. At dinner no peas, no cauliflower, no cabbage, no radishes, no carrots, no lettuce. Turnips, asparagus, celery, artichokes? Never heard of them. Tea or coffee? Absolutely unknown.

Something like this would have been the situation if the white race had had its origin in the New World, and the Old World had never been discovered. For all the plants which have been mentioned existed, before the days of Columbus, only in the Old World. Leaving out of consideration meat diet, we would under these conjectural conditions have corn meal mush for breakfast, with a nice slice of cooling *papaya,* or possibly some raspberries or blackberries. At dinner we might eat pokeweed for greens, and Jerusalem artichokes, corn fritters, potatoes, pumpkins or squash, sweet potatoes, tomatoes, kidney and lima beans, *chayotes* and chili peppers. Guava jelly might be served, and perhaps an avocado salad, and by way of beverages, chocolate, yerba maté, or possibly cassina tea. As dessert we would enjoy a few slices of pineapple and perhaps a *cherimoya.* For candy, we should have the peanuts to make peanut brittle, but it could not be made with cane or beet sugar. Such would be our circumscribed menu. There are, to be sure, certain wild fruits, edible roots and so forth, which could be gathered as we gather huckleberries and blueberries, but most of them cannot be profitably cultivated, and the plants which have been mentioned in our suppositional diet would be the only ones to be seen in our vegetable gardens.

When it comes to clothing, there would be cotton of the best but probably no linen, and for that matter, no silk, for our cultivated flax and the silkworm as well, are natives of the Old World. Sacks would not be made of hemp but of sisal. In the medicine chest would be no castor oil. Physicians would not be able to administer opiates, but there would be plenty of cocaine and quinine. Of precious timbers, rubbers and tobacco, we would lack nothing.

All this is romancing rather than science. But it serves its purpose—to suggest how racial a matter is agriculture. To-day we are living in a hemisphere where are native such useful plants as chayote, Surinam cherry, Indian rice, Indian cucumber, Indian fig, pokeweed, paw-paw and custard apple, yet their names fall strangely on our ears, and their tastes are foreign to our palates.

The reason for this is that the European, wherever he goes, prefers to take with him the plants and animals which he has inherited from his distant cultural ancestors, and with which he grew up from the infancy of his race. Even the Kentuckian's blue grass is a plant of European origin, and the daisy, proposed, oddly enough, by the American Legion for its emblem, is foreign born. Thus, by tracing to their native homes the plants which peoples have domesticated, we can spell out the origin of races.

Most people have heard of mummy wheat. (They have heard, too, that this grain, when sown, after more than two thousand years in a royal tomb, grew vigorously. This, however, is not true, and many times as it has been denied, the myth thrives perennially.) But, after all, Egypt itself is really recent. Wherever careful search is made, wheat and barley are found in the ruins or in the graves of peoples so much more ancient than the old Egyptians that their very names have been forgotten forever.

Since wheat and barley are found associated with our people as far back as can be traced, and since all cultivated plants must once have existed wholly in the wild in some restricted area, it is reasonable, surely, to suppose, that could we find the native locality of wheat and barley, we would have some index to the original habitat of our race. In looking over the list of plants grown by our cultural ancestors, one is struck by the fact that they are nearly all found in a wild state in the same general region. And that region is Central Asia, comprised in the modern states of Russia, Turkey, Afghanistan, Tibet and a few adjacent ones—that little known, peculiar, semi-desert country which lies around the Aral and Caspian Seas, near the Caucasus mountains, in Asia Minor, and on the far or northern slopes of the Himalayas.

In this region radish, garlic, onion, shallot, leek, garden cress, chevril, dock, spinach, alfalfa, chickling vetch, fenugreek, flax, hemp, mulberry, sweet cherry, plum, pomegranate, apple, quince, olive, bean and lentil are all indigenous. And there, too, garden pea, buckwheat and two-rowed barley are at home. Possibly wheat and common barley had their origin there, but of this it is harder to be certain. From this original center of distribution these economic plants must have been disseminated in every direction.

There is put one other spot which, as regards a center of distribution for crop plants, has been anything like a rival to Central Asia, and that is the Mediterranean basin. In early Egyptian times, contact with the continent of Eurasia was so slight as to exclude from the fields and gardens of those ancient Nile dwellers most of the plants just mentioned above. But from the southern and eastern shores of the Mediterranean the Nilotics could draw for cultivation such wild plants as parsnip, horseradish, pieplant, pea, cabbage, cauliflower, parsley, caraway, asparagus, Italian artichoke, alsike clover, crimson-top clover, saffron, fig, field pea, one-grained wheat, proso, Egyptian cotton and castor plant.

There are also plants apparently native *both* to Central Asia and the basin of the Mediterranean Sea. Among these are mustard, walnut, chestnut, turnip, grape, carrot, madder, chives, purslane, celery, lettuce, chickory, asparagus, sainfoin and here, too, perhaps, can be mentioned purple clover, vetch, hops, bird cherry, almond and carob. Of these the ancient peoples of Egypt and of Central and Mesopotamian Asia were equally free to make a choice for purposes of domestication, since they were growing wild in both cultural areas.

One cannot help feeling after going through this long and significant list that the greater part of the useful plants of the temperate zones has been mentioned. Is it any wonder that in regions so well stocked with the plants most necessary to man the first great cultures of the world grew up? In northern Europe there were at hand for primitive man probably little more than rye, oats and timothy, strawberries, blackberries, raspberries, carrots and sea kale. In this short list there is scarcely a first-class human food except oats and rye. There are no drug, dye or fiber plants of real importance native in northern Europe and no oil plants or fine fruits. It is not surprising, therefore, to learn through archæological remains that the peoples of northern Europe were still in the Stone Age when Egypt and Babylon first flourished. It is not that the northern races had less cultural ability but only that among the factors retarding their development was a dearth of useful plants.

If one looks over the list of great food plants of Central Asia and the Mediterranean, the most impressive thing, as De Candolle long ago pointed out, is that they are chiefly the annual plants—mainly grasses, that is to say, the cereals which five and ten thousand years ago were the staff of life, exactly as they remain to-day. It is no mere accident that ancient and modern food agriculture rests largely upon the annual grasses. An annual plant grows from seed to mature stature, passes through reproduction and returns to seed again in one season. So it comes about that as the annual grasses bear their grains abundantly, and as grains have particularly starchy content, they are the most nutritious of the world's seeds, and the most generally satisfactory food of the temperate zone. Moreover, an annual plant gives returns on the investment in time or money practically at once, that is, within the year. And lastly, as contrasted with the planting and harvesting of perennial plants, stands out the easy culture of an annual crop. If the field needs to be cleared for another kind of crop, no extra labor or loss of money is involved. An annual plant, too, is adapted to a climate with cold winters, as it does not have to remain in the ground during the dangerous season. It is likewise especially well fitted for an arid climate from the same cause—that it can be withheld from dangerous exposure when necessary. For these reasons, wild annuals are dominant in a few portions of the earth's vegetation. These are regions which have extremes of heat and cold and are marked by a semi-arid atmosphere. Such areas exist on every continent. Our own Great Plains are covered with indigenous annual plants, but, as it chances, few of them are useful to man. The largest of all such areas is that which stretches from the Mediterranean northward and eastward toward

Mongolia. And, as it happens, no mean portion of the plants of this region is especially adapted to the feeding and clothing of humans.

Necessity is the mother of civilization. The races which found themselves in the plant environment of which we have spoken, the great semi-arid steppes and prairies of Central Asia and the eastern end of the Mediterranean, found that while the annual grasses yielded particularly fine foods, they also required labor and forethought. An annual plant, here this year, may have its seeds transported far away, and next year it will be here no more. In the tropics the domestication of a tree, such as one of the useful palms, consists more in the domestication of its owner than of the tree; the tropical native merely settles in a grove of palms, and there he stays and enjoys its fruits. But the dwellers in the steppes and prairies found that seeds of their life-sustaining plants had to be saved, sown and tended. In this way, agriculture may be said to have originated, and indeed to have become quite naturally the preëminent possession of the so-called temperate zones. If by agriculture we mean what the word was intended to mean, that is, field culture, then the credit for its invention is more than likely due, in the Old World at least, to our own prehistoric ancestors.

When primitive man had once found a good assortment of useful plants, he came more than ever to look on vegetation from a human and utilitarian point of view. Plants of no use were quickly uprooted and cleared away to make room for plants

MAP TO ILLVSTRATE
OVR INHERITED CROPS

OUR INHERITED CROPS

that were. Some one has said that the best chance which a plant has in its struggle for survival is to be looked on with favor by man, for man will tend it, disseminate it and kill all its competitors. The modification of the natural flora of Europe is a striking example of this. The native vegetation has been partially or completely removed from all the best agricultural soil and remains only on mountains, bogs, sterile moors, salt marshes, sand dunes and roadside ditches. Even the forests have been in many cases completely altered by adaptation to grazing, hunting or fagot gathering and lumbering.

When the European went forth into new lands in the great expansive period of the last four centuries he took with him the plants with which, as a race, he had grown up. He learned, of course, to eat or utilize the vegetation of the new lands, too, but only in a limited degree. With much the same feelings that he entertained about the superiority of his blood, his weapons, his language and his religion, he took with him his native crops, convinced that they were better than could be found anywhere else.

The force of this conviction has been so strong that often against terrific odds, he has tirelessly and even relentlessly pushed his agriculture into every part of the world which is adapted to it, and only after repeated failures has he been willing to abandon the attempt in regions which will not support the type of agriculture to which he is accustomed. To show to what length a racial prejudice in agriculture will go, the case of a gang of engineers and laborers in Brazil may be cited. Imported from

the United States for construction work in the
Amazonian jungle, they were fed regularly on white
bread, meat, cornstarch and other common American
diets, all imported from the United States and
shipped up river at enormous expense. It might
have been thought that food as good as this would
be satisfactory, but fresh vegetables and fruits,
being perishable, had naturally been left out and
as a result beriberi soon began its ravages, until
the little white tombstones beyond the camp were
more numerous than the tents of the survivors.
Some one suggested that they should eat the fruits
and nuts on which the natives and animals fed in
the forest. But this idea was scornfully rejected
because no white man cared to eat "monkey food."
In fact, it was preferable to die. The same prejudice
against "substitutes" was felt during the food crisis
of the Great War.

Of all the plants which the white man has chosen
to regard as superior, by none does he set more store
than wheat. People who eat wheat are practically
in a caste, in the popular mind, a caste based on
wealth and implying superiority of taste and culture.
Many persons during the Great War felt, when
deprived of "white" bread, and forced to eat rye,
and other "substitute" breads, that they were not
only eating something that did not taste so good,
but that they were eating something intrinsically
inferior.

Rice, which feeds more millions of humanity than
any other plant in the world, is generally looked
upon in European lands as entirely a second-class

cereal—it is, in fact, generally thought of by the housewife as a "vegetable," that is, a side dish served occasionally like squash or sweet potatoes. The fact that rice is the food of the majority of the world is unimportant to her beside the fact that wheat is the food of the minority—the exclusive, small, upper crust of humanity.

In Russia it was, and probably still is, the custom for the peasant who grew wheat to subsist largely on breads made of rye, barley and other cereals. Wheat, in that land where formerly caste was so clearly marked, was especially the badge of aristocracy. Travelers say that "black bread" is still the commonest and cheapest bread in Russia and wheat is still the unique possession of the well-off, although traditional social barriers have broken down.

Even corn is generally thought of as constituting a distinctly informal dish, especially if served in the form of bread or meal, and its use is far more widespread in country districts than at urban tables.

The attempts of white man to carry his ancestral crops into every part of the earth, and his failures, have been noticed. These failures were due not only to trying to grow plants in regions too hot or too cold or too wet or too dry. They were due, too, to attempts to grow some of our most important crops on acid soils. It is a peculiar fact that a very generous proportion of the plants most esteemed for food require neutral or basic soils, and produce poorly or not at all on acid soils. There can be little doubt that this is because so many of our crop plants were brought originally from Central Asia, and the saline regions there and around the Mediterranean. They came from a region with much alkali, and they continue to demand it. As proof of this latter fact one has only to take a short ride near Washington, D. C. It is only two hours by motor from Washington to Frederick, Maryland. In those two hours one passes from acid soil and poor, thin farms with small barns, sagging gates and many abandoned houses, to the limestone valley around Frederick, where the turf is emerald green, the fields solid gold without a blemish, the apple trees loaded with fruit, the barns huge and freshly painted, the fences straight and whitewashed, the cattle superb, the farmers wealthy, the roads perfect and the banks flourishing. The farmers of Frederick are not better men than those of sandy eastern Maryland. They are merely settled in limestone country.

It has occurred to some people, like the younger Arrhenius, that it is a mere accident that our cultural ancestors originated in an alkaline region. Suppose they had originated in an acid soil region like parts of Sweden, Scotland, New England and the like. Would they not have domesticated plants growing naturally on acid soil? Should we not have an agriculture based on acids instead of bases? Imagine for a minute that this were true. The Middle West would be but a very indifferent farming region and would turn to industrialism; ultra-alkaline regions like the Great Basin and peninsular Florida would be practically deserts so far as crops are concerned and would be abandoned to wild vegetation. But New England, except where too rocky, would have the finest crops in the country, and the other Atlantic states would be close rivals.

Dr. Coville of the United States Department of Agriculture has entertained the idea of trying to construct an agriculture adapted to acid soils. He has commenced work with the plants which are found on that type of soil, the huckleberry, blueberry and cranberry. It is true that these are not at present fruits of the first importance, but it is at least worth while to try to breed some kinds that will be first class. As an experiment it is looked on with considerable interest.

It may be, of course, that it is chiefly from lime-loving plants that humans can derive nourishment. In that case the attempt to evolve a food crop agriculture from acid soil plants would be futile. In support of this view there is the idea that since ancient peoples discovered most of the common food plants, we may conceive of them as having tried and rejected as inferior a great many other sorts of crops—for certainly in the course of human migrations they had ample opportunity to sample foods from acid soils as well as basic. That they ultimately settled on lime-loving plants as the chief food crops would seem to point to an intrinsic superiority of this kind. This is a matter which deserves much more attention than it has ever received, and if we understood the theoretical aspects of the case we would be able to derive practical benefits.

From the investigation of the origin of cultivated species yet further value may come. The so-called "back-to-nature movement" is the result of a real problem. Plants, like animals and humans, become overcultivated. City dwellers become pale and subject to diseases, pampered in their tastes and unable to endure hardships. Animals, too, suffer from domestication; one of the almost ludicrous cases is the well-known one of many collies. People with jaded tastes have taken a fancy to very narrow-headed collies and have bred this caricature of a dog until his cranium is so small that he hasn't even good dog brains. Plants, too, have been overcivilized. In the case of the cereals, for instance, we breed them for large grains and grow them in pure cultures. As a result, when fungi or insects attack a wheat field they find something equivalent to a particularly fat, juicy person unable to defend himself in the presence of a hungry pack of wolves. A pure stand of wheat is just one vast pantry to its parasites. No such multiplication of spores or insects would be known in the wild, because the host plant would be scattered and the seeds not so large. And, moreover, and most important, wild plants are as a rule actually more hardy and disease resistant than cultivated ones. In some way not wholly explained cultivated plants actually do become weakened. Specially prepared soils, fertilizers, breeding for certain characters at the possible expense of others may partially account for this. But whatever the causes, the fact is the same, and plant breeders are beginning to go back to wild plants to infuse fresh vigor into the cultivated strains.

Obviously, if the wild ancestors of our "cultigens"

as they are called, are to be called in for hybridizing or stock purposes, it will have to be determined which are the wild ancestors and where they can be found. In this cause economic botanists have looked diligently for the original wild potato, wheat, barley, cotton, sweet potato, tobacco, corn and many others. This has proved a great deal more difficult than might be expected, and though it has frequently been claimed that wheat, tobacco, cotton and corn had been found in a truly wild state, it has generally been difficult to prove that the supposed ancestral plants were not merely cultivated plants which had escaped, which is not the same thing, by any means. In cases where the wild ancestor has been located with certainty it is generally found that these plants are much more puny or unproductive or otherwise inferior than their cultivated descendants except in regard to vegetative vigor. This certainly implies a compliment to the skill of primitive man who was able to accomplish such wonders in the conjury of plant breeding. The American Indian is sometimes credited with the most tremendous feat of hybridization and selection ever accomplished—the production of corn, a plant which has evolved so far from its original ancestor that it cannot now be recognized as close kin to any grass in the world.

But it is only fair to credit to other races some of the glories of plant dissemination. The Chinese not only drew from the Central Asia plateau their share of the crops of that region, as indeed they drew some elements of culture common with the

West, but in their own country they evolved in cultivation the modern orange, peach, persimmon, jujube, the plum, rice, millet, rhubarb and *yang-mae* or *yamamato* (just beginning to be known here), the bamboo shoot and other plants.

The Arabs have been responsible for the cultivation and more especially the dissemination of sugar, coffee, date, fig, pepper, cinnamon, cloves, nutmeg, hemp, opium, indigo, saffron, madder, frankincense, myrrh, rice and other plants. Curiously enough a good many of these plants do not grow in Arabia at all. The Arabs, in historic times, went from Spain to the Isles of Spice and from Persia to Madagascar and Guinea spreading about the plants in the lands where they conquered or traded.

Before the coming of the white man the Indian had disseminated from their original homes so many plants that they occupied vastly greater areas under cultivation than they had held in the wild. Chief among these were maize and tobacco, but manihot, beans, potato, cotton, squash and others had also been so extended that when the Spanish and English came they met some or other of these crops wherever they went.

To the Polynesians credit is probably due for the remarkable feat of spreading over thousands of miles of ocean (crossed in small, open boats) the breadfruit, the coconut, the taro, the yam and perhaps, too, the banana.

To the marvelous work of plant breeding and plant introduction nearly all peoples have contributed more or less. Such a contribution exceeds in practical importance many other forms of culture often ranked higher. A people's language may perish, their religion be forsaken, their precious works of art be broken or forgotten, and even their blood lost by intermixture with other races, but what they have done for agriculture remains their eternal contribution to human life. Historians, anthropologists and others often assign insufficient credit to races which have done so much for the world at large. The study of the ancient and even the archæologic history of agriculture is not only full of fascination and speculation; it is fraught with solutions of modern problems in this day when new demands are arising and fresh viewpoints are needed.

SUGGESTED READING

CANDOLLE, ALPHONSE DE, *Origin of Cultivated Plants,* second English translation, 1909. A classic work and a compact one, containing a study of a large number of plants. The concluding remarks are significant as generalities; the introduction displays the methods by which the author determined plant origins. The actual text is more valuable as reference than interesting as reading. Modern research has often shown this book to be in error, but the outlines remain true.

PICKERING, CHARLES, *A Chronological History of Plants,* 1879. A large, excursive book, compiled and written in a somewhat antiquated style. But full of interest although as indigestible from the standpoint of general reading as a dictionary.

JORET, CHARLES, *Les Plantes dans l'antiquité et au Moyen Age*, 1897–1904. An interesting historical work in two volumes, filled with facts. Devoted largely to pre-Greek civilizations and the archæological evidences of plant culture.

LAUFER, BERTHOLD, "Sino-Iranica; Chinese Contributions to the History of Civilization in Ancient Iran," *Field Museum Anthropological Series*, Publication 201, Vol. 25, No. 3, 1919. A learned large treatise on the social and agricultural links between the white and yellow races in ancient times. Its philological eruditions are beyond all but students of oriental languages, but much information can be derived from it by any one. The introduction contains an interesting criticism of De Candolle's *Origin of Cultivated Plants*.

CARRIER, LYMAN, *Beginnings of Agriculture in America*, 1923. Complete and interesting information on Indian crops and agricultural practices; shows along what lines agriculture was developing in pre-Columbian days and would have developed in the New World without the intervention of the Old.

BRUNHES, JEAN, *Human Geography*, English translation by T. C. Le Compte. 1920. Chap. IV. A classic in its subject, extremely suggestive if brief. Its generalities on man and his domesticated plants and animals are keen and trustworthy.

FORBES, R. H., "Plant Introduction," *Sultanic Agric. Soc.*, Egypt, Vol. 10, pp. 2–4, 1923. A brief but interesting account of the oldest agricultural land in the world. Contains a table of the origin of Egypt's cultivated plants.

EDGAR, WILLIAM C., *The Story of a Grain of Wheat*, 1925. An absorbing story of wheat and flour and of man's long-continued struggle to increase their production. The author carries his narrative from the earliest times to the present day.

CHAPTER XV

MUST WE STARVE?

A CULTIVATED, bright and charming English boy, just down from Cambridge, in the year 1797, was talking with his father in the quiet of their drawing-room about the sorrows and evils of the poor and the hopes and despairs of future society. The father, Daniel Malthus, was a correspondent of Rousseau, that quixotic optimist, and he did not agree with his son Thomas that we must have the poor always with us. But before the talk was done, Malthus senior had a vast deal more respect for his son's mental caliber than he had entertained when they sat down.

The young man had grounded himself in the realistic principles of Hume, Robert Wallace, Adam Smith, Richard Brice and Townsend's *Dissertation on the Poor Laws,* and he had come to the conclusion that human beings were increasing in ever greater and greater proportions, while the plants and animals on which they fed did not begin to keep pace with man's fecundity. In fact, he believed that agricultural land tends slowly to give poorer and poorer returns, so that the gulf between the birth rate and food production becomes yearly wider.

Malthus asked his son to reduce his thoughts to

writing, and when this had been done the old man was so thoroughly impressed that he sent the manuscript to a publisher. It was an amazed world which opened this book and read the statement that "population increases in a geometrical, food in an arithmetical ratio." But as even thinking people rarely doubt a statement which is sicklied over with a pale cast of mathematics, the world accepted this formula as a fact against which there was little use to rail or struggle. Even so eminent a reasoner as John Stuart Mill said that persons who did not believe it entirely were mere sentimentalists.

The French Revolution had witnessed the disillusionment of the romantic school of Rousseau. As is always the case during and after wars, the tories were in power and there had set in a period of reaction, of self-satisfaction, personal and national, and of excessive selfishness.

The moment was ripe for a fresh solution of the problem of the English Poor Relief system. At that time pauper children were cared for by public taxation. The result had been to subsidize pauperism. The evils of the industrial revolution were at their worst because cheap child labor was the only kind greatly in demand with manufacturers. As a result, adults of the laboring class, unable to get work, found it necessary to beget children in large numbers or to starve.

What Malthus realized from his reading and observations was that the Poor Relief must be stopped if the high birth rate of Europe was to be stopped. This would allow the "natural checks to population," such as disease, war and famine, to kill off the superfluous numbers of workmen. For the richer classes he recommended late marriages. These viewpoints were admirably suited to the tastes of people who had no material worries or privations and did not wish to feel responsible for relieving the difficulties of others.

Thus Malthus, who had in reality said little that had not been said before, came in on the crest of an anti-reform wave. The conclusions which were deduced from Malthus's work were that the poor found themselves in their miserable plight chiefly due to the vices which they themselves upheld—lack of thrift, shiftlessness, stupidity and unrestrained sexual relations. To raise their pay, clean up their streets and dwellings, or to educate them would only be to give them the material medium in which to spawn more rapidly; in the end worse poverty than ever would be the result. In the struggle for existence (a phrase which Darwin got from Malthus), the human race would soon be cutting throats right and left. Such were the sentiments with which the county gentry of Georgian times, their belts distended with mutton and beef, found it pleasant to console themselves for the empty bellies of their poorer brethren.

But not every one agreed with Malthus, and he discovered that he had not many facts to support him. He went abroad to collect contributory evidence, using the rather unscientific method of first forming a theory and then examining the facts for reference. Montesquieu and others had said before

all that Malthus had said; the only thing that he had
done which others had not was to phrase his thought
in a readable, revealing way. The ponderous methods of his predecessors had left the public cold. In
that day nobody was opening the covers of pamphlets
on vital statistics except statisticians and insom-
niacs. But in the revised later editions of Malthus's
work, a long statistical background had been con-
structed for his original startling thesis, so that the
reader was now not only excited by the fundamental
propositions, but awed by the indigestible mass of
figures.

It is strange that nobody detected the glaring
errors among these figures and in these propositions.
For instance, Malthus made an imperfect distinction
between the sexual impulse, which is universal among
people between certain ages, and the reproductive
instinct which may be anything from nil to a huge
force. Nor did he distinguish between potential
increase, which assumes a woman to bear living
children throughout her reproductive years and is
incalculable in a few generations, and actual increase
which is always much less than potential.

Further, Malthus was absolutely ignorant about
the facts of actual increase among domestic animals
and plants. He based his thesis upon the food
scarcity in such countries as England, France and
Holland, where every one was leaving the landlord-
throttled farms for the industrial centers. These
conditions he naïvely placed side by side with the
tremendous increase in population in America,
where with superabundant space and food, almost

all the pioneers were able to have large families. He asks us to add these two facts together and deduce a result. It reminds one of the children's catch question: how much is ten ducks and five chickens?

Eventually Malthus suffered an eclipse of popular fame. This, it is to be feared, was not because anybody realized his mistakes. But it was after the fall of Napoleon, when the "natural check" of war had reduced the crowding numbers of Europe, when the birth rate in France and England was falling, and when there was no indication that the English aristocracy would lose their heads as the French had done. People slept better at night and lost less weight by day now that every one could be selfish in comfort. Roast beef was still plentiful, in spite of everything Malthus had predicted, and his name was no longer to be heard in drawing-room arguments.

By the Seventies botanists and agricultural experts, and notably the great biologist Francis Galton, began to take up some of Malthus's statements in real earnest; in fact, they attacked the crux of the problem, ignoring with scientific impersonality all the inference to be drawn about the proper conduct of the well-to-do toward the poor, and calmly examined his statements about biological increase. The result of a few decades of investigation was to pronounce utterly false and unsupported by any facts the statement that "population increases in geometrical, food in arithmetical ratio." Biologists would not even permit the Malthusians to say that "population has a *tendency* to increase faster than food," for the ambiguity of the word "tendency" was naturally challenged at the outset. Moreover, it can easily be shown at any time that, though there are spots in the world where population increases faster than food, there are many others where there is far more food than the population requires.

The theories of Malthus had reached their nadir of importance and were just about to go to the museum of scientific relics, when, during the reign of high prices, hard times and reaction which followed the Great War, there arose the school of the neo-Malthusians who number among them such economists as Ely, Pearl, Marshall and Taussig. The most recent exponent of this thought is the eminent Professor East of Harvard University. His biological training, the regiments of statistics which he musters under his banner, and the penetration of his thought make everything he says worth listening to, and men who are younger or less experienced are diffident about disagreeing with him. In his book, *Mankind at the Crossroads* (1923), he has written in a very readable style one of the arresting philosophical works of our times.

It is possible that Professor East would deny that he is a neo-Malthusian. He is too broad-minded to be easily classified. But to form any judgment one must try to grasp his viewpoint. In essence, Professor East appears to be saying that the days of plenty of food for every one are over. The abundance in which we in America have always lived has been an abundance of natural resources comparable to a discovered chest of gold. This is

now almost spent, and the pinch of want must soon
be felt, especially as immigration is forever adding
new mouths that must be fed.

Professor East points, as nearly all people of
Malthusian trend are prone to do, to China as a
land where, even with the most intensive agricultural methods and every phase of thrift, even of
the most penurious economy, the number of the poor
comprises most of the population, and the saturation
point of population in relation to food is not only
always imminent but frequently surpassed. Every
few years some part of that land is depopulated by
a terrible visitation—first famine, then starvation
and finally disease among the weakened survivors.
But as soon as the crisis is over and there are fewer
mouths and better crops, up goes the birth rate
again, mounting as steadily as summer temperatures in Hongkong, until the breaking point is
reached once more.

Professor East compares this to the birth rate of
animals who in abundant seasons bring forth and
raise many young, while in periods of scarcity of
food the whole reproductive process—sexual impulse, fecundity and ability to nourish offspring—
is slowed down or stopped. Professor East regards the human as an animal, one who struggles to
live yet in the end must die; and who is therefore
subject to just such a rigorous environment as any
other animal, is as much the servant of sex instincts
and is in short, however distinguished from other
animals by intellect and civilization, still trapped in
the paw of Nature's laws of supply and demand—a

paw which opens and closes by a volition certainly not man's.

To think of man as an animal conditioned by an environment is a point of view which recommends itself to a biologist—in other words, to a man who cares only for the *facts* about life and death. But there are some other points in the thoughts of the neo-Malthusians which need to be taken apart and examined critically. First of all, there is the matter of China—the most quoted example of the evils of crowding. China is pointed out as a land in which civilization is exceedingly old, and the land has been forced for indefinite thousands of years to support the population. By some sort of an intellectual broad jump it is reasoned that other and younger countries will at length become equally crowded, and other younger farm lands will be taxed in the same way, and that inevitably we must come to the same pass. Then only the infinitesimal rich class will be able to live in comfort and rear children with advantages, but the rest of the population, we are told, will be at the mercy of crop failures and famines.

There is a story that a missionary was giving an earnest address on how to save babies' lives. His audience was a Chinese one, and while he was talking an old man arose and interrupted him.

"But, sir," said the venerable sage, "what we need in China is not more babies but fewer."

There seemed to be nothing to say to this profound observation, and the missionary said it. We can only imagine that, in order to reconcile his high-minded purpose with the awful truth of the old man's statement, he must have adopted the slogan of "Fewer, but *better* babies!"

But to return to Chinese agriculture, the truth is that there is nothing to show that China produces her maximum. The oft asserted "cultivation of every square inch of ground" in China is very impressive to the sort of person who makes a hasty tour of a country and writes up his impressions in some favorite travel magazine, with a profusion of pictures and a paucity of correct interpretation. The cultivation of every square inch of ground would not necessarily mean superior yields. In thinking of Chinese agricultural production we must bear in mind the following points, (1) the unknown, uncalculated, but necessarily huge toll of plant diseases —a matter only beginning to be understood in western lands, much less in oriental ones; (2) the appalling lack of transportation facilities in China which enables one province to starve to death while an adjacent one has plenty; (3) the small farm system of agriculture tenaciously clung to and revered by the farmers because it descends from classic times when feudalism made it necessary; that the modern Chinese nation should depend on such a Liliputian and obsolete system presents the spectacle of a big man riding a pony; (4) the lack of organization of farming and marketing, which could keep the farmer in relation to the centers of demand, or where they do exist, the insufficiency of such organizations to meet the exigencies; (5) the lack of mineral fertilizers; (6) the lack of general agricultural science of the modern sort.

These are other points one could enumerate, but these are quite enough. What is more significant is that these agricultural problems cannot be duplicated in any great degree among those of other densely crowded lands in the west, like Belgium. Only India approaches the conditions of China. Our own country may lose its youthful exuberance, become crowded, and in many ways display the ills of overcivilization, but with the western genius for organization, who can say that our agricultural life will ever resemble the Chinese?

Professor East anticipates this question, "Cannot our agricultural explorers and economic botanists contribute to the problems of new or better-yielding crops by foreign introductions of food plants?" To use Professor East's own words: *"They haven't a chance."* He argues that every food plant of value in the world was known to primitive man, hence we have nothing to hope for in the way of lucky discoveries in food species. Without taking the space for a lengthy refutation of this last statement (one which could not by any means be supported) it is proper to ask whether *all* the foods known to primitive man have been given a fair trial throughout the lands of civilized man. The answer is an emphatic *no*. Had agricultural explorers accepted this point of view, not one of the improved, hardy, resistant or superior-yielding species, now generally being disseminated, would ever have been known outside the local regions in which they were indigenous. Suppose, for instance, that the marvelous hard, durum wheats had been left in their native haunts, on the recommendation of Professor East that it would be futile to search for new useful plants. Some semicivilized peoples—a few millions at the most—would be enjoying the benefits of this superior wheat, and our country, our wheat states, would have $50,000,000 less annually than they do now.

And durum wheat is not the only example of this sort. In the last twenty-five years the agricultural explorer has brought to this country Peruvian alfalfa, which earns an annual increment of $5,000,000;[1] Professor East has apparently forgotten African dates, which return $275,000 a year to our country. The value of the recently introduced *feterita* is $18,000,000 every year, and Japanese rice, which can be raised in the Sacramento Valley, earns $13,000,000 for California every twelve months. The sorghums introduced by the Department of Agriculture net $10,000,000 for their growers, while the navel orange, which is generally believed to be an artifact by Burbank but which was in reality brought from Brazil in 1872, is worth increasing amounts every year; at present, it brings in $16,000,000 annually.

To meet Professor East's statement that all the economic species were known to and exploited by early man, there is the case of Sudan grass. Discovered by Professor Piper, it was absolutely unknown to man as a useful plant unless a few natives

---

[1] In the figures quoted the most recent maxima have been given. These figures have been compiled from data in the Office of Foreign Seed and Plant Introduction, Bureau of Plant Industry, Department of Agriculture.

may have used it. It only entered this country in 1909, but in the few years which have intervened it has forged ahead until it occupies a place as one of the foremost economic grasses of the United States. Its annual value to this country is $12,000,000. In view of these facts it is to be wondered how Professor East can maintain that the agricultural explorer "hasn't a chance." So vast an increase in the earnings of the American farmer as is represented by the total of even these few species (and there are many others) must represent a corresponding increase in the food production of the country. The population of the United States is growing, but so is the production of foodstuffs. Malthusians take note!

Referring to some of the recently introduced plants of this country Professor East asks what good it does the North Dakota farmer to tell him about mangoes and dasheens and more crops 'of which he has never heard. *His* agricultural crisis remains. Professor East is aiming a shot particularly at a book entitled *The World's Food Resources* by the distinguished geographer Joseph Russell Smith. This work Professor East regards as perniciously optimistic and he is not at all impressed with the list of Department of Agriculture introductions of foreign food plants from which Mr. Smith draws much of his confidence about the future. These thousands of introduction numbers, when their names fall unfamiliarly on Professor East's ears, are generally tropical.

Here, then, the heart of the question is reached.

Professor East is reckoning without the tropics and subtropics. The disinclination of the races of Europe, North America and Japan to dwell out of the temperate zones, blinds us to the fact that near the equator, nevertheless, is the spot in the world most favored for plant growth. It is a simple problem in physics. For practical purposes we may say that all energy is derived from the sun. Where does the sun shine most directly? Where does it provide the longest growing season? In the tropics. Richard Spruce, returning from the Amazon with its five-tiered forests, to the gray skies and long winter nights of England, said he could not imagine how a plant could *grow* with so little sunlight.

There is no escaping the fact that in the tropics and subtropics the greatest amount of energy can be stored in plant tissue in a given number of years or in a given number of acres. Food, at least food that constitutes nourishment, represents energy, energy to be released for human use. For this reason, in the lands which lie between Capricorn and Cancer, a great world larder exists, and will appear increasingly as the great forests are cleared and the savannahs are plowed. As compared with the temperate lands, where nearly all the area suitable to agriculture is being exploited, the tropics have not even skimmed the surface of their possible development. Of the jungles 90 per cent are said to be untouched.

So vast a figure as the tropics seems to have been left out of Professor East's statistical calculations. How big cannot of course be more than surmised;

it cannot be stated in numbers. But this only goes to prove how often figures lie. Statistics seldom tell the whole truth; it is the latent, unmeasurable forces which are the gods of the future. And they are fond of springing surprises. All this, of course, does not appear to help the North Dakota farmer directly. In fact, it might even be construed to mean that farming in North Dakota would suffer an eclipse. Such a thing is emphatically not the case. But what one can perceive is that the temperate zones are not going to be forced to bear the *whole* weight of the future food supply of the world.

It is in the temperate zones that manufacturing conditions are at their best. It is in the tropics that agriculture is most favored by incontrovertible astronomic facts. The future of the tropics is, therefore, chiefly agricultural, while that of the temperate zones, though destined to play a great rôle in agriculture, is also highly industrial. A rich industrial population can afford to buy its food from afar—witness England, where in normal times the price of food is not prohibitive. The New England housewife's table, too, is often loaded with what are almost exclusively tropical products, and no one regards this as surprising.

Professor East has chosen to speak in disparaging terms of the mango and the dasheen. He made a bad choice, for he forgets or he does not know that the dasheen is as nourishing as the potato, and the mango as delicious as the peach. It is true that, at present, they are almost unheard of in a state like North Dakota, and certainly they could not be grown there. But the day is not far off when they may appear on North Dakota tables. There was a time, too, when northern farmers knew nothing of coffee, tea, cocoa, pineapples, molasses and cane sugar, tapioca, coconut, orange, lemon, lime, banana, dates, figs, pepper, rice, vanilla, ginger, cinnamon, clove and many another tropical and subtropical product with which every pantry in northern countries is stocked. That chayotes, yams, yautias, taroes, plantains, mangoes, papayas, avocadoes and many other plants now rare in this country may become common in southern fields and northern markets it seems foolhardy to doubt.

Our distaste for the present living conditions in the tropics has nothing to do with the matter, nor is the case altered by the history of the white laborer in the tropics, weakened with drink which superstition taught him to regard as a guard against fevers and untrained to work in the hours suited to tropical climates. Whether farming in the tropics is all to be done by the races that are native to them, directed and capitalized, perhaps, by northern peoples, or whether at last northern labor may adapt itself to certain phases of tropical employment, it is still to the tropics that we may look for a larder to feed the hungry word.

Professor East rightly reminds us that the price of meat is going to go up. It has been said to require ten times as much acreage to graze cattle as it does to grow the best cereals, dollar for dollar, and calorie for calorie. It is probable that the cereals will encroach upon grazing lands in Argentina, Canada and Australia, as in parts of our own country. The Japanese, in their crowded island, centuries ago gave up meat for rice. Meat, of course, we shall always have, at a price, and the cost of fowl and fish may not advance materially.

But the time is coming when agriculture and certainly not stock raising will dominate the surface of the globe. Our most primitive ancestors were those who spent their time in chasing the deer. We mark an advance in human culture when first they cleared a space and planted seeds. A highly agricultural population is a highly advanced one, and not even a king, as the great Emperor Diocletian showed when he abdicated to grow cabbages, need be ashamed of the grand old name of farmer.

SUGGESTED READING

EAST, PROF. EDWARD M., *Mankind at the Crossroads*, 1923; Chap. IV, "The Population and the Food Supply," largely statistical; Chap. VI, "A Permanent Agriculture." Chiefly philosophical; the ideas are significant and suggestive; serious-minded reading but by no means difficult.

SMITH, JOSEPH RUSSELL, *The World's Food Supply*, 1919. A survey of many crops, with optimistic outlook. Short and easy.

REUTER, EDWARD BYRON, *Population Problems*, 1923. A modern evaluation of old and new Malthusianism. A serious but absorbing book.

POPENOE, WILSON, *Manual of Tropical and Subtropical Fruits*, 1920. Chap. I, "The Outlook for Tropical Fruits." Lucid and illuminating.

WILLIS, J. C., *Exploitation of Plants,* 1917, ed. F. W. Oliver. Chap. IV, "Tropical Exploitation." The importance of the tropics in human affairs is well set forth.

THOMPSON, WARREN S., *Population: A Study in Malthusianism,* 1915. Entertaining treatise, with a neo-Malthusian trend.

HEDRICK, W. C., *Economics of a Food Supply.* An interesting discussion of the devices and processes by which a sufficiency of food is brought to the hands of the consumer, popularly written.

WILCOX, EARLEY V., *Tropical Agriculture,* 1916. A sound, authoritative and readable volume on the climate, soils, cultural methods, crops, commercial importance and opportunities of the tropics.

INDEX

(1)

THE END

Donald Culross Peattie (1898–1964) was one of the most influential American nature writers of the twentieth century. Peattie was born in Chicago and grew up in the Smoky Mountains of North Carolina, a region that sparked his interest in the immense wonders of nature. He studied at the University of Chicago and Harvard University. After working for the U.S. Department of Agriculture, he decided to pursue a career as a writer. In 1925 he became a nature columnist for the *Washington Star* and went on to pen more than twenty fiction and nonfiction books over the next five decades. Widely acclaimed and popular in his day, Peattie's work has inspired a modern age of nature writing.